CAMBRIDGE LIBRARY COLLECTION

Books of enduring scholarly value

British and Irish History, Seventeenth and Eighteenth Centuries

The books in this series focus on the British Isles in the early modern period, as interpreted by eighteenth- and nineteenth-century historians, and show the shift to 'scientific' historiography. Several of them are devoted exclusively to the history of Ireland, while others cover topics including economic history, foreign and colonial policy, agriculture and the industrial revolution. There are also works in political thought and social theory, which address subjects such as human rights, the role of women, and criminal justice.

Wakefield Manor Book, 1709

William Elmsall was the deputy steward of Wakefield manor in 1709. He is taken to be the compiler of this comprehensive record of the state of the manor and its accounts in that year. After the work's value to the study of eighteenth-century English social and economic history was recognised by the Yorkshire Archaeological Society, publication followed in 1939. The book was edited by John Charlesworth (b. 1865), a fellow of the Society of Antiquaries, who transcribed and edited parish registers and other documents of historical importance. Contained in this work are lists of the names of the lords, freeholders, officers, bailiffs, and all the towns and villages within the manor. The book also includes decrees covering rent and fines and the fees of gaolers and bailiffs, as well as information on the succession of the lords of Wakefield manor.

Cambridge University Press has long been a pioneer in the reissuing of out-of-print titles from its own backlist, producing digital reprints of books that are still sought after by scholars and students but could not be reprinted economically using traditional technology. The Cambridge Library Collection extends this activity to a wider range of books which are still of importance to researchers and professionals, either for the source material they contain, or as landmarks in the history of their academic discipline.

Drawing from the world-renowned collections in the Cambridge University Library and other partner libraries, and guided by the advice of experts in each subject area, Cambridge University Press is using state-of-the-art scanning machines in its own Printing House to capture the content of each book selected for inclusion. The files are processed to give a consistently clear, crisp image, and the books finished to the high quality standard for which the Press is recognised around the world. The latest print-on-demand technology ensures that the books will remain available indefinitely, and that orders for single or multiple copies can quickly be supplied.

The Cambridge Library Collection brings back to life books of enduring scholarly value (including out-of-copyright works originally issued by other publishers) across a wide range of disciplines in the humanities and social sciences and in science and technology.

Wakefield Manor Book 1709

Edited by
John Charlesworth

CAMBRIDGE UNIVERSITY PRESS

Cambridge, New York, Melbourne, Madrid, Cape Town,
Singapore, São Paolo, Delhi, Mexico City

Published in the United States of America by Cambridge University Press, New York

www.cambridge.org
Information on this title: www.cambridge.org/9781108058841

This edition first published 1939
This digitally printed version 2013

ISBN 978-1-108-05884-1 Paperback

The Anniversary Reissue of Volumes from the Record Series of the Yorkshire Archaeological Society

To celebrate the 150th anniversary of the foundation of the leading society for the study of the archaeology and history of England's largest historic county, Cambridge University Press has reissued a selection of the most notable of the publications in the Record Series of the Yorkshire Archaeological Society. Founded in 1863, the Society soon established itself as the major publisher in its field, and has remained so ever since. The *Yorkshire Archaeological Journal* has been published annually since 1869, and in 1885 the Society launched the Record Series, a succession of volumes containing transcriptions of diverse original records relating to the history of Yorkshire, edited by numerous distinguished scholars. In 1932 a special division of the Record Series was created which, up to 1965, published a considerable number of early medieval charters relating to Yorkshire. The vast majority of these publications have never been superseded, remaining an important primary source for historical scholarship.

Current volumes in the Record Series are published for the Society by Boydell and Brewer. The Society also publishes parish register transcripts; since 1897, over 180 volumes have appeared in print. In 1974, the Society established a programme to publish calendars of over 650 court rolls of the manor of Wakefield, the originals of which, dating from 1274 to 1925, have been in the safekeeping of the Society's archives since 1943; by the end of 2012, fifteen volumes had appeared. In 2011, the importance of the Wakefield court rolls was formally acknowledged by the UK committee of UNESCO, which entered them on its National Register of the Memory of the World.

The Society possesses a library and archives which constitute a major resource for the study of the county; they are housed in its headquarters, a Georgian villa in Leeds. These facilities, initially provided solely for members, are now available to all researchers. Lists of the full range of the Society's scholarly resources and publications can be found on its website, www.yas.org.uk.

Wakefield Manor Book, 1709

(Record Series volume 101)

The manor of Wakefield was one of the largest in England, covering a huge area of the West Riding of Yorkshire, and the records of its property transactions, agricultural business and law enforcement are an important source for legal, social and economic historians. The Wakefield manor court book for 1709 was transcribed from a copy in the possession of Colonel J. Parker of Browsholme Hall, Clitheroe (formerly in the West Riding of Yorkshire and now in Lancashire). Colonel Parker was president of the Yorkshire Archaeological Society from 1913 until his death in 1938. In that year, his son presented his late father's copy of the court book to the Society, where it has the archival reference DD46. There is also a copy among the records of the manor of Wakefield, which has the reference MD225/4/1. Five earlier volumes in the Record Series (29, 36, 57, 78 and 109) containing translations of medieval court rolls of the manor of Wakefield are also now reissued in the Cambridge Library Collection, and the Society continues to publish editions of further material from this rich archive.

WAKEFIELD MANOR BOOK,

1709

THE YORKSHIRE
ARCHÆOLOGICAL SOCIETY

FOUNDED 1863 INCORPORATED 1893

RECORD SERIES

VOL. CI

FOR THE YEAR 1939

WAKEFIELD MANOR BOOK, 1709

EDITED BY

JOHN CHARLESWORTH, F.S.A.

PRINTED FOR THE SOCIETY

1939

Printed by

THE WEST YORKSHIRE PRINTING CO. LIMITED,

WAKEFIELD.

PREFACE.

The MS. Book now published was, it is assumed, compiled by William Elmsall, Deputy Steward of the Manor of Wakefield in 1709—probably for the Duke of Leeds, who had recently acquired the Manor.

The account is very comprehensive, yet whilst enumerating the collieries, quarries, etc., it omits all reference to the Lords' Corn Mills in Horbury, Newmillerdam, Ossett, Wakefield and in other places in the Manor, although the rents from them were considerable.

As the decree states there was no record of the fines, rents, etc., paid by Copyholders, etc., except the Rolls themselves, and a search through these would entail the expenditure of much time and labour.

The thanks of the Society are due to the owners of the Book, the late Col. John Parker, Major Robert Parker and Miss Parker for kindly lending the volume for transcription and allowing its publication.

I desire to express gratitude to all who helped with the many difficulties met with in editing.

The following abbreviations are used in the footnotes :—

C.D.—*Dugdale's Visitation of Yorkshire with additions*, edited by J. W. Clay, F.S.A., privately printed, 1899-1917.

H.F.M.G.—*Hunter's Familiæ Minorum Gentium*, edited by J. W. Clay, Harleian Society, 1894-96.

H.P.—*Hunter's Pedigrees*, edited by J. W. Walker, O.B.E., F.S.A., Harleian Society, 1936.

Y.A.J.—Yorkshire Archæological Journal.

JNO. CHARLESWORTH.

Horbury,

November, 1939.

THE PRESENT STATE

OF

THE MANNOR OF WAKEFIELD

IN

THE COUNTY OF YORK

BELONGING TO

HIS GRACE THE DUKE OF LEEDS,

IN THE YEAR

1709.

OF ITS EXTENT AND ANTIQUITY.

The MANNOR OF WAKEFIELD in the County of York is one of the most large & extensive Mannors in England. The greatest part of the West Country from Normanton Four Miles East of Wakefield to Lancashire being parcell of it and noe less distance than 34 English Miles.

It contains 118 Townes, Villages or Hamletts of which Wakefield & Hallifax are the Chief.

This Mannor was p[ar]cell of Ancient Demesne & Surveyed under the Title of T[erra] R[egis] E[dwardi] before the Conquest & it continued as p[ar]cell of the possessions of the Kings of England till Henry the first who about the 6th year of his Raign Anno D[omi]ni 1107 did give this Mannor among others to Wm de Placetis Sonne of the first Wm Earl Warren in consideration of his service for taking Robert de Courtois The Kings Brother Prisoner in Normandy.

THE SUCCESSION OF THE LORDS OF THE MANNOR.

This William to whome this Grant was made had issue a Daughter named Issabel,[1] She first married to Will[ia]m Sonn of King Stephen with whome she had noe issue and after to Hamelin Plantaginet the naturall Sonn of Jeferay Plantagenet by whome she had issue Willm̃.

This Will[ia]m maryed the Daughter of Will[ia]m Earl of Norfolk[2] by whome he had issue John.

This John had issue William who married the Daughter of Robert Earl of Oxford but died in the life time of his Father leaveing his Wife with Child who had issue John who died without Issue in the 21st year of King Edward the Third.

This last John Earl Warren built the Castle of Sandall Scituate about a Mile South of Wakefield and made it the cheif Seat of the Mannor. He haveing diverse Bastards & noe lawfull Issue gave all his Honors Castles Mannors Lands & Tenements to King Edward the Second in the 9th year of his Raign of intent to have a Regrant to his Bastards intaile; the King the year after made a Grant to the Earl & to one Matilda de Mairford[3] his Concubine for Life, Remainder to John de Warren Sonn of the said Matilda and the heirs Male of his Body & Remainder to one Thomas de Warren, another Sonn of the said Matilda and the heirs

[1] Isabel was daughter of the 3rd earl.

[2] Pembroke, she was widow of Hugh earl of Norfolk.

[3] Nairford or Nerford.

Male of his Body, Remainder to the Heirs of the Body of the said Earl lawfully begotten and for want of such Issue to returne to the King. In the 12th year of the said King Edward the Second, This John Earl Warren by virtue of Lycence from the King did grant this mannor of Wakefield to Thomas Earl of Lancaster for & dureing the Tearme of the natural life of the said Earl Warren The Earl of Lancaster injoyed it but for a small time for he was beheaded at his owne Castle at Pontefract within three years after (vizt) in the 15 King Edward the 2d after the death of the Earl of Lancaster, this John Earl Warren had the Mannor of Wakefield again & injoyed it dureing his Life : He died the 21st year of Edward the Third & had marryed the said Matilda his Concubine before who survived him She lived untill the 33d Year of King Edward the Third & kept Courts at Wakefield in the name of Countis de Warren, and her Two Sons John & Thomas before mentioned dyed before her without Issue—Soe that from the first grant of the Mannor to the death of the Countis de Warren it apeareth to be 252 years.

After the death of Matilda Countis de Warren, King Edw[ar]d the Third in 36th Year of his Raign Created Edmund de Langley his Sonn Earl of Cambridge & gave him in Augmentation of his Revenies The Mannor of Wakefield. King Richard the Second created this Edmund Duke of Yorke who had issue Edmund Duke of Yorke who dyed at the Batle of Egen Court. His Second Sonne Richard Earl of Cambrige was father to Richard Duke of York who was slain at Wakefield feild Batle whose Sonn Edward the 4th after he had gotten the victory at Totonfeild builded Wakefield Bridge & a Stately Chapel thereupon in memory of his father & of those who lost their Lives with him. This Victory was in the year 1461. Soe that this Mannor of Wakefield was the Inheritance of the Dukes of Yorke for about the space of 100d. Years.

From the begining of Edward the 4th time it continued p[arcell] of the possessions of the Kings of England till the year 1554 at the mariage between King Philip & Queen Mary which at time it was united to the Dutchie of Lancaster.

In the 6th year of King Charles the First this Mannor of Wakefield was granted from the Crowne to the Earl of Holland soe that it apeareth to have been as p[arc]ell of the Possessions of The Crowne for the space of 170 years.

This Earl of Holland maryed his Daughter to S[i]r Gervas Clifton & gave him this Mannor of Wakefield as her mariage fortune.

About the Year 1665 This S[i]r Gervas Clifton sold it to S[i]r Chr[ist]ofer Clapham.

And the Heirs of S[i]r Chr[ist]ofer Clapham in the year 1700 sold it to His Grace The Duke of Leeds the present L[or]d of this Mannor.

A Discrip[ti]on of the Scituation of its severall Parts & its Boundaries.

This great Mannor of Wakefield is not altogether intire & contiguous for in severall places it is broke off by the Honor of Pontefract & other Mannors.

The most Eastern p[ar]te Four Miles from Wakefield lye Normanton & Woodhous a Towne & Hamlet which are boundred round with the Honor of Pontefract viz[t] Whitwood to the East, Snydall to the South, Warmfield to the West, & Altofts to the North, within this Division is the Mannor of Woodhous.

About Fourteen Miles North-West from Wakefield, lyeth Eclesell, another Branch of the Mannor, & is also incompassed by the Honor of Pontefract, & other mannors & break of at least Eight Miles from the nearest p[ar]te of any of the rest of the mannor and is bounder'd by Horsford, & Calverley to the East, Tongue, & Pudsey, to the South, Bradford, & Bolton to the West, & Idel to the North Its reputed one of The Inferior Mannors.

About Twelve Miles West of Wakefield lyeth Dalton another Branch of The Mannor & is incompassed by the Honor of Pontefract & other Mannors & broke off about Two Miles from the rest. Its bounded by Kirkheaton to the East, Almonbury to the South, Huthersfield to the West, & Dighton & Bradley to the North, its also reputed one of the Inferior Mannors.

The rest of the Mannor may properly be devided into Three Branches (vizt Wakefield Branch, Holmfirth Branch, & Hallifax Branch.

Wakefield Branch joyns on Holmfirth Branch & is in Length from the East end of Wakefield Outwood to Emley south west being the nearest p[ar]t of Holmfirth Branch about Ten miles, it's very irregular in it's forme, for in some places it is 7 or 8 miles broad & in others not above one. Within this Branch are the Graveships of Wakefield, Stanley, Alverthorp, Thornes, Sandall, Horbury and Osset and hath also within it The Mannors of Walton, Crigleston, Bretton, Soothill, Ardsley, Southwood. The Rectory Mannor of Wakefield, & the Rectory Mannor of Dewsbury. It is bounded by Medley, The River of Calder, Heath, Okenshaw, Crofton, & Chivit to the East, Wooley, Bretton Di[midium]? to the South, Emley (p[ar]t of Holmfirth Branch) Midgley, Nether Shitlington, Thornhill, Mirfield, Heckmondwike, and Batley to the West, Morley, Midleton, East Ardsley, Lofthous, & Carleton to the North.

Holmfirth Branch extends from North-East to the County Palatine of Chester, West being about 14 Miles, within this Branch is the Graveship of Holme. The Inferior Mannors of Emley, Burton, Cumberworth, Shelly, Shepley, & Thirstonland, It is bounded by Bretton (part of Wakefield Branch) & Midgley to the East. Clayton, Skelmanthorp, Denby, Thurlston, & Penniston, to the South, The County of Chester & Sadleworth, to the West, Marstin, Meltom,

Tongue, Honley, Farnley, Stors, High-Burton, Lepton, & Denby Grange to the North.

Hallifax Branch is disjoyned from the other Branches by the Honor of Pontefract & other Mannors, The nearest & most Eastern Part about 2 miles from Wakefield Branch begins at Hartchstead, and extends Westward to the County of Lancaster, being about 23 miles, within this Branch are The Graveships of Sowerby, Hip[per]holme, Scamonden, & Rastrick, The inferior Mannors of Hallifax, Brighous, Hipperholme-thorne, Shelf, Ovenden, Skircoat, Rottenstall, Stansfield, Wadsworth, Heptonstall, Midgley, Barkisland, Stainland, Rishworth, Norland, Goldcarr, Fixby, Crosland, Lindley, & Quarmby. It is bounded by High Town, Robert-Towne, & Mirfield, to the East, Kirkheaton, Bradley, Huthersfield, Lockwood, South Crosland, & Slaghwaite, to the South, Marsden, & Lancashire, to the West, Haworth, Thornton, Clayton, North Byerley, Wyke, & Scoles to the North.

THE NOMINA VILLARUM

or

The Names of The Townes Villages and Hamlets within the Mannor of Wakefield with The Distinction of which doe present service to His Grace The Duke of Leeds Lord of The whole, and which are claimed by Inferior Lords.

His Grace The Duke of Leeds.

Wakefield, Stanley, Ouchthorp, Newton, Wrenthorp, Woodside, Alverthorp, Flanshaw, Snapethorp, Thornes, Horbury, Sandall, Milnethorp, Woodthorp, Newbiggin, Pledwick, Kettlethorp, Painthorp, Chapelthorp, Boynehill, Dawgreen, Dirtcarr, Hollingthorp, Normanton, Dewsbury, Osset, Gawthorp, Chikinley, Earls-Heaton, Over Buthroyd, Nether Buthroyd, Hip[per]holme, Northowrom, Shipden, Harley Green, Myxenden, Warley, Shakleton, Wydophead, Eringden, Sowerby, Soyland, Blackwood, Luddenden, Ripponden, Rastrick, Tootill, Scamondin, Hartchstead, Holmfirth, Holme, Scholes, Woodall, Austonley, Hepworth, Foulston, Thwonge.

Inferior L[or]ds.

The right Hon[oura]ble The E[ar]l of Cardigan.[1]

1	Ardsley & Woodkirk	Haigh
	Westerton	Topcliff
	Dunningley	Overgreen

The Lord Irwin.[2]

2 Halifax

[1] *Complete Peerage*, III, 14.
[2] Clay, *Extinct and Dormant Peerages*, p. 110.

Sir George Savile Baronett.[1]

3 Soothill, Chidsill
Hanging Heaton
4 Skircoat
5 Shelf
6 Ovenden
7 Rawtonstall, Soltonstall
8 Heptonstall, Shakleton
9 Wadsworth
10 Stansfield, Langfield
11 Rushworth
12 Norland
13 Barkisland
14 Goldcarr, Millbridge
15 Stainland, Old Lindley
16 Emley, Bentley Grange

Thomas Thornhill Esq.[2]

17 Fixby, Lindley, Quarmby
18 Hip[per]holme Thorne

Sir John Armitage Baron[e]t.[3]

19 Kirklees, Clifton
20 Brighous
21 Midle, Shitlington

Sir Wm Wentworth Baron[e]t.[4]

22 Breton West
23 Vpper & Nether Cumberworth Half
24 Flockton Upper & Nether

James Farrer Esq.

25 Midgley

[John ?] Stanhop Esq.[5]

26 Eccleshill

Charles Waterton Esq.[6]

27 Walton

George Kay Esq.[7]

28 Kirkburton Highburton Ryley.

John Wilkinson Esq.[8]

29 Dalton

— Hide Esq.

30 Skelmanthorp

Dr John [?] Kirshaw[9]

31 Shelley Roydhous

John Horsfall Gent[10]

32 Thurstonland

The Freehold[e]rs in that Towne

33 Shepley

John Sylvester Gent

34 Woodhous

[1] *Loidis and Elmete,* I, 314.
[2] *C.D.,* I, 82.
[3] *ibid.,* II, 412.
[4] *ibid.,* II, 131.
[5] *C.D.,* I, 222.
[6] *Y.A.J.,* XXX, 411.
[7] *C.D.,* I, 78.
[8] *ibid.,* I, 85.
[9] *ibid.,* II, 149.
[10] *ibid.,* II, 204.

Edwd Allot Gent[1] 35 Crigleston

Wm Oates Gent[2] 36 Southwood green

Thomas Wilkinson Gent[3] 37 North Crosland, Longroyd brigg

Richard Witton Esq[4] 38 The Rectory Mannor of Wakefield

John Richardson Cl[ericus][5] 39 The Rectory Mannor of Dewsbury.

Wm Horton Esq[6] 40 Coley.

Totall of the Inferior Mannors 40

Totall of The Townes and Villages within The Mannor of Wakefield 118.

The Constableries.

Within The Mannor of Wakefield are holden Four Court Leets or Sheriff Turnes at Wakefield, Hallifax, Brighous, & Burton.

Vnder the Court Leet at Wakefield are the Constableris following vizt Wakefield, Sandall, Normanton, Osset, Horbury, Stanley, West-Ardsley, Walton cu[m] Bretton, Soothill, Dewsbury, & Eccleshill.

Vnder the Court Leet at Hallifax are, Hallifax, Sowerby, Skircoat, Ovenden, Warley, Wadsworth, Midgley, Rishworth cum Norland, Stansfield, Langfield, Heptonstall, & Erringden.

Vnder The Court Leet at Brighous are The Constableries following (vizt) Hip[per]holme, cu[m] Brighous, Rastrick, Fixby, Northowrom, Shelf, Quarmby, Dalton, Hartchstead cu[m] Clifton, Stainland, & Barkisland.

Vnder The Court Leet at Burton are the Constableries of Kirk Burton, Shelley, Shepley, Cumberworth, Emley, Flockton, Thurstonland, & Holme, with its villages of Fulstone, Scholes, Wooldale, Cartworth, Austonley, Hepworth & Thwong.

FREEHOLDERS WITHIN THE SAID CONSTABLRIES.

Wakefield.

Richard Witton Esq, Theophilus Shelton Esq,[7] Nicholas Fenay Esq,[8] Thomas Fairfax Esq,[9] Robert Browne, Joseph Hall, Thomas Blanshead, Peter Robinson Senr, Abr[aham] Wilson, Francis Allen, James Dickinson, John Liverseige, Tho[mas] Whittaker, Richard Shaw, John Pulleine, Robert Lumbe, John Hirst, Samuel Robinson, Thomas Lee, Thomas Beatson, John Hewitson, Joseph Beatson, Joseph Cook, Joseph Wood, Wm Brooksbanck, Richard Gargrave, Thomas Loxley, Thomas Johnson, John Roades, Peter Robinson Junr, Samuel Roades,

[1] *H.F.M.G.*, II, 496.
[2] *ibid.*, I, 290.
[3] *C.D.*, I, 86.
[4] *ibid.*, I, 107.
[5] *ibid.*, I, 310.
[6] *ibid.*, I, 310.
[7] *C.D.*, I, 107.
[8] *ibid.*, I, 135.
[9] *ibid.*, II, 195.

Thomas Bolgy[1], John Tilson, Samuel Hide, John Wood, Francis Wheatley, Allen Johnson, Michael Barstoe, Robert Wilson, John Waddington, John Scott, Joshua Green, Tho[mas] Hawkins, Francis Mawd, Tho[mas] Percivall, Jo: Watkinson Gent[2].

Wm Wormall, John Dawson, Barnabas Thomson, Robert Milnes, Ebenezar Buxton, John Hewit, James Harrison, Richard Dawson, James Brathwaite, Wm Doughty, Joseph Bolton, Wm Rawlin Senr, Wm Harrison, Jacob Rhodes, Joseph Shillitoe, Jer[emiah] Dickson, Jno Godley, Abr: Bevor, Wm Naylor, James Clayton, Jno Norton, Jno Pighells, Jer[emiah] Spinke, Robt Hopkinson, Geo. Dickson, Wm Oates, Tho: Birkhead, Rowland Barrough, Francis Pitt, Richard Armitage, Robert Watson, John Lord, Roger Gill, Jonas Mawreley, Geo: Walton, Matt: Robinson Senr, John Brumley, John Briggs, Wm Philips, Anthony Bolton, Richard Ackersley, Wm Spinke, John Walker, Butcher, James Scriviner, Benj: Sigston, Robert Scott, Ab: Barber, Robt Nicholson, Tho: Warberton, Wm Copendall, Henry Bradley, Tho: Bingley, John Nevinson, John Lomb, Joseph Naylor, John Pollard, Tho: Wilson, Tho: Potter Senr, Tho: Potter Jnr, Tho: Pollard, Tho: Gill, Samuel Knowles, Samuel Vsher, Willm Naylor, Butcher, George Rawlinson, John Walker, Shoemaker, Stephen Lawrence.

Sandall.

Lyon Pilkington Esq, Mr Joseph Wood Cl[erk], John Grice[3] Gent: Gervas Norton Gent:[4] Jno Wood Gent: Joseph Hall, Mich[ael] Wheelwright, Francis Leake, John Lambert, John Brook, John Chapman, John Webster, Henry Bradley, Robert Dickinson, Gervas Sigsworth, Geo: Beaumont, Gent: Edward Allot, Gent: Wm Beatson, Morrit Mathews, Richard Haigh, Jonas Burnet, Richard Cusworth, Robert Cusworth, Isaac Cusworth, Mr Henry Rayner,[5] Geo: Bingley, James Swallow, Mr Walker, Robt Elam, Joseph Bever.

Normanton.

James Favel, Gent.[6] Chr[isto]fer Favel Gent.[7] Richd Redman[8] Gent: Richd Wadsworth Gent. John Crawshaw, Wm Crawshaw, James Simpson, Martin Burnill, Wm Walker, Henry Halstead, Wm Barke, George Fletcher, Henry Martin, John Sylvester Gen: Samuel Dobson, Charles Dolston Esq.[9] Robert Cusworth.

Osset.

Wm Oates Gent:[5] Fra: Marsden, Richd Fostard, Wm Hirst, Josias Hepworth, Thomas Gill, Mark Whittaker, John Speight, John Robinson, John Scholefield, Joseph Smithson, Josias Oates

1 *H.P.*, 154.
2 *ibid.*, 130.
3 *H.P.*, 85.
4 *H.F.M.G.*, III, 911.
5 *H.P.*, 118.
6 *C.D.*, III, 392.
7 *ibid.*
8 *ibid.*, II, 198.
9 *ibid.*, II, 325.

Gent:[1] John Whitley, Thomas Birkhead Gent, James Spurr, Joseph Spurr, John Illingworth, James White, Dr Davinson, Michael Parker, Charles Nettleton, Cl[erk], John Peace, Anthony Milner, Richard Hemingway, John Milner, Thomas Wilby, Robert Shaw, Gent.[2] James White of Lights, John Smith Gent: John Gupwell, Joseph Hirst, Samuel Land, Richard Fostard Jn^r, Joshua Haigh, John Scholefield, James Shepley, Joseph Haigh, Wm Harrop, Wm Midlebrook, Sr Geo: Savile Baron[e]t John Harrup.

Horbury.

Thomas Leek Gent:[3] John Rhodes Gent: Richard Norfolk Gent. John Wadsworth, Wm Dennison, James Haigh Cl[erk][4] Danl Sill[5] Cl[erk] — Holstead Cl[erk] Elkana Coop, Thomas Pashley, Willm Wormall, Thomas White, Joshua Bargh, Richard Wormall, Wm Issot, David Coop, Geo: Cockill, Danl Thornes, Tho: Craven, Geo: Bracebrige, James Sill Gent[6] Benjamin Coop, Tho: Good[a]ll John Stringer, Thomas Pearson, Richard Thornton Esq: Thomas Beatson, Wm Pollard, Thomas Cart[er], John Cawthorne, John Binnes, Benjamin Briggs, Wm Copend[all] Gen:[7] Samuel Wadsworth, Josias Peace, Joshua Coop, Mathew Geld[er] Ralfe Walker, Thomas Hunt, Wm Dawson.

Stanley.

Sr Lyon Pilkingto[n] Baron^t, Robert Benson Esq.[8] John Savile Esq Oswold Hatfield[9] Gen: Wm Heword Gen: Danl Mawd Gen: John Lumbe, John Wilkes, Robert Harrison, John Shaw, John Sugden, Thomas Denton, Mr John Clarkson Cl[erk] Robert Munckton Esq, David Law, Daniel Oley Gen:[10] Samuel Peaker, Tho: Smith, Joseph Armitage Gen: Robert Wood, Wm Copind^ll Gen: Geo. Burnill, Robert Watson Gen: John Smith Esq: Robert Shaw Gen: John Wood Gen: Theophilus Calverley Gen: Richard Smirthwaite,[11] Mr Henry Robinson Cl[erk] Tho: Burkhead Gen: Wm Horton Esq: Wm Fenay, Robt Glover, John Wilkinson Esq:[12] Jo: Rayner, Fr: Dixon, Benj: Benton, Willm̃ Lee, Tho: Gill Gen:

West Ardsley.

Roland Mitchill, Gen: Chr[ist]ofer Hodgson Gen: Henry Shaw, Gen: Richd Nettleton Gen: John Wilks, Israel Rhodes, John Robinson Gen: John Brooksbank Gen: Saml Bradley, Joshua Brook, John Robinson, James Naylor, John Speight, Thomas Roebuck Gen.[13]

Walton cum Bretton.

Charles Waterton Esq: Sr Wm Wentworth Baron^t,[14] Ralfe Ireland Esq: Tym[othy] Rayner, Tim: Hirst, John Goodaire,

[1] *C.D.*, I, 290.
[2] *ibid.*, 20.
[3] *ibid.*, 133.
[4] *ibid.*, *C.D.*, II, 133.
[5] *ibid.*, II, 159.
[6] *H.P.*, 130.
[7] *ibid.*, 148.
[8] *H.P.*, 146.
[9] *ibid.*, 93.
[10] *ibid.*, 130.
[11] *H.P.*, 130.
[12] *ibid.*, 45.
[13] *C.D.*, II, 176.
[14] *C.D.*, II, 131.

John Barker, Hugh Shillitoe, John Twigg, Joseph Sympson, Tim: Rhodes, Robert Fretwell.

Soothill

Robert Waterhous Gent: Josias Oates Gent: Tho: Hyleley, Charles Netleton Cl[erk] John Scholefield.

Dewsbury.

John Murgatroyd Gent: Thomas Webster, Wm Elmsall Gent: Joseph Oldroyd, Abm̃ Greenwood Senr, Michael Whitley, Wm Hall, Abram: Thornes, Michael Parker, George Shepley, John Richardson Cl[erk] John Turner Gent: Jer: Chadwick, Abrm̃ Firth, John Wheelwright Gent: Robert Lee, Abm Greenwood Jnr, Robert Holdsw[o]rth, James Shepley, George Castle, Samuel Chaister, Tymothy Wheatley, John Chaister, James Willans, John Knowles, Thomas Speight, Richard Whitley, Thomas Whitley.

Eccleshill.

— Stanhop Esq: Abrm: Nichols, Wm Swaine Gent: Edwd Swaine, Jeramia Sowden, Wm Sowdin, Josias Sowdin, Wm Hutton Senr, Wm Hutton Jnr, John Jowet, Wm Gaith, Wm Nichols, James Fletcher, George Barraclough, Zacra Rayner, Nathan Jowet, Jno Deane, Abrm: Barraclough, John Steel, Thomas Pearson, Wm Norton, Joseph Vickars.

Hallifax.

John Butterfield, Robert Butterfield, John Batley, Fra: Bentley, Saml Stead, John Hodgson, Nathan Feilding, John Holdroyd, Jessey Lodge, John Moore, Richard Newton, Wm Procktor, Joshua Marcer, Elias Robinson, Wm Chamberlain, Jonathan Stead, John Cock, Thomas Grice, John Prescot, John Wilkinson, James Sagar, Jer: Hook, Gent: Robert Whitehead, Joseph Hodgson, James Lister Gen:[1] John Dolive, John Mawd Gent: John Allenson Gent: — Antrobus Gent: John Bothomley Gent: Henry Dawson, — Benson Gent: Rid Baraclough Gent: Jno Baraclough Gent: Jno Barrat, Jno Bryercliff Gent: Gabriel Bentley, Wm Currer Gent: Wm Drake Esq: Joshua Dunn Gent: Joseph Drake, Henry Dryver, Tho: Darley Gent: John Driver, John Elam, Wm Ellis, Robt Parker Esq: John Fournes Gent: Dd Ryley, George Farrar, Dd Prescot, Dd Farrar, Richd Scarborough, Gent: Wm Hollingworth, George Hargraves, Nathanl Holden Gent: Timothy Hirst, Joseph Holdroyd Gent: George Holdroyd Gen: Jonathan Tattersall, Myles Walker, Jonathan Longbothom, Saml Lord — Murgatroyd Gent: Jno Manknowles, Jno Smith, Gent: Jno Nalson, Jno Milns, George Noble, Jonathan Oldfield, John Pool, Bart[holmew] Wooler, Wm Scott, — Preistley Gent: Henry Ramsden, Gent: John Savile Esq: Joshua Sugden,

[1] *C.D.*, I, 117.

John Stell, Wm Thomson, John Wadsworth, John Woodhead, Richard Wade, Jonathan Windle, Mr Heald cl[erk] Mr Wilkinson Cl[erk] Vicr of Hallifax, John Waterhous, Richard Walker, John Hillas, Rot Barraclough, Gen: Joseph Philips, Richard Ramsden Gen: Thomas Rigg.

Sowerby.

John Greenwood, Tho: Sunderland, Josia Normanton, Wm Greenwood Senr, Thomas Swaine, Wm Normanton, James Stansfield, Josias Stansfield, Jeremia Ryley, John Dickson, John Walker, Mathew Wadsworth, Michl Sydall, Jeremia Crosley, Richd Firth Gent: Richd Holdroid, Elkana Hoyl, Gent: John Gawkroger, John Ryley, James Ryley, John Crosley, John Sutcliff, Wm Sutcliff, Nathan Whiteley, James Hill, Symeon Crosley, Israel Wilde, John Normanton, Joshua Horton Esq: Saml Stansfield, John Cockcroft Gent: Henry Cockcroft Gent: Richard Stearne Esq: Wm Horton Esq: Thomas Dobson Gent: John Patchet, John Dearden Gent: James Ogden, Geo: Clegg, John Wheelwright Gent: John Hoyl, John Kenworthy, John Preistley, Richard Dearden, Jonathan Hanson, Thomas Townley, — Bradshaw Gent: Henry Feilding, Willm Leigh Esq: Michael Crosley, Elkana Horton Gent: Abrm Firth, Michael Firth Gent: John Whiteley, Joseph Clapham, Toby Ryley, Thomas Mitton, Samuel Hill, Henry Whitworth, Richard Royd, John Shaw, Robert Hatfield.

Skircoat.

Richard Sterne Esq: Edwd Wainhous Gent: Richard Towne, Henry Gream, James Greame, Wm Kitchingman, Wm Dean, John Wainhous, Robert Barraclough, John Waterhous, John Coggill, Joseph Godley, Joseph Wood, Tho: Rigg Gent: Joshua Laycock, Richd Ramsden, Michl Wainhous.

Ovenden.

John Fournes Gent:[1] John Wilkinson, Robert Barstow, Joseph Fournes Gent.[2] James Ryley, Thomas York Esq: John Wadsworth, Mathew Smith, Nathaniel Preistley, Thomas Ibotson, Thomas Rigg, Thomas Oldfield, John Stott, John Marsden, Luke Hoyle, Willm Illingworth, James Dodson, Saml Tasker.

Warley.

John Murgatroyd Gent: Benj: Wade, Robert Brigg, John Dearden Gent: Anth[ony] Waller, John Trueman, John Farrer, Geo: Oldfield, Richard Tattersall, Wm Murgatroyd, John Greenwood, Thomas Barker, Thomas Longbothom, John Midgley, John Cockcroft Gen: Paul Greenwood, Joseph Holme John Brooksbanck, Thomas Oldfield, Robert Towne, Richard Smith, John Wadsworth, John Bryercliff, John Crosley Gent: Wm Blaimires, John Beanland, Ambrose Patchit, Robert Midgley, Josias Stansfield, Joshua

[1] *H.F.M.G.*, I, 93. [2] *ibid.*

Farrar, David Greenwood, John Walker, Thomas Midgley, Wm Leigh Esq: John Brear, Willm Hollingworth, John Wainhous, Isaac Farrar, Joseph Nichalson, Anthony Naylor, John Patchit, Eleazar Tetlow, Nathaniel Murgatroyd, Willm Murgatroyd, Edmund Tattersall, John Riley, Arthur Maud, Jeremia Ryley, Henry Butterfield, James Murgatroyd.

Wadsworth.

Henry Cockcroft Gent:[1] Wm Cockcroft Gent:[2] Tho: Cockcroft Gent: Tho: Lister, David Brigg, Joseph Sutcliffe, Jonas Shakleton, Symeon Redmon, John Greenwood, Wm Sutcliffe, Paul Hoyle, John Cockcroft, Jno Eastwood, Wm Midgley Gen: James Greenwood, Ralph Bryerley, Paul Greenwood, Abr^m^ Sunderland, John Horsfall, John Redmon, Josias Hoyle, Wm Hellewel, Wm Hanson, John Kay, John Ingham, Richard Thomas, — King Gent: Mich[ael] Crosley, Jno Pickles, Symeon Buckley, Saml Tilson, John Townend, Robt Thomas Abr^m^ Wood, Jno Longbothom, Abr^m^ Eastwood, Ambrose Greenwood.

Midgley.

James Farrer Esq: John Crosley Gent: Richard Midgley, John Lockwood, James Murgatroyd, Edwd Sutcliffe, Jonas Turner, Henry Hellewell, Thomas Sydall, Henry Plurett, Wm Shakleton, Jonathan Brigg, Wm Lockwood, Jonas Beardsall, Wm Brigg, Timothy Allenson, Robert Wade, Henry Keighley, John Wainhouse, John Murgatroyd, Joseph Sunderland, Richard Sterne Esq: Richard Patchit, Joshu Laycock.

Rushworth cu[m] Norland.

John Smith, Richard Tayler, Benj Holdroyd Senr, Saml Lassy, Benj Holdroyd Junr, Samuel Gawkrojer, Henry Dyson, John Godley, Jno Dyson, Jno Haigh, Jno Nortcliff, Henry Ramsden, Henry Scholefield, James Whiteley, John Whiteley, Henry Wilson, Joseph Ramsden, Saml Crowther, Gabriel Bentley, Mich[ae]l Bentley, Henry Clay, Daniel Hoyle, Mich^l^ Bates, Isaac Bates, John Taylor Gen: Henry Barrow, Nathan Carter, Nathan^l^ Chadwick, Charles Clay, James Berry, Josias Stansfield, Isaac Holdroyd, Abrm Read, Robert Towne, Wm Brooksbank.

Stansfield.

Wm Sutcliff Gent:[3] Edm^d^ Barker, Richard Naylor, Richard Scholefield, James Gibson, John Horsfall, Richd Gibson, James Mitchel, Luke Townend, John Horsfall Junr, Edm^d^ Ashworth, Mich^l^ Bentley, Henry Banister, Tho: Barker, Ab^r^m Clegg, Anthony Crosley, John Stansfield, James Crabtree, James Clayton, Adam Holden, Amos Eastwood, John Eastwood, Richd Sutcliff, Wm Shackleton, James Stansfield, Gen: Richard Naylor, Richard Stansfield, John Sutcliffe, Henry Sagar, John Sagar, John Booth,

[1] *H.F.M.G.*, II, 543. [2] *ibid.*, 541. [3] *H.F.M.G.*, II, 541.

Edm^{d} Stansfield, Jno Greenwood, Richard Thomas, John Thomas, Wm Foster, Richard Wadsworth, Jno Hitch, Paul Middop, Jno Lord, James Gibson, Richard Gibson, Henry Walton, Richard Eastwood, Lawrence Ashworth, Richard Mason, Jno Speake, Lawrence Ashworth, Wm Barker, Jno Holden.

Langfield.

John Law Gent: John Vtley, John Gibson, John Sutcliff, Henry Cockcroft Gent: Wm Sutcliffe, John Normanton, Wm Sunderland, Symion Crosley.

Heptonstall.

Wm Mitchill, Henry Mitchill, Thomas Greenwood, Thomas Greenwood Junr, Henry Cockcroft Gent: James Ogden, John Sugden, John Greenwood, John Sutcliffe, Thomas Bentley, James Bentley, Richard Crabtree, Wm Sutcliffe, Symeon Crabtree, Wm Cockcroft Gent: Richard Thomas, Joseph Sutcliffe, Mich^{l} Eastwood, Richard Ramsden, Paul Greenwood, Thomas Greenwood, Jno Nowel, Richard Horsfall, John Halstead, Wm Hutley, Robert Halstead, Jno: Kendall, Josias Hoyle, Luke Horsfall, Wm Pilling, John Shackleton, James Rawson, Jno Chapman, Thomas Shackleton, Simeon Townend, Richard Wadsworth, Nathan^{l} Sutcliff.

Erringden.

Wm Sutcliffe, Robert Sutcliffe, Thomas Pilling, Henry Sunderland, John Greenwood, Jonathan Greenwood, Chr[ist]ofer Thomas, Ely Crosley, Isaac Farrar — Bradshaw Esqꝫ: Robert Halstead, George Halstead, John Sutcliff, John Walker, Wiłłm Thomas, Richard Halstead, Richard Thomas, John Greenwood, Henry Cawcroft Gent: Wm Cawcroft Gent: John Cawcroft Gen: Richard Naylor, Jonathan Greenwood.

Hip[per]holme cum Brighous.

Edwd Langley Gent: Wm Walker Gent: Wm Walker Junr, John Green Gen: John Bedford Gen: Michael Gibson Gent: Edwd Gibson, Jonathan Preistley, John Wright, James Tetlow, Henry Gill, Joseph Holmes, John Hanson, John Sharp, Saml: Rudlesden, Tho: Kitson, Eleazar Tetlow, John Simpson, John Nichols, John Barraclough, Nathan Whitley, Richard Walker.

Rastrick.

John Nichols, Henry Haigh, Thomas Pollard, John Murgatroyd Gent: Robert Laycock Cl[erk]

Fixby.

Thomas Thornhill Esq. John Wilkinson Esqꝫ

Northowrom.

Joseph Crowther Gent: Abrm Hall Gent: Joseph Wood Gent: Christofer Dade Gent: Thomas Holdsworth Gent: John Preistley,

Jeremia Baxter, Robt: Northend, John Clay, James Lister Gent: Robert Ramsden Gent: Wm Drake Esq: John Bryercliff Gent: Michael Woodhead, Miles Ingham, Jeramia Brigg Gent: John Barke, John Wildman, John Fournes Gen: John Staincliffe.

Shelfe.

John Sugden, Tho: Poole, Saml Bentley, Thomas Swaine Gen: John Burnley Gen: John Smith Gent: Mr Clifford, Cl[erk], Samuel Starkey, William Walker Gen: Richard Walker, Gent: Samuel Wade, Mr Ellison Cl[erk] Will[ia]m Hird, Wm Horton Esq: Jno: Apleyard, Jno Best, Michl Best, — Law Gen: John Rookes Esq Abrm: Lumbe, Edwd Slater, — Sunderland Gent: Jer[emiah] Rosendall, Mathw Thorpe, Nathan Whiteley, Joseph Crofftes.

Quarmby.

John Dyson Senr, Wm Dyson, Jno Dyson Jun: Wm Dawson, John Haigh, John Haigh Junr, Isaac Holdroid, Geo: Woodhead, Jeremia Walton, Joseph Bothomley, Wm Ratcliff Gent: — Roe Gent: Thomas Wilkinson Gent: John Bothomley, James Dyson: — Haigh, Thomas Gleadhill, Edwd Lee, Abr[aha]m Lockwood, Hugh Ramsden, John Walker, Rich: Thornton Esq: Jo: Whitwham, Wm Ainley, Thomas France.

Dalton.

John Wilkinson Esq: John Longley Gent: Richd Beaumont Esq:[1] Sir Wm Ramsden Baront[2] Chr[isto]fer Shaw, Gent: Richd Beaumont, Joseph Thewlis, Richd Hepworth, John Horsfall,[3] Wm Horsfall, Thomas Horsfall, Thomas Walker, Jos: Eastwood, Wm Ratcliff Gen: — Armitage Gent: Thomas Darley Gent: George Hirst, Thomas Slack, — Reyner, Wm Brookesbanck, Thomas Bray, Michl Blackburn, Mathew Hirst.

Hartchstead.

Sr John Armitage Baronet.

Stainland.

Thomas Hanson, Thomas Denton, George Fairburne, Henry Crowther, Jno Cooper, Wm Denton, Jno Denton, James Dyson, Jno Holdroyd, Edwd Hellewell, Richard Denton, Martin Gleadhill, George Hey, James Hirst, James Haigh, Tho: Hellewell, John Garthside, Jno Mawde, John Moore, Joseph Preistley, Thomas Preistley, Henry Ramsden Gent: Danl Meller, John Meller, Richard Whiteley, Jefferey Ramsden, Edmd Townend, Randolfe Whiteley, James Gleadhill, Edwd Jackson, — Wilman Gent:

Barkisland.

Wm Horton Esq Mich Firth Gent: Isaac Holdroyd, John Ramsden, Geo: Holdroyd, John Firth, Thomas Taylor, Moses Foxcroft, Jno Dean Gent: Isaac Whiteley, Jno Gleadhill, Richd Musgrave Esq:

[1] *C.D.*, III, 224. [2] *ibid.*, I, 86. [3] *ibid.*, II, 204.

Kirkburton.

Geo: Kay Esq, Geo: Roebuck, Martin Wimpenny, Joseph Briggs Cl[erk], Robt Fitton.

Shelley.

— Kirshaw D, Wm Ratcliff Gen: Edwd Senier, Thomas Coldwell, Tedbur Wallis, George Green, Caleb Roebuck, John Roebuck, James Moxon.

Cumberworth.

Sir Wm Wentworth Baronet, Edwd Kenyon, Joseph Firth, John Coldwell, Joshua Shawe, Richard Hutchinson, Godfrey Horne, Abrm: Hepworth, Joseph Oxley, Wm Green, Jno Ritch.

Shepley.

Richard Mathewman, John Firth, John Archer.

Flockton.

Sir Wm Wentworth Bart, George Kay Esq: Sr Arthur Kay Baront,[1] John Rhodes Gent: Joseph Senier, Thomas Brook, John Brook Gent:

Emley.

Sr Geo: Savile Baront, Thomas Wheatley Gent:[2] John Allot Gent:[3] Richard Wilkinson, — Allot, Geo: Parker, Mathew Marshall, Richard Blacker, Wm Feild, Jno Walshaw, Martin Hepworth, — Robinson Gent: Tho: Holden, John Wilkinson, Richard Wilkinson Junr

Thurstonland.

Wm Horsfall Gent: John Lockwood Gent: Joshua Newton, John Newton.

Holmefirth.

Jonas Kay Gent: James Earnshaw Gent: Godfrey Crosland, Luke Wilson, Henry Jackson, John Newton, John Tinker, Philip Bray, John Green, Christofer Green, Robert France, Danl Broadhead, James Hinchliff, Henry Jackson Junr, David Dickson, Jno Roebuck, Richard Crosland, Thomas Cuttill, John Haigh, Geo: Moorhous, John Wilson, John Tyas, Philip Earnshaw, John Green, Jon Tyas of Sleadbrook, Abrm̃ Wood, John Garlick Cl[erk], Abrm: Firth, Humphrey Roebuck, John Mathewman, Richard Morton, Tho: Derby Gent: Samuel Wagstaff Gent: Abrm: Ratcliff Gen: Thomas Booth, John Roberts, John Creswick.

N.B. By a reasonable computation above 1000d men have out of the Mannor of Wakefield Votes for the Election of The Knights of the County.

[1] *C.D.*, I, 78.
[2] *H.F.M.G.*, II, 599.
[3] *C.D.*, II, 56.

FREEHOLDERS TO BE ADDED W[HI]CH ARE SINCE FOUND TO BE OMITTED AS FOLLOW:

To West Ardsley.

John Harrison, John Boyle, Timothy Kitson, Joseph Dawson, Timothy Raynor, Henry Weightman, William Westerman, Dan[l] Glover, John Scott, John Harrison, W[m] Harrison, John Nelson, James Hudson, John Barker, Robert Shaw Gen: Peter Robinson, — Watson, — Brooksbanck Gent:

To Horbury.

W[m] Craven, John Haigh, Geo: Cockill, W[m] Carr, John Hunt, John Walker, Jer[emy] Serg[ean]t, Sam[l] Wadsworth Ju[r], Temp[est] Pollard, Francis Rhodes, Francis Blacker, W[m] Sunderland, Jo: Thornes, Tho: Wood, Robt: Thornes, W[m] Thornes, Nathan[l] Hunt, W[m] Pollard Ju[r], John Dickson.

To Dewsbury.

John Nettleton, Gent: W[m] Turner Gent: John Ashley, Tho: Hemingway, Sam[l] Beckit, Joseph Auty, Simeon Buckler, Joseph Jepson, John Ellis, Joshua Ellis, Tho: Chaister, Geo: Chaister, Martin Willans, Joseph Thornes, Abrm: Hemingway.

Hartchstead cum Clifton.

Abr: Horsley, Richard Poplewel, Jn[o] Clapham, Jonathan Wilby, W[m] Childe, Jonas Drake.

ROYALTIES, PROPERTIES & CUSTOMES OF THE WHOLE MANNOR OF WAKEFIELD IN GENERALL

The Mannor of Wakefield hath within it all the officers in Common process of a County. The Sheriff of the County of Yorke wherein it lyes, nor his officers have any authority to infringe it except in Criminall Cases. The Lord of the Mannor hath all the charge on him as a Sheriff. He Deputes a Retur[na] Breviu[m]. The Bayliffs in the severall divisions of the Mannor & a Geoler to Receive the Prisoners, he keeping a Geole for that purpose within the Mannor. Also by the Patent of this Mannor noe inferior process ought to be executed within it from the County Court but (excepting The Inferior Mannors within themselves) all inferior process sho'd be only issued out of the Courts kept for The Lord of the Mannor.

All Treasure Trove, Deodands, Felones Goods, The Goods of all Outlaw'd Persons & the Goods of Felo's de se throughout the whole Mannor belong the Lord thereof And all Waifs & Estrays except in some Feew Inferior Mannors who hold them by Patent or Prescription. And the Lord of the Mannor hath Free Warren throughout the whole Mannor.

There are noe Demesne Lands nor Messuages now ap[per]taining to the Mannor being all granted off since the Mannor was in the possession of the Earl Warrens, save the Moot Hall & Common Bakehous in Wakefield. But there are some small quantities of Land which have been forfeited from such as have been convicted of Capital Crimes, and some feow Intacks off the Commons & Wast Grounds. All which shall be spoke off in their places.

All the forementioned Lords of the Inferior Mannors doe hold of the cheif Lord of the Mannor and they & severall other Freeholders doe pay Cheif rents which are called Earles Rents suposed from the Earl Warrens And which is to be noted that these Rents have been always lett w[it]h the Baylywicks & collected by the Four Bayliffs. Though there are a great many other Free rents collected by the Graves which are the Officers for the Collecting of the Copyhold Rents, with last mentioned Free rents The Lands they issue out of doe all Offices as Copyhold Lands doe which makes a traditionall account among the Tennants that whilst the Copyhold Lands were all at the will of The Lord and long before the Composition grant & Dicree to make the Fines certain did these later Freeholders compound with the Crowne (in whose hands the Mannor then was) to infranchise their Copyholds that they might thereby be freed from such arbitrary Fines and bare Tenure as was in those days. Yet covenanted that their Lands should continue to serve the office of Grave in their turne as when Copyhold. This Covenant is not found in among the Records yet by all the Customs of the Graves collecting those Rents among the Copyhold Rents hitherto seems likely that it was soe.

There are in this Mannor about 1400[d] Copiehold Tennants the most of which by a Dicree out of the Dutchy Court & another out of the Exchequer Court in the 7th Year of King James the 1st inrolled in the Court Rolls of the Mannor of Wakefield compounded & gave 35 years the Lord Rent purchase to make their Fines certain Severall have since & the rest are at the will of the Lord.

The Compounded Lands pay at every alianation or death Three years Lords Rent, Every Rent Charge or Annuitie one Penny at the Shilling Every Lease for a Terme of years, a Year and a half Lords rent as also for Life or the grant of a Reversion as by the Dicree here at large taken out of the Roll of the 9[o] King James the 1[st] is set downe.

A COPY OF THE COMPOSITION DICREE OUT OF THE DUTCHY COURT RECORDED IN THE WAKEFIELD ROLLS 9[o] K. JAMES 1[st]—19[o] JULY.

Ad hanc cur[iam] vener[unt] Thomas Pilkington ar[miger] Will[iel]mus Ramsden ar[miger] Henricus Grice ar[miger]

Ric[ard]us Sunderland gen[erosus] Georgius Ratcliffe gen[erosus] Joh[ann]es Hanson de Woodhous Henricus Preistley de Baytings Joh[ann]es Batty Joh[ann]es Mawd Philemon Speight Rogerus Audsley et Joh[ann]es Firth de Firthhous customarij Tenentes D[omi]ni Regis in sepa[ara]lib[us] prepo[s]ituris p[ar]cell[is] manerii p[re]d[icti] coram Joh[ann]e Savile et Ed[ward]o Cary Militib[us] capitalib[us] senes[ca]llis d[i]cti D[omi]ni Regis manerii sive d[omi]nii sui de Wakefeld et petier[unt] tam p[ro] seipsis quam pro o[mni]b[us] al[ii]s tenent[i]b[us] ejusdem manerij; quod duo Decreta un[um] sub sigillo Ducatus Lancastr[iae] et alterum sub sigillo Sc[accari]i unacu[m] sep[ara] l[i]b[us] rentallibus sive Schedulis p[re]d[icto] decreto dicti Ducat[us] Lancastr[iae] annexat[is] s[e]c[un]d[u]m tenor[em] ejusd[e]m decreti irrotularentur et recorderent[ur] hic in Rot[u]lis Cur[iæ] manerij p[re]d[icti] ad ist[a]m eand[e]m Cur[iam] Que o[mn]ia ad instancia[m] et requisicionem predictorum tenentiu[m] sup[er]ius no[m]i[n]at[orum] et s[e]c[un]d[u]m tenorem predicti decreti irrotulari fecimus p[ro]ut sequitur videl[ice]t.

Jacobus Dei gra[tia] Anglie Scotie Francie et Hib[er]nie Rex Fidei Defensor Etc Omnibus ad quos p[re]sentes l[ite]ras nostras p[er]venerint Sal[u]t[e]m Inspeximus tenorem cujusdam decret[i] in Camera Ducat[us] Lancast[riae] apud Westm[o]nasterium inter record[a] ejusd[e]m Ducat[us] ib[ide]m remanen[tia] et Existen[tia] in hec verba **Whereas** S[r] John Brograve Knt His Maj[es]ties Attorney Generall of the Dutchy of Lancaster hath exhibited an Information into this Court against Diverse Copyholders and Tenn[an]ts of his Maj[es]ties Mannor or Lordship of Wakefield in the County of Yorke which are hereafter p[ar]ticularly named videlicet ("NB for Brevity sake I omitt Copieing out the names of all The Copieholders in every Graveship which are p[ar]ticularly set downe in the Decree only that it was against 57 in Wakefield. 71 in Stanley, 55 in Alverthorp, 50 in Thornes. 91 in Sandall, 71 in Horbury. 93 in Osset, 274 in Sowerby, 119 in Hi[pper]holme, 74 in Holmfirth, 12 in Scamonden, & 15 in Rastrick)" **By which** Information his Maj[es]tie said Attorney hath alleaged that whereas The Kings highness is and ever since the begining of his Raign of his Realm of England and his most Noble Progenitors for a long time have been lawfully seized in his and their Demesne as of Fee respectively of the mannor or Lordship of Wakefield in the County of York being annexed unto the Dutchy of Lancaster and within the Rule Order & Jurisdiction & Survey thereof whith in the precincts of which Mannor or Lordship The Graveships of Wakefield Stanley, Alverthorp Thornes Sandall, Horbury, Osset, Sowerby, Hip[per]holme, Holmfirth, Scamonden, & Rastrick being members and parcells of the said Mannor or Lordship are & doe lye & the greatest p[ar]te of all the Lands Tenem[en]ts & hereditam[en]ts lyeing & extending in or into the said Mannor or Lordship and severall Graveships are and by all the time whereof the mamory of man is not to the contrary have bene Copyhold Lands p[ar]cell of the said Mannor or Lordship & demysed or demysable by Copy of Court Roll of the said Mannor or Lordship to any p[er]son or p[er]sons willing to take the same in Fee Simple or Fee Tail or for Term of life or lifes at the will of the Lord of the said Mannor or Lordship for the time being according to the Custome of the said Mannor or Lordship at and for the Fines uncertain & arbitrable at the will of the Lord for the time being or his Steward thereof to be paid to the Lord of the said Mannor or Lordship for the time being for & upon every grant & admittance of & unto the said Copyhold premises & every p[ar]te thereof And showing further that the Copieholders of the said Mannor or Lordship have by all the time whereof the memory of man is not to the contrary used & accustomed att and in the Court of the said Mannor or Lordship by way of Surrender to grant Rents out of their Copyhold Tennements to any person or persons whatsoever with power to distrain for the same rents in & upon such Lands & Tenements charged with the same Rents for & upon every which Grant soe made The Lord of the said Mannor or Lordship for the time being hath used to have & ought to have such a Sum of money for and in the name of a Fine for his assent to the same grant as hath been assessed & taxed by the said Lord or his Steward of the said Mannor or Lordship for the time being which Fines or Summes of money being soe arbitrable and uncertain as is aforesaid have been heretofore a great yearly revenue to the said Kings maj[es]tie & his most noble Progenitors Lords of The said Mannor or Lordship And further alleaging by the said information that the Def[endan]ts have combined & confederated together to defrawd the Kings Maj[es]tie of his said Fines and to that end the same Def[endan]ts did pr[e]tend & give out that by the custome of the said mannor the said Fines were not arbitrable or uncertain but were and ought to be certain vid[elice]t: For and upon every admittance by Surr[ender] or discent to any Estate of inheritance in possession according to the custome of the said Mannor or Lordship one years rent & an half according to the Rents paid to his Maj[es]tie for the Lands & Tenements whereunto the same Admittance is made and for a Messuage without any Lands Fourpence & for a Cottage without Lands Twopence and for & upon every such grant of Rent as is afores[ai]d twenty pence for every Twenty Shillings rent soe granted & soe according to the rate for a greater or lesser Sum[m]e, and for and upon every admittance to any estate for life lives or years in possession or reversion or to any estates of inheritance in Reversion depending upon such p[ar]ticular Estates half soe much as is before mentioned and pretended to be paid for and upon the said admittances to Estates of Inheritance in possession And for & upon admittances thereupon after Seisors accustomed there to be made for bettring of assurances three years rent according to the rents paid to his Majestie for the

Lands & Tenements whereunto the said admittances upon seisures are made or at leastwise not to exceed the rates aforesaid and that the Lord of the said Mannor or Lordship or his Steward for the time being ought to admitt every person to whome any of the said Copyhold premises sho[ul]d or did discend or come by discent Surrender or otherwise or which should give or comitt caus of Seisure for betring of assurances or to whome any such grant of Rent should be made as is aforesaid at and for such certain Fine & Rate as is last before mentioned, Showing further that although the said pretended Customs were very faign'd and untrue yet the said Copyholders did labour & endeavour by all means possibly to make good & strengthen the same and wold doubtless in short time give & procure great countenance & allowance unto the said pretended Customs as wel for presentmnts to be thereof made in the Court of the said Mannor or Lordship by the Copieholders thereof as also by the Connivency of the under Stewards and other inferior Officers of the said Mannor or Lordship unless they were prevented in their said Courses by some order to be therein taken by this Court And showing further that there were divers parts of the Wastes of the said Mannor or Lordship which were Demesnes of the same Mannor or Lordship and had not been demised or demiseable by Coppie of Court Roll of the said Mannor or Lordship untill of late that some part thereof by Commission & some part thereof by the Stewards of the said Mannor or Lordship with[ou]t warr[an]t had bene incroched improved & rented & demised by Copy yet Divers of the said Defendants had unlawfully entred & intruded into the said Waste grownds soe incroached or improved & had procured divers grants by copy of Court Roll of the said Mannor or Lordship to be made unto them thereof as if the same were or had been ancient Copyhold or customary Lands Ten[emen]ts & hereditaments & that by pretence thereof the same Defend[an]ts had taken & received the issues & profits of the said Waste grownds soe improved or incroched without any good Right or title soe to doe and did make like pretence & claime for the certainty of the Fines of and for grants & admittances made of the said Waste grownds so rented demised & improved or incroched as is before mentioned to be by them made for and concerning the fore[sai]d grantes & Admittances of and unto the aforesaid ancient Copyhold Lands Tenm[en]ts & hereditam[en]ts wherein his Highnes said Attorney praid the advice of this Court and due remydie in the premises as in and by the said Information more at large apeareth **To which** said information the said Def[endan]ts apeared & made their answers & thereby did confes that his Maj[es]tie was & is as they veryly think lawfully seised in his Demesne as of Fee in Right of his Highness Dutchie of Lancaster of and in the Mannor or Lordship of Wakefield in the Information mentioned & that the said Graveships were within the precincts of the said Lordship or Mannor & members & parcells thereof and that a great part of the Lands Ten[e]m[en]ts & hereditm[en]ts in the said Mannor or Lordship & severall Graveships are & by all the time whereof the memory of man is not to the contrary have been Copyhold Lands p[ar]cell of the said mannor or Lordship and demised & demiseable by Copy of Court Roll of the said Mannor or Lordship according to the Custome of the said Mannor in Fee simple or in Fee Tail or otherwise and that the Copyholders of the said mannor or Lordship had by all the time whereof the memory of man is not to the contrary used & accustomed at & in the Court of the said mannor or Lordship by way of surrender to grant Rents out of their Copyhold Tenements to any p[er]son or p[er]sons w[ha]tsoever with power to distraine for the same Rents in & upon the Lands & Ten[emen]ts charged with the same Rents and did aleage further that they the said Defendants did severally & respectively hold some of them in fee simple & some in Tail with Remainders over by Copy of Court Roll according to the Custome of the said Mannor divers of the said Copyhold Lands Tenements & hereditments parcell of the said Mannor or Lordship of our said soveraign Lord the Kings majestie paying & doeing therefore dyvers severall rents Customes & charges & services to his Majestie & that they did take it that the Fines to be paid & upon every Grant & admittance of & unto the said Copyhold Lands Ten[emen]ts hereditm[en]ts and Rents was not uncertanie and arbitrary at the will & pleasure of The Lord of the said mannor or Lordship for the time being or his Steward thereof as in and by the said Information is supposed but certain & had bene usually assessed & taxed as followeth That is to say for and upon every admittance or discent to any estate of inheritance in possession according to the Custom of the said mannor or Lordship one years rent & a half according to the Rent paid to his Maj[es]tie for the lands & Tenm[en]ts whereunto the same admittance is or hath bene made and for a messuage without any Lands Fourpence and for a Cottage without Lands Twopence And for & upon every such grant of Rents as is aforesaid Twenty pence for every Twenty shilling rent soe granted and soe according to that rate of and for a greater or lesser Som[m]e & for & upon every admittance to any Estate for life or lives or years in possession or Reversion or to any estate of inheritance in Reversion depending upon such particular estates half soe much as is before mentioned to be paid for and upon the said admittances to estates of inheritance in possession And for any upon admittancis after seisures according to the custome usually there made for betring of assurances three years Rent according to the Rent paid to his Majestie for the Lands and Tenements whereunto the same admittance upon seisure are or have been made or at lestwise had not exceeded the Rates aforesaid and the said Def[endan]ts by their said answers did further say that they did take it to be true that divers p[ar]cells of the waste grownds of the said mannor or Lordship had bene at divers severall times by virtue of divers severall Commissions & by other Lawfull Attorneys and meanes inclosed and improved for the greater p[ro]fitt & benefit of our said Soveraign Lord and his most Noble Progenitors Lords of the said Mannor or Lordship which said p[ar]cell of Wastes after such improve[men]ts as is aforesaid had been granted & demised by Copy of Court Roll of the said Mannor or Lordship for certain yearly Rents Customs & Services and for such Estates and in such manner and forme as the said ancient Copyhold premises had bene used to be granted And the said p[ar]cells of wast soe being granted by Copy as is aforesaid had passed by way of Surr[ender] & discente & otherwise in such maner & forme to all intents & purposes as the said ancient Copyhold premises had passed And that his Majestie and his Noble Progenitors lords of the said Mannor or Lordship had bene duly answered of such like Fines and Sums of money in every Decree for and upon all and every the grants admitt[an]ces and charges of the said improved premises as they had been answer'd for the said ancient Copyhold premises And the said Def[endan]ts did further aleage by their said answers that divers of them the said Def[endan]ts did severally hold divers p[ar]cells of the said wasts soe improved and granted by copies as is aforesaid and that they and their Ancestors & those whose estates they had therein had bestowed & disbursed great Sum̄s of money as wel in takeing and purchaseing the said improved premises as also in building thereupon and hedgeing & fenceing the same In consideration of all which premises the said Def[endan]ts did humbly pray by their said answers that the said severall Lands Rents & hereditam[en]ts heretofore p[ar]cell of the said waste & holden by them the said Def[endan]ts or any of them by virtue or pretence of any grant or grants by Copy of Court Roll of the said mannor or of any Surr[ende]r made according to the custom of the said Mannor and then or theretofore in the severall tenures or occupations of the said Def[endan]ts or any of them or of their or any of their ancestors or of any other by from or under whome they or any of them had or claimed or p[re]tended to have the same or any of the same as Copyhold[e]rs of said mannor or Lordship might be by his Maj[es]tie most gracious consideration of the premises & com[m]iseration of the pore Estate of soe great a number of this most humble faithfull & obedient subjects the Def[endan]ts & Copyholders thereof and of their wifes & children families & posterities and by the favour of this Hon[ora]ble Court Judicially & finally declared & decreed in & by this Hon[ora]ble Court to be and have bene and soe for ever hereafter to continue Copyhold Lands Ten[emen]ts and Hereditments lawfully demised & demiseable by Copy of Court Roll according to the Custome of the said Mannor or Lordship upon such said certain severall and annuall yearly rents and for and upon such Fines and for every of the same soe demised or demiseable premises upon every such grant admittance &

charge as is before mentioned to be paid for the same or such other reasonable fines as shold be thought meet to this Hon[ora]ble Court And also that such certain Fines for and upon all grants admittances & charges of the said ancient copyhold premises might be set downe and decreed by this honorable Court to be thereafter paid for the same as had bene paid for the same or as this hon'ble Court shold think meet & convenient or otherwise that the said Defendants might be excused by the favor of this honorable Court & without any offence to the same to p[re]fer a Petition for and upon the behalfe of themselves their wifes children & families to ye Kings most excellent Maj[es]tie thereby to p[ro]cure some signification of his Majesties gracious pleasure for the further confirmation assurance & continuance as which of the said certainty of Fines as also of all and every such devises & grants as at anytime theretofore had bene or at anytime thereafter sho'd be had or made for or concerning the said improved premises or any p[ar]te or p[ar]cell thereof and upon such signification had or made that then the same to be finally & Judicially decreed in & by this Hon[ora]ble Court as in & by the said Answers more at large appeareth **After** w[h]ich answers soe made the said Def[endan]ts preferrd their humble Petition to the Kings most Excellent maj[es]tie setting forth thereby in effect all the said matters conteyned in their said answers and that their Estates & customs were likely to be impeached as wel by the said Information as also by one other like Information exhibited against The Def[endan]ts in his Maj[es]ties Court of Exchequer and therefore most humbly praying that his Maj[es]tie wo'd be pleased to give Warrant as wel to ye Lord Treasurer of England and the Chancellor of his Maj[es]ties said Court of Exchequer & the Lord Cheif Baron & other Barons of the same Court as also unto his Highness Chancelor and Counsel of this Court as wel for the inabling, continuance and confirmation of the said Estates by Copy of Court Roll of the said p[ar]cell of Wast for ever to be and continue and soe to be accepted and injoyed by the Petitioners & their heirs and assigns as Copyhold Lands in the same sort nature & qualitie as the same ancient Copyhold Lands of ye said Mannor are according to the custom of the said Mannor at and for the usuall yearly Rents service & customs now paid & done for the same as also for the Establishing of such a certainty of and for the aforesaid Fines to be paid to his Highness his heirs & Successors for and upon every such Grant and admittance of and unto any of the said Copyhold Messuages Lands Tenem[en]ts Rents & Wasts so improved as are before mentioned as by this Court and the said Court of Exchequer sho'd be respectively thought meet and that the same might be soe ordered and Decreed by the severall Decrees of the same Court with such reasonable & convenient lib[er]ties and in such maner and forme as to the same Courts shold seme convenient & to grant his Maj[es]ties Royale assent for the passing of an Act of

Parliament for the full & p[er]fect confirmation and corroboration of the said Decrees and also for the full & absolute establishing and assurance as well for the said Copyhold estates of and in the said Messuages Lands Tenments Rents and p[ar]cells of Wast as also for the said certainty of the Fines In most humble & due Consideration whereof and in most loyall a[u]gm[entat]ion & declaration of their due gratitude for the same The said Petitioners did not only humblie tender & present to his Highness so much money as should amount to Thirty five years rent of all the Rents by them paid to his Maj[es]tie for the premises to be paid to his Highness at such days as by the said Lord Treasurer & Chancellor of this Court sho[ul]d be set downe but also did most humbly offer that from thenceforth they & their heirs & assignes for ever should & would pay to his maj[es]tie his Heirs & Successors the severall Fines hereafter mentioned upon their severall Admittances (That is to say) upon admittance of every Copyhold[e]r by discent & also upon Surrenders of Estates of Inheritance in possession & upon Seisures there used for betring of assurances for all messuages with Lands all Cottages with Lands all mills be the Fulling mills or Corne mills & all Lands w[ha]tsoever and Courses of water three years Rent according to the Copyhold Rents now paid to his Highness for the same, For a mess[uage] without Lands Eightpence & for a Cottage without Lands Fourpence and also for every rent charge that shold be granted by Surrender by any Copyholder Twenty pence in the Pound & soe after that rate be it more or less And further upon Admittances for Life Lives or years in Possession or Reversion or to any Estate of inheritance in Reversion depending upon such p[ar]ticler Estates one year & an half rent respectively according to the p[ro]portion of the Rents then paid to His Highness for the same as in and by the same Petition may apear **Whereupon** it pleased his Maj[es]tie to direct his highness Letters of Privy Seall unto the Lord Treasurer of England and the Chancellor of the Exchequer and Dutchie of Lancaster and to the Cheif Baron of the said Court of Exchequer and other Barons of the same Court together with his Maj[es]ties Councel of this Court for the time being by which said L[ette]rs (His Maj[es]ties reciteing the effect of the said Petition) is conteined the effect following. That in Consideration of the said Fines & Sums of money to His Highness offered by the said Petitioners and out of his Highness abundant care and zeal of an equall administration of equitie & Justice & of His Maj[es]ties Princely disposition rather to desist from such his owne Right then to demand or admitt any extraordinary extremity of Law And out of the generall favor, and affections he beareth to the good estates of all his loveing subjects and especially of his Tenants who by their tenures doe more imediatly & peculierly depend upon his Maj[es]tie and principally of such as doe make any especiall demonstration of their duties and loyalties unto him and upon an advised & diliberate Consideration of the premises His Maj[es]ties right trusty & right wel beloved Chancellor Thomas Lord Ellesmere L[ord] Chancelor of England and with his Maj[es]ties right trusty & Right wel beloved cosens & Councellors Robert Earl of Salsbury Lord Treasurer of England Henry Earl of Northamton Lord Keeper of the Privy Seall Thomas Earl of Suffolk L[ord] Chamberlain of the King's maj[es]ties most Honorable houshold Thomas, Earl of Exeter & George, Earl of Dunbarr and of his trusty & welbeloved Councellors Edward L[or]d Wotton Sr John Harbert, Kn^t his Maj[es]ties Second Secretary, Sr Julius Caesar, Knight, Chancelor of the said Exchequer & Sr Thomas Parry Knight Chancelor of the said Dutchie of Lancaster who by his Maj[es]ties direction had treated with the said Petitioners concerning the premises and in Consideration of the Estates of the said Petitioners being fully resolved & determined to give and grant all such aid & assistance as to his Royall Estate & power apertaineth both for the confirmation and corroboration of the said Petitioners Estates in the said Copyhold Messuages Lands Tenements & p[ar]cells of Wast Grounds And also for the establishing of a certainty of & for the said ffines and for that such his Majesties resolution and determination could not be his Mejestie was informed fully perfectly & absolutly performed or accomplished otherwise or by any other means than by an Act of P[ar]l[ia]m[en]t His Maj[es]tie did by his said Letters fully assure the said Petitioners to grant his Royall assent to such a Bill as to that intent should at any time hereafter pass both houses of the said high Court of P[ar]l[ia]m[en]t **And** his Highness Did thereby in the meantime in p[ar]te of accomplishment of his Maj[es]ties said resolution and for the better preparation of the passage of the said Bill in P[ar]l[ia]m[en]t[1] for his Highness his heirs & successors give unto the said Lord Treasurer and Chancelors of the Courts of the Exchequer & Dutchie And the cheif Baron and other Barons of the Exchequer togather with his Maj[es]ties Councel of this Court for the time being And to every of them respectively express charge power & authority amply fully & finally to p[er]forme and doe all and every such Act Acts and things by severall orders or Decrees of the said severall Courts of Exchequer & Dutchy Chamber or otherwise as by or for the said Petitioners or by their Learned Council should be advised and desired as wel for the absolute enabling confirmation & corroboration of their said Copyhold Estates of and in the premises and of and in the said p[ar]cells of waste grownds and to and for a p[er]fect creation of good & p[er]fect Copyhold Estates therein by Copy of Court Roll and to and for the inabling of the same p[ar]cell of Wast Groun'd to be p[er]petually demised and

[1] An act for confirmation of several Decrees made in the Court of Exchequer Chamber and Duchy Chamber between the King's Majesty and divers Copyholders of His Majesty's Manor of Wakefield in the County of York, 7 James I, chapter 1, private acts.

demiseable by Copy of Court Roll of the said Mannor or Lordship according to the Custom of the same Mannor or Lordship at and for such yearly rents Customs & services to be paid and done for the same to his Highness his heirs & Successors as were then paid and done for the same As also for the establishing of a certainty of such ffines to be paid upon all admittances as wel for the said ancient Copyhold premises as also for the said p[ar]cells of Wast as is before mentioned to be offer'd unto his Maj[es]tie by the said Petitioners with such further liberties according to the tenure of the said Petition as to them the said Lord Treasurer Chancellor cheif Baron, Barons of his Highness Exchequer & Councel of His Dutchy aforesaid for the time being and every of them respectively should seeme convenient or expedient And that in all and every such Decree & Decrees soe to be made in his Maj[es]ties several Courts aforesaid which shall be declared and p[ro]vided that the same Decrees & every claus therein contained should be for ever good & effectuall in Law & equity ag[ains]t his Highness & Successors and without any saveings or other reservation therein to to be had or made of any right or title in Law or equity unto his Maj[es]tie his heirs or successors contrary to the tenure and purport of the same Decree or Decrees any Law use or custome or other matter whatsoever to the contray in any such cases used due or accustomed notw[i]thstanding And for and concerning The Sum̃e of money according to the rate of Thirty ffive years Rent of such Rents as now paid to his Maj[es]tie by the said Petitioners & by them tendred to be paid unto his Maj[es]tie ffor and in Consideration thereof his Highness did further thereby will & require the said Lord Treasurer of England and Chancelor of this Court for the time being to take such order to and for the paym[en]t and satisfac[ti]on thereof by the said Petitioners and to his Maj[es]tie his heirs or successors according to the tenure of the said tender as to them should seme convenient as in and by the said Letters of Privy Seall remaining of Record in this Hon[ora]ble Court more at large apeareth **Vpon** the due Consideration of all which premises & for ye consideration and Causes afore recyted & declared by the Kings most excellent Maj[es]tie in & by his said Warr[an]t under his said privy seall as aforesaid & to and for the absolute enabling confirmation corroboration and better p[re]servation and continuation of the said tenures Estates and possessions of all and every the said Defendants Petitioners Tenents being Copyholders and of their heirs and assignes and of all other p[er]son & p[er]sons claiming by from or under them or any of them or to the use or uses of the said Def[endan]ts or any of them and also of all other p[er]son and p[er]sons to whose use or uses the said Def[endan]ts or any of them doe claime as Guardions or ffeofees in trust of and in all and sing[u]ler the severall Messuages Cottages Mills Lands Ten[emen]ts & hereditaments mentioned and expressed or intended to be granted conveyed and now injoyed in or by all or any of their said Coppies Surrendrs or admittances which are granted or mentioned or intended to be granted or passed in or by all or any such Copie or Copies Surrender or Surrenders Admittance or Admittances or used & now injoyed as p[ar]t or p[ar]cell hereof and of all and every the Comons feedings Pastures p[ro]fitts apprender & other benefits and hereditaments therein or thereunto belonging or apertaining or in any wise used granted reputed or occupied and now injoyed as thereunto in any wise ap[per]taining or belonging And for the better preparation of the said Bill in P[ar]l[ia]ment whereunto his Ma[jes]tie is soe graciously resolved & determined to give his said Royall assent and hath accordingly made such declaration and given such reall assurance of the p[er]formance thereof as aforesaid and for and towards the p[er]formance and accomplishment of his Maj[es]ties most gracious Will and pleasure and of his express charge and Comandment declared & delivered in and by his said Warrant under his said privy Seall **And** by the authority of this Court **It is** by the Chancellor & Councel of this Court the 27th Day of November in the Seaventh year of his Maj[es]ties Reigne of England France & Ireland & of Scotland the 43[d] declared ordered & finally and absolutly decreed That all the said Messuages Cottages Mills Lands Ten[emen]ts & hereditments whether they have been heretofore parcell of the said Wasts or no which are now holden and injoyed & now compounded for by the said Def[endan]ts or any of them or by any other p[er]son or p[er]sons claiming by from or under them or any of them or to the use or uses of them the same Def[endan]ts or any of them or by any other p[er]son or p[er]sons to whose use or uses the said Def[endan]ts or any of them doe clame as Guardians or ffeofees in trust by virtue or p[re]tence of any grant or grants by Copy of Court Roll or of any Surr[ender] or Surrend[ers] Admittance or admittances made according to or by Coulor of the Custom of the said Mannor, and now or heretofore in the severall tenures or occupations of the said Def[endan]ts or of any of them or of any other p[er]son or p[er]sons clameing by from or under him or any of them or to the use or uses of them or any of them or in the severall tenures or occupations of any of them or any of the ancestors of the said Def[endan]ts or of any p[er]son or p[er]sons by from or under whom the said Def[endan]ts or any of [them] do claime or p[re]tend to have or hold the said Messuages Cottages Mills Lands Tenem[en]ts or hereditments now compounded for or any p[ar]te thereof as Copyholders of the said Mannor or Lordship and all and every the Comons feeding Pastures p[ro]fitts aprender and other benefits & hereditaments therein or thereunto or to any p[ar]te or p[ar]cell thereof in anywise belonging or therew[th]all now or heretofore granted used or occupied and now injoyed for and under divers severall yearly rents Customes and services now yielded & paid to his Maj[es]tie for the same (except such **buildings** & Lands as are demised or mentioned to be demised to Nathaniel Duckit Gent by the Kings Maj[es]tie by Indenture dated the 26th day of June in the 3d Year of his Highness Raign only excepted) now are and for ever hereafter shall be & shall be esteemed accounted & adjudged eversithence the granting thereof respectively to have been and for ever hereafter to be and remain good and p[er]fect Copyhold Messuages Cottages Mills Lands Tenements & hereditaments severally & respectively demised & demiseable in ffee simple ffee Tail for life lives years or otherwise by Copy of Court Roll according to the Custome of the said Mannor or L[or]dship any defect of or concerning the antiquity validitie sufficiency continuance or Custome thereof or interuption of p[re]scription or any other exceptions that may be taken thereunto or any Law or usage or not usage or any other matter or thing w[ha]tsoever to the contrary in anywise notwithstanding and that all and Singuler the said Messuages Cottages Mills Lands Tenements & hereditaments and every p[ar]te therof and the said Comons ffeedings pastures and profits apprender & other benefits and hereditam[en]ts aforesaid (except before excepted) shall be demised & demiseable and shall be esteemed taken and admitted to have bene and for ever hereafter to be demised & demiseable by Copy of Court Roll according to the Custome of the said Mannor or Lordship of Wakefield at and for such end the same severall yearly Customes and Services as have heretofore been done for the same and at for and under such and the same severall yearly Rents as in that behalf are now paid as wel for the said p[ar]cells of Wasts as also for all other Copyhold Messuages, Cottages, Mills, Lands, Ten[emen]ts & hereditm[en]ts, of or within the said Mannor or Lordship holden or injoyed by the Def[endan]ts or any of them or by any person or persons clameing by from or under them or to the use or uses of them or any of them or by any other p[er]son or p[er]sons to whose use the said Def[endan]ts or any of them doe claim as Guardians or Feofees in trust and according to the rate & proportion of the same Rents now paid as aforesaid **And** it is further ord[r]d & decreed that from henceforth there shall be paid to his highness his [? heirs] and Successors for ever and upon every grant & admittance to be had or made as wel of or unto all and every the said Copyhold Messuages, Cottages, Mills, Lands, Tenements, & hereditments now compounded for of or within the said mannor or Lordship as also of or unto the said Messuages, Cottages, Lands, Ten[e]ments, & hereditments heretofore p[ar]cell of the said Wasts now compounded for w[hi]ch Copyhold and p[ar]cells of wast are now enjoyed & holden by the Defendants or any of them or by any other p[er]son or p[er]sons clayming by from or under them or any of them or to the use or uses of them or any of them or by any other p[er]son or p[er]sons to whose use or uses the said Def[endan]ts or any of them doe claim as Guardians or ffeofees in trust by virtue or pretence of any Copy or Copies of Court Roll of the said Mannor

Surrender or Surrenders Admittance or admittances & also of or unto any rent or Rents issuing or granted or to be granted or issueing out of the same severall Messuages, Cottages, Mills, Lands, Ten[emen]ts & hereditam[en]ts, or any p[art]s thereof the several Fines or Sum̃s of money herein & hereby limitted & noe more or less (that is to say) upon admittance of every Copyholder to Estates of inheritance in possession by discent and also upon Surrend[er] of Estates of inheritance in possession & upon Seisures for betring of assurances for all Messuages with Lands All Cottages with Lands All mills be they Fulling mills or Corne Mills and all Lands Ten[emen]ts & hereditam[en]ts whatsoever with all and singuler their appurtenances w[ha]tsoever & courses of water Three years rent according to the Copyhold Rents now paid to His Highness for the same & noe more or less & for a Messuage without Lands Eightpence & noe more or less and for a Cottage without Lands. Fourpence & noe more or less and also for every rent charge whereof any grant shall be made upon discent Surrender or seisure for bettring of assurances to be made Twenty pence in the pound and noe more or less and soe according to that rate for a greater or lesser Sum[m]e And further upon every admittance to any Estate for life or lives or years in possession or reversion to any Estate of inheritance in Reversion or Remainder depending upon such p[ar]ticular Estates One year & a half rent respectively according to the p[ro]portion of the rents now paid to his Highness for the same **Provided** that noe p[ar]ticular Estate for lives or Reversion or remainder shall be made or surrendred joyntly to any more than to Two p[er]sons only whereby his Maj[es]ties Princely favor for admittances for such Estates according to this Decree may not be abused in the Fines **And** it is further ordered and decreed that if at any time hereafter any of the said Messuages Cottages Mills Lands Tenements or heredit[amen]ts for which there is answered and payd to his Maj[es]tie one entire Rent and for which the said fines are hereby agreed to be paid shall be p[ar]celled severed or devyded either for or upon any Estate of Inheritance or for life lives or years whereby the certainty of the rent & fine to be payable for such Lands Ten[emen]ts or hereditam[en]ts soe p[ar]celled severed or devided from the residue of the same shall not or may not apear that then & in every such case there shall be a just & equall aportionm[en]t of the rent to be paid as wel for the said Messuages Cottages Mills, Lands, Ten[emen]ts and hereditaments to be p[ar]cell'd severed or devided from the residue of the same as also for the residue of the Copyhold Tenem[en]ts & hereditam[en]ts soe p[ar]celled severed or devided during the Estates or times of such p[ar]celling severing or devideing which aportionment & shall be made by the Oathes of the Grave for the time being and Two Copyholders of and within such of the Graveships aforesaid within which the said Lands Ten[emen]ts or hereditam[en]ts soe to be p[ar]cell'd severed or devided as is aforesaid shall respectively be scituate lyeing & being at the Court to be holden for the said Graveship before the Steward of the said Mannor for the time being or his Deputy when the admittance or admittances to any such Messuages Cottages Mills Lands Tenem[en]ts & hereditam[en]ts soe p[ar]celled severed and devided shall be made & then & there shall be entred by the Steward or his Deputy or the Clarke of the said Court in the Court Rolls of the same Court after which aporconm[en]t presentment & entrie made such rents shall be paid as wel for the said Messuages Cottages Mills Lands Tenements & hereditments soe to be parcell'd severed or devided as for the said residue of such Messuages Cottages Mills Lands or Tenements parcell'd severed or devided as is aforesaid as shall be soe aportioned presented & entred to be paid for the same as is aforesaid and noe more or other rent whatsoever dureing the estates or times of such p[ar]celling severing or deviding and that then and from thenceforth the Fynes to be paid for and in respect of the said Messuages, Mills, Cottages, Lands, Tenem[en]ts & hereditm[en]ts soe to be p[ar]cell'd severed or devided & of the said residue of such Messuages, Cottages, Mills, Lands, Tenements, & hereditm[en]ts soe p[ar]cell'd severed or devided (as is aforesaid) shall be rated taxed & paid according to the rate of the said Rent soe to be apportioned presented & entred as is aforesaid & not otherwise nor after any other Rate **And** it is also ord[r]d & decreed that all and every Rent by the right claim entrye possession seisin tenure estate & interest of any p[er]son or p[er]sons whatsoever of in or unto all or any of the said Messuages, Cottages, Mills, Lands, Tenements or hereditam[en]ts before mentioned in this Decree and Compounded for as aforesaid shall be & shall be esteemed accounted and adjudged to have been & for ever hereafter to be of such nature qualitie & condition to all intents constructions and purposes as if the same Messuages, Cottages, Mills, Lands, Tenements & hereditm[en]ts & every p[ar]te thereof had been & were good & p[er]fect copyhold Messuages, Cottages, Mills, Lands, Tenem[en]ts & hereditaments demised & demiseable time out of minde & by Copy of Court Roll severalie & respectivelie according to the custom of the said Mannor or Lordship of Wakefield upon such said certain Fines & Rents as aforesaid and noe other & that all & every Grants demises Surr[en]ders admittances p[re]sentm[en]ts Inquisetions Court Rolls actions playntes suits process pleas verdicts Judgments Executions Conveyances & Assurances and all & every other act & acts thing & things heretofore had made done or suffered or hereafter to be had made done or suffered of for or concerning all or any of the same Messuages, Cottages, Mills, Lands, Tenem[en]ts, & hereditm[en]ts & every p[ar]te thereof shall be & shall be esteemed accounted & adjudged to have bene time out of minde of man heretofore and for ever hereafter to be of such nature quality & condition to all intents constructions

& purposes as if the same Messuages, Cottages, Mills, Lands, Tenements, & hereditam[en]ts & every p[ar]te thereof had been and were good & p[er]fect Copyhold Messuages, Cottages, Mills, Lands, Tenem[en]ts & hereditam[en]ts anciently for & dureing all the time whereof the memory of man is not to the contrary demised & demiseable by Copy of Court Roll according to the Custom of the said Mannor And that all and every the Tenn[en]ts and Copyholders of all & every the said p[ar]cells of waste & all the residue of the Def[endan]ts & every of them & their & every of their heirs & assignes & all & every other p[er]son & p[er]sons claimeing by from or under them or any of them or to the use or uses of them or any of them and all and every other p[er]son & p[er]sons to whose use or uses the said Def[endan]ts or any of them doe claim as Guardians or Feofees in Trust & their heirs & assignes shall & may for ever hereafter respectively according to his or their intrests of or in the same p[ar]cell of wasts & other the p[re]mises have hold possesse inherit & injoy all & every p[ar]te of the said wasts & premises & all & every such Com[m]ons of Pasture, Turbary, & other Com[m]ons, Ways, Paths, gates, waters, & watercourses lib[er]ties of digging, getting of Turves, Slate, Stone, Sand, Gravel, Marle, & all such other Lib[er]ties, privileges, benefitts, Freedoms, & immunities in & upon all & every of the Wasts, Comons & Moors, of the said mannor & other wasts & moors whatsoever in such like manner & forme as now is or at any time heretofore hath bene injoyed, used, or accustomed, by the Tennentes Copieholders or occupiers for the time being of the said premises or any p[ar]te thereof or used or injoyed as p[ar]te or p[ar]cell of the same premises **And** it is furthermore finallie Decreed by the said Court that this Decree & all and every the Clauses thereof & therein shall be & so for ever hereafter shall be taken & adjudged to be good and effectuall in Law and Equity against the Kings Maj[es]tie his heirs & successors & their & every of their Assignee & Assignes according to the true intent tenure & purport of this Decree And that every Claus article & sentence herein contained for the better accomplishment of his gracious & Princely favour & the continuall peace & quietness of his said Customarie Tenn[an]ts shall be taken & expounded most beneficially for the said Def[endan]ts their heirs & assignes & every of them & most stricktly against the Kings Highness his heirs & successors any prerogative claime title or demand or other matter or thing whatsoever to the contrary notwithstanding and that if at any time hereafter any manner of action suit Bill or Plaint shall be commenced or prosecuted or any manner of information allegation Plea or objection shall be had or made for or upon the behalf of the Kings Majestie his heirs or Successors or of any other p[er]son or p[er]sons claiming by from or under him them or any of them that all or any p[ar]te of the said p[ar]cell of Wast or of any other the premises whatsoever compounded for as is before mentioned is not or ought not to be esteemed accounted or adjudged good & p[er]fect copiehold Messuages Cottages, Mills, Lands, Tenem[en]ts, & hereditam[en]ts to all intents constructions and purposes as aforesaid for or becaus of any such defect or insuficiency, or Contynuance prescription or Custome as aforesaid as in that behalf may be urged or objected by the strict course of the Com[m]on Law or for any other defect imperfection or insufficiency, w[ha]tsoever That then it shall be lawfull & sufficient to and for all or any p[er]son or p[er]sons that now are or at any time hereafter shall be Tenn[an]ts or Copieholders of the premises or of any p[art]s thereof soe compounded for as aforesaid & for their & every of their heirs & assignes And all other occupiers or possessors in their right to aleage plead show in barr generally effectually & substancially of any such action suite Bill, Plaint Information allegation Plea or objection this present order or Decree & not to be compelled to plead allege or show the same in strict cours & forme of Law and to demand Judgment whether any such action, suite, Bill, Plaint, Information, allegation, Plea, or Objection soe made or to be made for ever upon the behalf of the Kings Majestie his heirs or Successors or any of any other p[er]son or p[er]sons claiming by from or under him them or any of them shall be admitted received or allowed contrary to this present Decree to have or comence any such action Suite, Bill, Plaint Information Allegation Plea or objection soe had or made as aforesaid contrary to this said Decree & that thereupon every p[er]son & p[er]sons plea & pleas allegation & allegations soe made and used in affirmation that the premisses or any p[ar]te thereof are not or is not customary or copiehold Lands shall be utterly and absolutly barred disalowed & disanulled & be for ever esteemed deemed & adjudged voide in Law & Equitie to all intents constructions & purposes **And** it is further ordered and decreed that if it shall hapen that any p[er]son or p[er]sons which have compounded as aforesaid & which are intented to be comprehended within the benefit of this Decree shall be by negligence or otherwise om̃itted out of this Decree or misnamed therein That then & in every such case upon due profe thereof made in this Court all and every such p[er]son or p[er]sons so om̃itted or misnamed shall be nevertheless & shall be taken & adjudged to be within the benefit of this Decree to all intents constructions & purposes and in as large ample & beneficiall manner & forme as if such p[er]son or p[er]sons so omitted or misnamed had bene truly specially & p[ar]ticlarly named & mentioned in this present Decree **And** it is further ordered & decreed by the authoritie aforesaid that as wel from time to time & at all times hereafter whensoever any Surrender shall be made of the premises or any p[ar]te thereof or any such cause of Seisure for the bettring of assurances shall be given of or concerning the same premises or any p[ar]te thereof as is aforesaid as also in case where any Surrender or Surrenders hath or have bene made of the premises or any p[ar]te thereof or any discent hath hapened or fallen of the premises or any p[ar]te thereof or any caus of seisure for betring of assurances hath bene given of or concerning the said premises or any p[ar]te thereof soe compounded for as is aforesaid whereof the Fine or Fines have not hitherto bene assessed taxed & levied by reason of any order or restraint the Steward, Deputie Steward, or Clarke of the Courte or Courts of and within the same mannor shall upon request to him or them or any of them in that behalf made make grants & admittan[ce]s upon and according to all & every such Surrenders discents & causes of seisure respectively according to the course & true intent of the same Surrenders discents & causes of Seasure and of the p[ar]tes thereunto at and for such Fines as are in and by this Decree in that behalf respectively limitted and apointed & noe more or less and that all & every such Fine & Fines upon Surrenders discents, & seasures hereafter to be made shall be assessed at the same Court when the admittance or admittances to the said premises or any p[ar]te thereof shall be made & that they shall do the same without exacting or takeing any Fee at all upon any such Seisure or upon any such admittance or Surrender or any other Sum̃e of money or reward for or in respect thereof other than such usuall Fee as have bene heretofore lawfully taken by the said Steward, Deputie Stewards, and Clarke, for makeing & writeing copies and inrollments of admittances & examining of women Coverte only **And** it is further ordered & decreed That in every grant, Copie, & admittance, so to be made as aforesaid of any of the Lands Ten[emen]ts heredit[a]m[en]ts & other the premises conteyned in this Decree express mencon shall be made that the same Lands, Ten[emen]ts, hereditam[en]ts, & other the premises contayned in this Decree & for what Rent or Rents and Fynes are to be paid for the same **And** it is further ordered & decreed That the Steward, Deputie Steward, & Clarke of the said mannor Court & Courts shall from time to time p[er]mitt & suffer the Def[endan]ts heirs & assignes and all p[er]sons lawfully clameing from by or under them or any of them to search & take Copies of the Court Rolls of the said Mannor & every of them for and touching the premises compounded for as aforesaid at and for such Fees as have bene heretofore lawfully used to be taken for such searches & copies & no more **And whereas** by virtue of a Com̃ission awarded out of this Court severall Rentalls or Schedules have bene made upon the presentments & Oaths of divers severall Juries of his Maj[es]ties Copyholders within the said Mannor and returned into Court conteyning all the severall Copyhold Rents now paid to his Majestie for the premisses which said Rentalls or Schedules doe now remain w[ith] his Majesties auditor of this Court for the North p[ar]tes and are very requisite to be transcribed & soe remaine amongst The Court Rolls of the said Mannor of Wakefield for the better direction of the Stewards & other officers of the said Mannor for the time being to assess & tax the Fines aforesaid according to the intent & true meaning of this Decree & according to the Rents herein expressed **It is** therefore ordered & decreed by the authority aforesaid that the said severall Rentalls shall be transcribed by his Maj[es]ties said auditors into this Court & that thereupon as wel the tenor of this Decree as also the said Rentalls or Schedules shall be transcribed & Sealled with the Seall of this Court & sent unto the said Court of the said Mannor of Wakefield to be there inrolled and safely kept amongst other the Records & Court Rolls of the said mannor for the better direction of the Stewards, Deputy Stewards, Clarks, officers, ministers, & the said Copyholders of the said Mannor which have compounded as aforesaid & of all & every other p[er]son & p[er]sons w[ha]tsoever whome it shall or may in anywise concerne for the due p[er]formance of this Decree And that the said Def[endan]ts & every of them their & every of their heirs & assigns & all & every other p[er]son & p[er]sons w[hat]soever intended & meant to be comprehended within this Decree & then & every of their heirs & assignes at all & every time & times for ever hereafter at every time of search there used shall have free lib[er]tie and access to search and see the said transcripts of this Decree and Rentalls & Schedules to be sealled & sent to the said Courte of the said Mannor of Wakefield as aforesaid And the Inrollm[en]ts thereof there in that Court and to take Copies or notes thereof as they or any of them shall think fitt & have occasion without paying any Fee or Fees or other reward for the search of the same **And** it is further ord[erdere]d & decreed by This Court that all and every p[er]son & p[er]sons which now have or hath any Estate of Inheritance according to the Custome of the said Mannor of or in any such Rent as is before mentioned issueing or payable out of the premises or any p[ar]te thereof (saveing & excepting Rents given & granted to charitable uses) shall bear pay and satisfie such an equall p[ar]te & portion of the said Thirty five years Rent paid to his Maj[es]tie with the Charges of the Composition with His Maj[es]tie & the p[roc]ureing of this Decree & other assurances therefore according to the rate & vallew of his & their said Estates and interests to be paid to such p[er]son & p[er]sons as have disbursed & laid out the same as by the auditor of this Court for the time being or the Chancelor & Councel of the Dutchy of Lancaster shall be thought mete And for and concerning the said Sum of Five & Thirty years rents & all and every the premisses tendred by the said Petitioners in and by their said Petition to his Highness for the consideration in the said Petition mentioned to be paid in manner & forme therein expressed amounting in the whole to the Sum̃e of [*blank*] The Security & assurance of the due payment & satisfaction whereof was referred to by his Highness to the order & Consideration of the said Lord Treasurer & the said Chancelor of the Dutchie forasmuch as it apeareth to this Court That the same &

every p[ar]te & p[ar]cell thereof is already paid to the hands of His Maj[es]ties generall Receiver of his Dutchy of Lancaster by the order & direction of the said Lord Treasurer & Chancelor of the Dutchy **It** is ordered & Decreed that all and every of the said Def[endan]ts their & every of their heirs & assignes & all and every other p[er]son & p[er]sons whatsoever intended and mente to be comprehended within this Decree and their & every of their heirs and assignes as also all and every their Lands, Ten[emen]ts, goods, & chattels whatsoever shall be thereof and of every p[er]te and p[ar]cell thereof clerely & absolutly acquitted exonerated & discharged ag[ains]t the Kings Maj[es]tie his heirs & Successors for ever **Inspeximus** etiam tenor[em] pred[icti] Rentall[s] sive Schedul[e] sup[er]ius in pr[ese]ratibus specificat[e] manu auditor[is] n[ost]ri pr[e]d[icti] signate ac in Cam[er]a Ducatus n[ost]ri pred[icti] in ter recorda ejusd[e]m Ducatus ib[ide]m reman[entis] et existen[tis] quo[rum] veri tenores sequunt[ur] in Schedul[e] presentib[us] annexat[e]

N.B. **The Rentalls** above mentioned are recorded in the same Roll but only mentions the Tennants names and the Rent they paid & not nameing the Lands those Rents issued out on makes those Rentalls soe useless at this distance of time that it wo[ul]d be of noe use here in this Book to Copy them out

Severall Copieholders who did not compound when the foregoing Decree was made have [compounded] since with the Lord of the Mannor but at a much greater Rate

The rest who have not compounded hold their mes[uages], Lands and Tenements, in all respects under the same tenure with the Compounded saveing that their Fines are at the will of the Lord which are usually set by the Steward at a year and a half Rent The Full vallew

THE OFFICERS OF THE MANNOR

First The Learned Steward who is always an able Lawier and sits Judge at the Moot hall in Wakefield every Court Day in all Copyhold Causes whatever whether by Coñon Law or Equity, as also in all mañer of actions under 40[s] where the Contract or damage ariseth in any p[ar]te of The Mannor In all matters relateing to the Lord of The Mannor he is his Councel and advises the vnder-steward in any point of Law for which his Gratuity or Sallary is £10 p[er] Annu[m] But if he be called abrode to attend he has his Councel Fee The pr[e]sent Learned Steward is Richard Witton Esq

The Vndersteward or Clarke of the Courts, he attends every Court as wel upon any occasionall adjournmt in any p[ar]te of the Mannor as at Moothall and keeps all the Forraine Court Leets & Court Barrons (viz[t]) Hallifax, Brighous & Burton, He takes & records all Surrenders makes up the Court Rolls & gives out Copies,

For the advantages of The Fees he pays £40 p[er] Anum̃ wh[i]ch are as follow [viz[t]]

Fees upon Surrenders

	£	s.	d.
For every Absolute Surrender inrolling	0	1	0
D[o] upon Discent	0	1	0
For every Conditionall Surrender inrolling the least..	0	1	6
For every Conditionall Surrender where the Grant is longe & for every Surrender of Lands with remaind[r]s &c according to their length but generally	0	3	4
For every Copy of an absolute Surr[ender] or a H[er]iott	0	1	0
For every Copy of Com̃on Conditionall Surrender ..	0	1	6
For every Copy where the Grant is large or where the Lands therein are intailed ..	0	3	4

	£	s.	d.
Vpon a seisure the Indenture inrolling ..	0	1	0
The seisure Warrant	0	1	0
The Three p[ro]clamations makeing & inrolling	0	11	0
The Regrant	0	1	0
The Seisure Coppy	0	3	4
The Clark's fee	0	1	0

	£	s.	d.
	0	18	4
The Examination of every Woman under Covert ..	0	2	0
Every Tuition Bond Drawing & Duty	0	10	0
The Tuition Copy	0	1	0
The Oath of Fealty	0	1	0

Fees upon Comon p[ro]cess in the Court Baron

	£	s.	d.
For entring every plaint except in Replevin Eject[men]t or Dower	0	0	4
For every Distringas	0	1	4
For every Alias & Plur[ies] Distress	0	0	8
For Warr[an]t of Attorney from the Pl[ainti]ffs Attorney	0	0	4
For every appearance Entring	0	0	4
For every Decl[aration] of affileing	0	0	4
For entring Imparlance	0	1	0
For coppying the Decl[aration] & duty	0	0	8
For every Plea affileing or entring	0	0	4
For copying the Plea & Duty	0	0	6
For affileing or entring Replycation	0	0	4
For the copyeing thereof and duty	0	0	6
For a ffileing or entring Rejoynder or Surrejoynder..	0	0	4
For the Copy thereof & Duty	0	0	6
For entring every Rule	0	0	4

For entring a Defalt	0	0	4
For entring a non Suit	0	1	0
For entring every Judgm[en]t or Verdict	0	1	0
For a Venire Facias	0	1	0
For a Subpoena	0	0	8
For a Jury Swearing	0	1	0
For every Witness Swearing	0	0	4
For a Levari Facias	0	2	0
For every al[ias] Levari Facias	0	0	4

In Replevin

For a Replevin granting	0	1	0
For a Bond drawing thereupon & Duty	0	2	1
For entring the Plaint	0	0	6
For an Attachment	0	0	6
For retvrn[o] habend[o]	0	1	0
For an apearance entring	0	0	6
For a Decl[aration] a ffileing or entring	0	0	6
For Coppying Decl[aration] & Duty	0	0	6
For Rule entring	0	0	6
For avowry affileing or entring	0	0	6
For Coppying avowry & Duty	0	1	2
For Plea affileing or entring	0	0	6

In Ejectment

For entring the Plaint	0	1	0
For Declaration affileing or entring	0	0	6
For apearance entring	0	0	6
For entring a Rule	0	0	6
For affileing or entring a Plea	0	0	6
For habere facias Possession[em]	0	1	0

In Dower

For Summons & action entring	0	0	8
For Declaration affileing or entring	0	0	6
For View in Dower	0	1	0
For every Grand Cape or Petit Cape	0	1	0

Generall Fees in any Cause

For reading every Copy of Court Roll or other Writeing at the Tryalls	0	0	6
For every Accedas ad Curia[m] allowing	0	6	8
For every Bill of Costs Taxing	0	0	4

Here may properly follow what Fees the Vndersteward allows the Attorneys upon his Taxing their Bills of Costs

Fees To The Attorney in Comon Causes

Every Summons or First Distringas	0	0	4

The Fee thereon	0	2	0
For every Alias Distringas	0	2	0
Fee on The Def[endan]ts apearance	0	2	0
For Decl[aration] drawing and duty	0	2	0
Fee thereon	0	2	0
Copy of Declaration & Duty	0	1	2
Plea Drawing on non assumpsit non cal[endis] etc.	0	0	8
Copy of Plea & Duty	0	0	6
A Replication Rejoinder Surrejoinder &c each ..	0	1	0
Councel ffee to any speciall pleading	0	5	0
Drawing Bre[vi]at (Brief) & Copy	0	2	0
For a Bre[vi]at drawing if any Councel or Attorney assist	0	1	0
For every Court day wherein the p[ro]ceed[ings] in the Action after apearance entred his Fee	0	2	0
For Bill of Costs drawing	0	0	4
For every Tickit	0	0	2
For a witness who lives w[i]thin the p[ar]ish of Wakefield	0	0	6
For a witness who lives out of the parish	0	1	0

In Replevin

For every Action entring	0	2	0
Declaration Drawing & Duty	0	1	2
For an Attachment or Retorn[o] habend[o] ..	0	2	0
Avowry drawing	0	3	4
Copy thereof & Duty	0	1	2

In Ejectment

Fee upon action entring..	0	2	0
For Decl[aration] drawing	0	2	0
Copy thereof & Duty	0	2	2
Plea drawing & Duty	0	1	2

In Dower

Fee upon Sumons	0	2	0
For Decl[aration] drawing & duty	0	2	2
Fee upon View	0	2	0
Fee upon every Grand Cape or Petit Cape	0	2	0
Plea drawing & Duty	0	1	2

An Attorneys Fee that comes to plead a Caus not being Solicitor	0	3	4
A Counsel Fee	0	5	0
Attendance takeing out Execution & Costs Taxing	0	2	0

The Collecting Steward or The L[or]ds Receivor

He setts fines & all manner of Rents, is the Accomptant &

overlooks all The Concerns of The Mannor, His Sallary is £15 p[er] Annu[m] & 1[s] p[er] £ for the vallew of all Vncompounded Fines, Felons goods, the Goods of Felo de se, Treasure trove & Deodands. Both the last Officers (viz) The Vnder Stewardship & The Collecting Stewardshp̄ have bene for many years under the managem[t] of one Person, now of William Elmsall Gent[1]

The Return[atur] Brevium. He makes a return of all Bail Bonds &c to the Courts of Queens Bench & Com̄on Pleas—He is imployed as The Lord of The Mannors Attorney in all causes relating to the Royalties of the Mannor where the Lord is a Party and has but the only Fee of 3[s] 4[d] for the return of every Bail Bond. The present officer is Thomas Gill, Gent:

The Geoler. He Farms the Geolehous & houseing which his Grace The Duke of Leeds the present L[or]d of the Mannor purchased in Hallifax & thereon made a convenient Geole under the yearly rent of £27 for accomodating all Degrees of Prisoners. He receives from the Bayliffs of the Mannor all p[er]sons under their arreast into his Charge at the said Geole in Hallifax and as the Lord of the Mannor is charged with every Prisoner and all escapes whatsoever out of the said Geole soe the Geoler findes good Security to indempnity the L[or]d from all and every escape that may hapen The present Geoler is Thomas Watmough & his Securities are John Beaumont of Himsworth Gent, Richard Midgley, of Hallifax, Gent, John Ramsden, of Clifton, yeom[an], & Wil-l[ia]m Ramsden of the same, yeoman. His Fees as they were setled & abriged by Richard Musgrave Esq, William Lowther Esq, Fra: Lindley Esq, Walter Calverley Esq, & W[m] Nevile Esq Justices of the Peace for the West Rideing of the County of Yorke on the 26th day of Aprill 1709 are as follow :

	£	s.	d.
The Geole Fee after 24 hours Custody	0	6	8
D[o] after 40 hours Custody the 6[s] 8[d] being included	0	17	4
Garnish	0	1	0
The Turnkey Fee	0	1	0
The first week dyet in the hous	0	10	0
Every week following	0	5	0
The Chamber Rent over the Low Geole—Every p[er]son that findes his owne bedding p[er] week	0	1	0
And a man & his wife the same	0	1	0
The same Chamber when the Geoler finds bedding	0	1	6
D[o] every man & his wife there that he finds bedding too	0	2	0

The Whole Mannor is devided into Four Baylywicks (viz) The Bayliff of Wakefield, the Bayliff of Hallifax, the Bayliff of The Fee of Wakefield & The Bayliff of Holme. They have all severall

[1] *H.F.M.G.*, III, 905.

Deputies & executes all such Process within the Mannor as the Sheriff Bayleys doe in the rest of the County as also carry the Persons under their arreast to the L[or]ds Geole at Hallifax if they be not baild within 48 hours, as the Sheriffs Bayliffs doe the Persons under their arreast to the County Geole. Vnder their respective Rents they have & receive to their owne uses in their several Divisions all the Freehold Rents called Earl Warren's rents. All Amerciaments of Courts All waifs and Estrays. And all Fees of Writts Executions & Court Baron Warr[an]ts whatsoever which are as follow.

Bayliffs Fees

	£	s.	d.
Every Arreast	0	2	0
Every Quo Minus writ serveing	0	6	8
Every Execution 1ˢ p[er] pound to £100 and if the execution be for above £100 whatever it exceeds that Sume their Fee for the Exceed is after 6ᵈ p[er] pound			
Conduct money for ye carryeing of Prisoners to the Geole their Fee is 1ˢ a mile			

In the Court Baron

	£	s.	d.
Every Sum̃ons executing	0	0	4
Every Distringas executing	0	1	0
Every Replevin executing	0	2	0
Every Venire Facias Executing	0	1	0
Every Scire Facias Executing	0	1	0
Every Nonsuit calling	0	0	6
Vpon every Verdict takeing	0	0	6
Every Writt of Possession executing	0	2	0
Every accedas Curia[m] allowing	0	6	8
Every Oath upon a Surr[ende]r Fealty	0	0	4
The Fee for calling the jury upon Findeing an heir & admittance	0	0	6

The present Bayliffe of Wakefield is Christofer Hargraves who farmes The Baylywick under the yearly Rent of £40, The Townes Villages & Hamlets following are within his Division (vizt) Wakefield, Stanley, Ouchthorp, Newton, Wrenthorp, Alverthorp, Flanshaw, Snapethorp, Thornes, Horbury, Sandall, Milnthorp, Woodthorp, Newbiggin, Pledwick, Crigleston, Ketlethorp, Painthorp, Chapelthorp, Boynhill, Dawgreen, Dirtcarr, Hollingthorp, Walton, Westbretton, Normanton & Woodhous. He has within this Farm of the Baylywick all the Freehold Rents called Earls Rents and also the Burges Rents of the Towne of Wakefield, He's paid for Stallage in the Comon Street, and has the Toll of Aples for their standing upon a Wast called Bitchill in the Towne which he repairs. He has the Tolls of all Quick Goods that are bought & drive downe the Street called Kirkgate on the Two Fairdays (vizt) Midsum̄r & All Saints. He keeps the Standards of Weights & Measures—All who come to Wakefield with Shows or any Quack Professions, before they be admitted p[ro]duce their Lycence or Pa[ten]ts for his allowance & pay him some small gratuity. He inhabits at Moothall in Wakefield which with a Garth & Orchard thereto belonging is another apurtinant to this ffarm, He keeps the Courthous Keys there when the Justices doe, as wel keep their Sessions as The L[or]ds Stewards doe His Courts. His securities are William Harrison, Cloth buyer, Jeramia Dickson, Stapler, & Nathaniel Hargreaves, Yeoman, all of Wakefield. The perticular of the Earls Rents & Burges Rents which he receives are as follow

The Free Rents called Earls Rents under the Collection within The Farme of the Bayliff of Wakefield (vizt)

	£	s.	d.
The Governors of The Free School for Ing-holme ..	0	2	0
Geo: Kighley	0	3	6
John Thomson..	0	3	4
Robert Benson Esq	0	6	5
Richard Smirthwait	0	10	0
James Swallow	0	3	2
John Sugden	0	1	4
Charles Waterton Esq	0	7	0
John Nevile Esq[1]	0	2	0
John Law	0	7	0
Jo: Hall Junr	0	0	10
Wm Hall	0	1	9
Wm Dickson	0	2	7
Mr Leek & Mr Vsher for Grice Land	0	17	10
Mr Daniel Mawd[2]	0	1	6
Jno Lumb	0	1	6
Jno Lord	0	1	0
Henry Rayner	0	2	0
Mr Shaw	0	2	0
Mary Kent	0	1	3
Normanton			
Will[ia]m Crawshaw	0	0	4
Martin Burnit	0	1	0
Wm Barke	0	0	3
Patrick hous	0	0	8
George Fletcher	0	0	4
Mrs Nighols	0	1	6
Mr Favile	0	5	6
Mrs Wood	0	1	2
Henry Martin	0	1	2

[1] *C.D.*, II, 159.
[2] *H.F.M.G.*, II, 621.

	£	s	d
James Sympson	0	0	10
Mr Sylvester	0	0	10
Mrs Levit	0	1	0
Widw Walker	0	1	10
Chr[ist]ofer Favile[1]	0	0	6
Saml Dobson	0	0	6
Charles Dolston Esq	0	1	3
Robert Cusworth	0	0	8
Totall	4	17	4

WAKEFIELD BURGES RENTS

Westgate

	£	s	d
Theophilus Shelton Esq[2]	0	0	6
Rowland Burrough	0	0	3
Mrs Sill	0	0	6
Mr Capps	0	0	9
Sr Fr: Burdit hous[3]	0	0	6
Mr Birkhead	0	0	6
Mr Geo: Dickson	0	0	6
Mr Hopkinson	0	0	6
Widw Walker	0	0	4¼
Mr Wm Naylor	0	0	6
Mr Spinke	0	0	6
Richard Lambert	0	0	6
Robt Munckton Esq	0	0	6
James Scholey	0	0	6
Thomas Bragg	0	0	6
Mrs Rooth	0	0	6
Widw Allen	0	0	6
Mr Clayton	0	0	6
Natt: Hargreaves	0	0	9
Mrs Naylor	0	0	9
Mr Cherryholme	0	1	0
Mr Beevers	0	0	6
Jno Godley	0	0	6
Jno Wood	0	0	3
James Braithwaite	0	0	3
Mr Smith Senr & Junr	0	0	9
Jonathan Oldfield	0	0	3
Jer: Dickson	0	0	3
Jo: Shillitoe	0	0	4½
Jacob Rhodes	0	0	3
Jno Burton	0	0	4½
Jno Dewhirst	0	0	6

[1] *C.D.*, II, 459.
[2] *ibid.*, I, 107.
[3] *C.D.*, I, 349.

Mr Gilbert Mann	0	0	9
Wid^{w} Francks	0	0	6
Hanna Chapel	0	0	$1\frac{1}{2}$
Benj Thomson	0	0	$1\frac{1}{2}$
George Askew	0	0	$1\frac{1}{2}$
Jno Robertshaw	0	0	$4\frac{1}{2}$
Mr Charnock	0	0	6
Benj: Frubisher	0	0	3
Wm Towlerton	0	0	$1\frac{1}{2}$
Wm Harrison	0	0	3
Jo: Lindley	0	0	3
Wm Rawlin Senio^{r}	0	0	$1\frac{1}{2}$
Jonathan Serjant	0	0	3
Isaac Serj[an]t	0	0	3
Mrs Horne	0	0	6
Wid^{w} Heald	0	0	3
Wm Shaw	0	0	3
Joshua Jessup	0	0	3
Humphrey Walker	0	0	$1\frac{1}{2}$
Stephen Holdsworth	0	0	3
Jo: Boulton	0	0	3
Mrs Sagar	0	0	6
Wm Doughty	0	0	6
Richard Stringer	0	0	3
Thomas Illingworth	0	0	$7\frac{1}{2}$
Mr Richard Dawson	0	0	6
Edm^{d} Sykes	0	0	3
Wid^{w} Thackerah	0	0	3
Mr Sagar	0	0	6
Mr Benson	0	0	3
James Harrison	0	0	3
Thomas Harris	0	0	3
Mr Milnes	0	0	6
Barnaby Thomson	0	0	$4\frac{1}{2}$
Jno Dawson	0	0	6
Wid^{w} Gunson	0	0	3
Saml Fockscroft	0	0	3
James Best	0	0	3
Widw Hewit	0	0	3
James Norton	0	0	6
Saml Morley	0	0	3
Jo: Priestley	0	0	3
Wm Wormald	0	0	3
Charitie Schoole, The Trustees of it	0	0	3
Widw Higham	0	0	3
Saml Taylor & Thomas Harrison	0	0	3
Chr[ist]ofer Audsley	0	0	$1\frac{1}{2}$
Willm̃ Rawlin	0	0	3

Mr Watkinson	0	0	9
Francis Allen	0	0	6
Mr Parcivall	0	0	3
M^{r} Fr: Mawd	0	0	9
Saml Greaves	0	0	3
Thomas Hawkins	0	0	3
Mr Green	0	0	6
Mr Robert Naylor	0	0	6
Mr Jno Scott	0	0	6
Mr Waddington	0	0	6
Mr Robert Wilson	0	0	4½
Mrs Wollen	0	0	6
Mr Bastoe	0	0	6
Mr Richard Crowther	0	0	6
Mr Johnson	0	0	3
M^{r} Fr: Wheatley	0	0	3
Mr Rhodes	0	1	0
Mrs Oley	0	1	0
Mr Saml Hides	0	0	6
Mr Tilson	0	1	0
Widw: Britner	0	0	4½
Saml Harrison	0	0	3
Jo: Dyson	0	1	0
Mr Watkinson	0	0	1½
Jo: Dyson	0	0	9
Benjn Ward	0	0	6

Kirkgate

Jno Huebanck	0	0	4½
Tho: Johnson	0	0	3
Tho: Plowes	0	0	4½
Marke Pullon	0	0	1½
Thomas Tomlinson	0	0	3
Edwd Beckit	0	0	1½
James Fowlard	0	0	3
David Oakes	0	0	6
Wid^{w} Fox	0	0	6
Widw Guddinson	0	0	9
Mrs Lee	0	0	4½
Mr Roebuck	0	0	6
Thomas Wofendale	0	0	3
Widw Hirst	0	0	3
Mrs Fleeming	0	0	4½
Thomas Loxley	0	0	6
Samuel Bennit	0	0	3
Willm̃ Thomson	0	0	6
Mr Pollard	0	1	0
Richard Gargrave	0	1	0

Mr Pullon	0	0	3
Wm Brooksbank	0	0	3
Robert Gunson houses	0	0	6
Widw Bollain	0	0	3
Widw Westerman	0	0	3
Jo. Wood	0	0	3
Mrs Walker	0	0	6
Tho: Allot	0	0	3
Jno Adcock	0	0	3
Simion Roberts	0	0	3
Jno Cooke	0	0	3
Jo: Cooke	0	0	3
Mr Norton	0	0	3
Jo: Beatson	0	0	3
Tho: Johnson	0	0	3
Mr Brumley	0	0	3
Mr Saml Vsher	0	0	4½
Mr Thos Wilson	0	0	6
Mrs Wood	0	0	6
Jno Shephard	0	0	6
Tho: Beatson	0	0	3
Mary Oakes	0	0	3
George Whiteley	0	0	3
Jo: Thornton houses	0	0	6
Robt Lumbe	0	0	6
Mr Pullon	0	0	6
John Hague	0	0	3
Lyon Wilmon	0	0	3
Abel Kirshaw	0	0	3
Mr Shaw	0	0	4½
Tho: Allot	0	0	3
Tho: Whittaker	0	0	3
Sarah Peace	0	0	3
Robert Dransfield	0	0	3
Mr Ward	0	0	3
Jo: Chambers	0	0	1½
Mr Hey	0	0	4½
Wid^{w} Wofendale	0	0	1½
Thomas Allen	0	0	3
Willm̃ Armitage	0	0	3
Wid^{w} Woodhous	0	0	3
Jno Healey	0	0	3
Jo: Cook	0	0	6
Henry Gudger	0	0	6
Mrs Wilson	0	0	6
James Dickinson	0	0	6
Francis Allen	0	0	3
Abr[aha]m Clegg	0	0	3

Ab[raha]m Wilson	0	0	6
Wm Hewit	0	0	3
Peter Robinson	0	0	3
Mr Wilman	0	0	3
Tho: Lee	0	0	6
Jno Lockwood	0	0	3
Benj: Lockwood	0	0	3
Wm Twist	0	0	6
Wm Coldwel	0	0	3
Mrs Norton	0	0	6
Thomas Harris	0	0	6
Mary Ward	0	0	6
Mr Thomas Pollard	0	0	4
Henry Sharp	0	0	3
Jo: Byrom	0	0	3
Charles Rodley	0	0	6
Edw[ar]d Langster	0	0	3
Nathanl Healey	0	0	3
Jo: Hall & Thomas Blanch	0	0	6
Jno Holmes	0	0	6

Northgate

Wm Scholey	0	0	3
Anthony Bland	0	0	3
Mr Pitt	0	1	0
Mr Armitage	0	0	9
Mr Watson	0	1	0
Jno Lord	0	1	0
Roger Gill	0	0	3
Jno Chipchace	0	0	6
Hugh Yates	0	0	3
Thomas Westerman	0	0	3
Mr Ingram	0	0	6
Mrs Winne house	0	0	3
Mrs Robinson	0	0	3
Matthew Robinson	0	0	3
Anthony Boulton	0	0	6
Richard Pearson	0	0	3
Mrs Wood	0	0	3
Wm Stringer	0	0	3
Jo: Birch	0	0	3
Jo: Hall houses	0	0	6
Geo: Walton	0	0	3
Richard Lewis	0	0	3
John Redy hous	0	0	3
Mr Fenay	0	0	6
Joshua Walker	0	0	3
Mrs Kirke	0	0	6

Thomas Stenton	0	0	3
Jn° Helliwell	0	0	3
Wm Phylips	0	0	6
Anthony Boulton	0	0	6
Thomas Wood	0	0	6
Mr Bastow	0	0	6
Mr Spinke	0	0	6
Gabriel Bartill (?)	0	0	6
Ralph Callet	0	0	6
Butcher Row			
Willm Naylor	0	0	3
Mr Vsher	0	0	3
Thomas Marshall	0	0	3
Widw Robinson	0	0	3
New Shambles	0	0	3
Jo: Hast	0	0	3
Tho: Gill	0	0	3
Widw Bradsbury	0	0	3
Geo: Rallinson	0	0	3
Widw Wright	0	0	3
Mr Copendall	0	0	3
Mr Warberton	0	0	3
Omitted in Westgate			
Widw Barke	0	0	6
John Hewit	0	0	6
Eben. Buxton	0	0	6
Jn° Armstead	0	0	3
David Smith	0	0	6
Wm Ryley	0	0	3
Dor: Harrison	0	0	3
Totall	4	15	8½

Fees for Weights & Measures

For measuring a Load of Corne	0	0	4
For sealling every drye measure	0	0	4
For cutting a yeard wand	0	0	4
For stamping a Pinte or other small measure	0	0	0¼

Weights and Measures in his custody (belonging His Grace The Duke of Leeds The present L[or]d of the Mannor

Weights vizt	**Measures**
A Stone weight of Brass	a Brass Winchester Bushell
a pair of Brass Scales	a Brass drye Measure Pinte
a Brass Pound	a Pewther Wine quart
A Sett of Brass Weights of £4	a Brass Yeard
	A Pewther Wine Jack

OFFICERS—THE BAYLIFF OF THE FEE OF WAKEFIELD OR THE BAYLIFFE OF DEWSBURY

The pr[e]sent Bayliffe of The Fee of Wakefield or the Bayliff of Dewsbury is Michael Parker who Farmes The Profitts of the sane under the yearly Rent of £16. The Townes Villages & Hamlets following are within his division (vizt) Dewsbury, Osset, Southwood-Green, Gawthorp, Soothill, Chickinley, Chidsell, Hanging-Heaton, Earles Heaton, Over Buthroyd, Nether Buthroyd, West Ardsley, Woodkirke, Westerton, Dunningley, Haigh, Topliffe, Overgreen & Eccleshill. His Securities are Robert Bedford Gent, Mathew Parker & John Naylor, Yeom[en]. He has within his ffarme The Earls Rents following (vizt)

Dewsbury	£	s.	d.
John Murgatroyd Gent	0	14	9
Wm Elmsall, Gent	0	9	0
The Towne of Ecclesall	0	10	0
Jnº Speight	0	0	2
Jeramia Chadwick	0	0	4
Michael Whitley	0	1	6
Abr[aha]m Firth	0	2	0
John Wheelwright Gent	0	2	0
George Shepley	0	3	0
Robert Lee	0	1	6
The heirs of [*blank*] Ramsdin Esq	0	3	4
The heirs of Robert Craven	0	2	0
James Green for Mr Ramsden Land	0	3	0
Joseph Oldroyd	0	9	4
Dº p[er] Chaster Farme	0	1	6
Joseph Oldroyd Junr	0	1	8
Abrm̃ Greenwood	0	11	2
Abrm̃ Greenwood Junr	0	1	6
Dº for Green Land	0	4	4
Robert Holdsworth & widw Brook	0	6	0
Richard Parker	0	0	2
James Shepley	0	1	0
Geo: Castle	0	5	1
Samuel Chaister	0	1	4
Tymothy Wheatley	0	0	6
John Chaister	0	0	6
James Willans	0	0	6
John Knowles for Weightman Land	0	2	2
Thomas Speight	0	1	3
Richard Whitley	0	0	6
Thomas Whitley	0	0	6
Osset			
John Whitley for Mr Kirk Land	0	17	0

James Spurr	0	2	6
Tho: Fox for Hallifax Freeschool Land	0	6	9
Joseph Spurr for M[r] Birkhead	0	4	0
John Illingworth for Kirshaw Land	0	3	6
Richard Foster	0	3	10
James White	0	2	6
Willm̃ Oates Gent	0	4	0
Joshua Bower for Oates Land	0	1	7
John Bradford for M[r] Davinson Land	0	4	6

Hanging Heaton

Robert Waterhous Gent	0	3	3
S[r] Geo: Savile p[er] Tho: Greenwood ffarm ..	0	0	6
D[o] p[er] Charles Greenfield	0	1	7
Mark Whittakers	0	3	0
John Breary	0	1	10
Anthony Fearnley	0	2	0
Wm Darnbrough	0	1	0
Wid[w] Speight	0	0	4
Joseph Dey	0	0	6
James Buckley	0	0	3
James Hirst	0	0	4
W[m] Ridlesden	0	0	4
Sam[l] Hodgson	0	0	4
Jo: Thackera for Dickson ffarme	0	0	4
Nathan[l] Rhodes	0	0	3
Henry Hemingway & James Speight	0	0	6
John Holdsworth	0	0	4

Earlsheaton

M[r] Charles Netleton Cl[erk]	0	0	4½
M[r] Josias Oates	0	2	10
M[rs] Wadsworth	0	1	2
John Scholefield	0	0	10

OFFICERS—THE BAYLIFF OF HALLIFAX

This Officer in the time of The Forrist of Hardwick when the Forrist Laws were in force was then call'd the Cheif Bayliff of Hallifax or Sheriff of Sowerby Shire and in all matters relateing to the Execution of Criminals acted as Sheriff and to this Day keeps the Gibbit Ax with which Malefactors were formerly executed at Hallifax

The pr[e]sent Bayliff is the aforesaid Geoler Thomas Watmough he haveing both the offices under his charge & Security and farmes the Profits of both under the yearly rent of £50. The Townes Villages and Hamlets following are within his division (vizt)

Hallifax, Skircoat, Shelf, Hip[per]holme, Northowrome, Shipdin, Hartley Green, Brighous, Ovenden, Myxenden, Warley, Saltonstall, Midgley, Heptonstall, Wadsworth, Shakleton, Wydophead, Erringden. **Sowerby,** Soyland, Stansfeild, Blackwood, Rawtonstall, Rushworth, Norlend, Langfield, Rastrick, Totehill, Fixby, Barkisland, Quarnby, Lindley, Scamonden, Ripponden, Ludenden, Milsbrigg, Longroyd brigg, North Crosland, Golcarr, Stainland, Old Lindley, Hartchstead, Clifton, Kirklees & Dalton. He has also within his ffarme a Stone Quarrie on Micklemoss in Northowrome and the Earl Warren Rents following (vizt)

Earles Rents

	£	s.	d.
Fixby			
Tho: Thornhill Esq	0	11	0
Clifton : John Armitage for Constable Lands ..	1	0	0
Northowram			
Mr Samuel Fournes for Longbottom	0	8	0
John Stancliffe	0	3	0
John Bentley & Edwd Northend	0	0	10
Wm Drake Esq	0	8	0
Joshua Horton Esq	0	0	8
Skircoat			
John Dransfield for Savile Land	0	0	3
Samuel King	0	1	0
Henry Milner	0	0	3
Do for Humphrey Milner Land	0	1	0
John Lockwood of Midgley	0	0	3
John Crowther for James Milner Land	0	0	1½
Stephen Milner	0	0	7
Do for Horsley Land	0	0	3
Midgley, Sowerby & Shelf			
John Batley for Shelf Hall	0	0	9
Willm Hodge	0	0	9
Willm Walker & James Chadwick for Tempest Lands	0	0	9
Mr Armitage of Kesworth Hill	0	0	9
Susan Brook for Waterhous Land	0	0	9
Hip[per]holme			
Nathan Whitley	0	0	4
John Barraclough for Lands at Hellewell Sike ..	0	0	1
Ovenden			
Dennis Illingworth for Wharton Lands	0	0	4½
Abrm̃ Illingworth	0	0	3
Willm̃ Illingworth for Land at Forsley	0	0	3½
Mr Fournes for Hayley Lands	0	0	3
Jer: Wilkinson & Robert Tillotson	0	0	4

Mr John Lister	0	0	1½
Bryon Farrer	0	0	3
Robert Doughty	0	0	3
Henry Wadsworth for Cockcroft Lands	0	0	1½
Barstow & Best Lands	0	0	2
Luke Hoyle for Mich[1] Hasleden Lands	0	0	1½
Robert Barstow for ffurnes Lands	0	0	1½
Henry Best	0	0	2
Mr Lister for Cockcroft Lands	0	0	1½
Rushworth & Norland			
Sr George Savile	0	13	4
Isaac Farrer for Woodhead Lands	0	2	0
Nathaniel Wadsworth and Chadwick	0	0	2
John Hopkinson	0	0	1½
John Milner of Norland for Woodhead	0	0	1½
Thomas Oldfield for Norland Hall	0	0	1½
Robert Towne for Raynor Lands	0	0	1½
Rushworth Hall	0	0	6½
John Godley	0	0	4
George Firth for the Oakes	0	0	1½
John Ramsden for the Booth	0	0	1½

OFFICERS—THE BAYLIFFE OF HOLME

The present Bayliff of Holme is Henry Wilson who Farmes the profits thereof under the yearly Rent of £10. The Townes Villages and Hamlets following are within his division (vizt:) Holmfirth, Holme, Scholes, Woodall, Cartworth Austonley, Hepworth, Foulstone, Tongue Kirkburton, Highburton, Ryley, Cumberworth half, upper & nether, Skelmanthorp, Shelley, Shepley, Thurstonland, Roydhouse, Emley, Bentley Grange Woodhous, & p[ar]te of Flocktons the upper & nether. He has also within his ffarme The Earl Warren Rents following. And his securities are Francis Matthewman Yeom[an] & Joseph Woodhead Yeom[an.]

Earls Rents

	£	s.	d.
Holmfirth			
Mr Henry Jackson	0	1	8
Thomas Hinchliffe	0	2	0
Thomas Booth	0	0	6
Jno Booth	0	0	6
Philip Bray	0	0	6
Mr Jno Pickard	0	0	2
Burton			
Geo: Kay Esqr	1	5	0
Emley			
Widw Allot p[er] Thorncliff	0	2	0

Richard Haire Lands	0	1	0
Geo: Parker	0	0	8
Mathew Marshall	0	0	2
Chr[ist]ofer Allot	0	0	3
Richard Blacker	0	0	8
Willm Feild	0	0	8
Jn° Walshaw	0	0	8
Jn° Gleadhill	0	0	8
Martin Hepworth	0	0	8
Mrs Robinson	0	0	8
Jn° Hepworth	0	0	8
Jn° Wilkinson	0	0	2
Skelmanthorp, Cumberworth			
Geo: Green	0	0	8
Joseph Firth	0	0	6
Jn° Coldwell	0	0	4
Joshua Shaw	0	0	2
Richard Hutchinson	0	0	2
Godfrey Horne	0	0	3½
Widw Longley	0	0	4½
Jn° Rich	0	0	8
Abrm̃ Hepworth	0	0	4
Totall	2	2	9

OFFICERS—THE TOLL GATHERER

The Tolls of Wakefield arise out of Cloth Wool Corne & Cattle and what only are bought and sold in The Towne of Wakefield. The present Farmer of these is James Braithwate under the yearly Rent of £50. The usuall Tolls & Fees are as follow

	£	s.	d.
Every Pack of Cloth sold in The Towne	0	0	6
Every Pack of Wool	0	0	4
Every 4 Bushells of Malt barly or otes	0	0	0½
Every 3 Bushels of all other sort of Graine	0	0	0½
Every Pack of Woodwist	0	0	0½
Every Sack of Aples or other Fruit	0	0	0½
Every Beast	0	0	2
Every Swine	0	0	0½
Every Pack of Cloth that is bought in the Towne & driven out any back way to defraud the Toll	2	0	0
D° Every Pack of Wool or Load of Corne	0	13	4

N.B There are severall Townes though formerly have paid yet now refuse & for severall years have bene allowed as free (vizt) Knaresbrough Beverley & Yorke

Also Townes within the Mannor (vizt) Osset Dewsbury, Lightcliffe & Hallifax

OFFICERS—THE BAKER

The Bakehous is erected near The Middle of the Towne of Wakefield and all Publique houses and such as bake to sell are obliged to bake there. The present Farmer of the Bakehous is M[r] Abrm̃ Beevers who holds it by Lease under the yearly Rent of £25. The Fees are as follow

Fees of The Bakehous

	£	s.	d.
The Com̃on Bakers who bake to sell have Twenty Pennyworth of bread or other things baked for	0	0	1
The bakeing of a Load of Meale into Bread for any Housekeeper in Wakefield.. ..	0	1	0
A large Pye	0	0	1
A large Pudding	0	0	0½
Six Tarts	0	0	1
A Large Stue of Hoghel	0	0	1
A small one	0	0	0¼
A small Pye	0	0	¼

THE GRAVESHIPS AND THE OFFICERS

There are Twelve Graveships w[i]thin The Mannor (vizt) Wakefield, Thornes, Sandall, Horbury, Alverthorp, Stanley, Osset, Rastrick, Holme, Sowerby, Hipperholme, & Scamonden, every of which hath yearly an Officer called The Grave such officers execute all manner of Precepts which issue out of the L[or]ds Courts and are directed to them from the Stewards, & collect the Freehold Copyhold Rents within their respective Graveships and pay the same to the L[or]ds Receivor. It is generally reckoned (as was said before) that the Freehold Lands are helpfull in this service & that noe Copiehold whatsoever are exempt from it but either finde Principall or Helper being that equall service one to another in their turnes wil thereby be reciprically administred for who ever hath occasion to seise and thereby cutt of an Intail or to make any better assurance, it can not be done without The Grave, And if such sho[ul]d be exempt from service noe returne wil be made to their fellow Copyholders (who doe serve such Offices) when they have such occasion soe that though many at this juncture refuse to help becaus the Principalls Co[ul]d not finde their Land's (soe overlookt in their turnes) doe seem to stand out and p[re]tend that their Lands are exempt from such service Yet the Custome seems reasonable & whenever tried at Law it's suposed wil be confirmed And for the regulateing these things and for the finding out The Copyhold Rents which have a considerable p[ar]t of them been lost by wrong recitement in surrenders given into Court of The L[or]ds Rents thereby to lessen the Fines which are ruled by the Rents mentioned in the Surrenders. His Grace

The Duke of Leeds the present Lord of the Mannor in the year 1709 by his Stewards called Courts in most of the Graveships and swore the most Substantiall Freeholders & Copyholders in those respective Graveships to enquire & finde out all the Lands his Rents issues out on And the Lands which yearly found the Graves and the Lands that help't respectively as they are all hereafter Sett downe being copied from their respective Verdicts

THE ROYALTIES IN PERTICULAR AND FIRST THE COPIEHOLD AND FREEHOLD RENTS ARISEING OUT OF THE GRAVESHIP OF WAKEFIELD

The Graveship of Wakefield is bounder'd by Stanley Graveship to the North, & East by Thornes Graveship to the South, & by Alverthorp Graveship to the West, And hath within it The Freehold & Copyhold Tennants following who Pay Rents &c according to the Verdict taken out of The Court Rolls of the Mannor as followeth.

Maner[ium] de Wakefeld } Ad Magn[am] Cur[iam] Baron[em] Nobilissimi Thome Ducis de Leeds pr[ae]nobilis Ordinis Garterij Militis D[omi]ni Manerij de Wakefield tent[am] ib-[idem] p[er] adjournament[um] Vicesimo Secundo die Septembr Anno Regni D[omin]e n[ostre] Anne Dei gra[tia] nunc Reginae Magne Britannie &c Octavo [22 Sept: 1709]

The Verdict of Thomas Birkhead, Thomas Wilson, Francis Pitt, Thomas Pollard, Thomas Warberton, Samuel Vsher, John Nevinson, Benjamin Sigston, John Dawson, Anthony Bland, Robert Scott, James Braithwaite & John Pollard being Freeholders & Copyholders within the Graveship of Wakefield of and concerning the Freehold & Copyhold Lands & Tenements within the said Graveship which pay Rents & doe servic to the Lord of the said Mannor of Wakefield

WAKEFIELD GRAVESHIP

1st	James Browne Gent in the Right of his wife for a Close called Base Flatt in the possession of Mrs Fleming .. } And hath help of John Wood of Woodthorp in right of his wife for houses in Ratton row & the rest of his Lands in Wakefield .. .. .. }	0	3	10
	Willm Copendall Gent for his hous in Rattan Row .. .. }	0	1	9
	Richard Fostard, Senior for a close at Rengate head .. .. }	0	1	3

	Thomas Beatson for a house & croft at Kirkgate End	0	1	5			
	The Governors of The Poor for the new Shambles	0	1	9			
	John Robinson of Barnby Moor for a Butcher Stall in the occ[upation] of Wm Ward	0	0	6			
	Forward				0	10	6
2d	Hannah Horne, widdow for a house in the Market place in the poss[ession] of Thomas Gill	0	0	10			
	And hath help of Richard Armitage Gent for a house in the poss[ession] of James Scorey called the Golden Cock	0	4	0			
	The Heirs of Thomas Brooke Gent: for a house in the poss[ession] of Thomas Warberton and one other house in the Churchyard in the poss[ession] of Michl Stears	0	2	6			
	Margaret Hall for a House in the Ratten row	0	0	6			
	John Walker for a House in Northgate in his own poss[ession] ..	0	0	6			
	Robert Green for a house in the Ratten row in his own possession ..	0	0	3			
	The Earl of Cardigan for a House in the poss[ession] of Robt Beevers ..	0	0	4			
	Willm Awdsley for a House att Westgate end	0	0	10½			
	John Nevison for two Houses in Northgate in his own Mr Garnet and Mr Woolen poss[ession]	0	0	9			
					0	10	6½
3d	The Governours of the Free School of Wakefield for one half of their Lands in Wakefield	0	2	7½			
	And hath help of Benjamin Sigston for Houseing near the Church Yeard late Mawdleys	0	3	0			
	Thomas Pollard for his house in the Market Place	0	2	5			

	The Heirs of Wm Lawson for a house att Ratten row end in the poss[ession] of Swail Hall, Tho: Booth, Richard Denton, and James Sidney	0	2	1			
	Obadiah Redhead for a Cottage Vnder the Brigg near the churchyeard	0	0	0¾			
	Mrs Kay for a House in the churchyeard	0	0	1½			
	William Nayler, Butcher for his house in the [*blank*]	0	0	8			
					0	10	11¾
	The Hon[ora]ble the Lord Raby for one fourth parte of all his Lands & Tenem[en]ts in Wakefield p[ar]te being the Milneroyds	0	5	2¾			
	And hath help of Joseph Prance for a house and Croft att the bottom of Kirkgate	0	0	10½			
	John Liverseidge for a House in the Silver Street in the occupation of Widdow Gold	0	0	6			
	Abraham Barber for a house in the Churchyeard	0	0	2½			
	John Dawson for a house att Bitchill	0	1	6			
	Robert & John Scott for a little Close att Northgate Head	0	0	3			
	Mary Oley, widdow for a House in Rattan Row in the Occupation of Widow Byewater and Jonathan Hargreaves	0	2	0			
					0	10	6¾
5th	The Hon[ora]ble The Lord Raby for an other fourth p[ar]te of all his Lands & Tenem[en]ts in Wakefield p[ar]te being the Milne royds	0	5	2¾			
	And hath help of Charles Faile Gent. in the right of his wife for Pinchen well Close & others	0	1	0			
	Thomas Tofield for a House in the Church yard in the poss[ession] of John Ward, Butcher ..	0	0	10½			
	William Nayler, Butcher for two houses in the Church yard	0	0	6			
	Anthony Bland for a house in Northgate	0	0	1			

	Christopher Lee for a house in Silver street in the Occupation of Widdow Swinden	0	0	6			
	Richard Shaw, Gent for a house in the poss[ession] of Edward Green ..	0	0	8			
	Ditto for a house in the poss[ession] of Joseph Hart	0	0	6			
	Mary Raper, widd[o]w for a house in Northgate adjoyning vpon the Fish Shambles	0	0	10			
	Mary Banister, Spinster for a house in Silver Street in the poss[ession] of Richard March	0	0	3			
					0	10	5½
6	Susannah Sill, widow[1] for one close of Land called Siddall Close & other Lands in Wakefield	0	6	6			
	Also for a close of Land called Horn-castle Close	0	1	0			
	And hath help of Doctor Clayton for a house in the Silver Street in the poss-[ession] of Samuel Hancock, Toby Sill[2] & others	0	2	10			
	John Walker for a Chamber in the Churchyeard	0	0	0¾			
	The Heirs of Daniel Greenwood for a Cott[age] vnder the Bridge adjoyning to the Church yeard	0	0	0¾			
	James Thornton for a Cottage in the Church yeard	0	0	0¾			
					0	10	6¼
7	Sr John Dalston, Barronett for one half of a Close of Land called Hall Ing	0	3	1½			
	And hath help of the Heirs of Mr Kirby of Siddall Hills in Patterdale ..	0	3	4			
	Samuel Vsher, Gent in the Right of his wife for New house att Bitchill..	0	1	9			
	William Middlebrook for a house at Bitchill	0	0	9			
	Mary Barrhouse, widow for a house in her own possession	0	1	4			

[1] *H.P.*, 130.
[2] *H.P.*, 130.

	The Heirs of Sara Browne for a little house att Broksbank att Westgate End	0	0	2	
					0 10 5½
8	William Hodgson, Clerk, for one half of his Lands in Wakefield, p[ar]te being one close called Horsefield Close ..	0	1	8	
	And hath Help of Charles Rimington, Gent in Right of his wife for Lands late Wallers	0	3	3	
	The Heirs of John Walker, Gent. for Lands late Wallers	0	0	4	
	Elianor Fleeming wid[ow] for a Close att Eastmoor	0	0	6	
	Samuel Firth for a house in Ratten Row in the occupation of Stephen Lawrence & for the Fish Shambles Chamber	0	01	3½	
	James Scrivener for a house in Northgate in his own poss[ession] ..	0	1	0	
	Samuel Hide for a house in Westgate in the poss[ession] of Geo: Hull ..	0	0	10	
	Francis Mawd, Gent: for Lands near Cliff Tree Hill	0	1	1½	
	James Braithwaite for p[ar]te of his House in Westgate	0	0	6	
					0 10 6
9	S[r] John Dalston Barronet for the other half of a Close of Land called Fall Ing	0	3	1½	
	And hath help of the Heirs of Joseph Bargh for a house att Bitchill in the poss[ession] of Anthony Bland..	0	2	0	
	Thomas Loxley for a house in Kirkgate late Standrows	0	0	8	
	Willm Naylor, Gent: for a house in Northgate in the house of Henry Bradley, Gent:	0	2	7	
	Ditto for a house in the church-yard ..	0	2	2½	
	Francis Pitt, Gent: for a house att Rengate Head	0	0	4½	
	Richard Norfolke, Gent. for a house in the poss[ession] of Toby Sill, Gent.	0	0	9	
	Rachel Kirke, widdow for p[ar]te of a house in the poss[ession] of Susannah Wright, widdow	0	0	9½	
					0 10 6

10	The Hon[ora]ble The Lord Raby for an other fourth p[ar]te of all his Lands & Tenem[en]ts in Wakefield p[ar]te being the Milneroyds	0	5	2¾			
	And hath help of Robt Monnckton Esq for his Lands in Wakefield ..	0	2	6			
	The Heirs of John Mawdsley for a House att Church Steel	0	0	4			
	Ciril Arthington for Cottages in the Church yeard	0	0	8			
	John Batty Esq[r] for a House in the poss[ession] of Francis Lister ..	0	1	10			
					0	10	6¾
11	The Hon[ora]ble The Lord Raby for the Last fourth p[ar]te of all his Lands & tenem[en]ts in Wakefield p[ar]te being in the Milneroyds ..	0	5	2½			
	And hath help of Thomas Birkhead, Gent. for Milneroyds and Kirkgate Closes	0	3	8			
	John Pollard in right of his wife for a house in the Rattan row in his own & Thomas Duffin poss[ession] ..	0	1	8			
					0	10	6¾
12	Will. Hodgson, Clerk, for the other half of his Lands in Wakefield p[ar]te being one Close called Little Fall Ing ..	0	1	8			
	And hath help of John Nevile Esq[r] for the Lower Mills & his Lands & tene-m[en]ts in Wakefield	0	6	7			
	Willm Wormall for a Close att Rengate Head	0	0	4			
	Thomas Warberton Gent for Newhouse in the Rattan row	0	1	10½			
					0	10	5½
13	The Governors of the ffree School of Wakefield for the other half of their Lands in Wakefield	0	2	7½			
	And hath help of Joseph Watkinson, Gent for two Houses in the Market Place	0	4	0			
	Thomas wilson, Gent. for his house in the Market Place	0	1	4			

No.	Entry	£ s. d.	£ s. d.
	John Bramley for a House in Northgate in the Poss[ession] of Samuel Knowles & Thomas Marshall & a Close called Oliver Ing & for a House in Westgate in the poss[ession] of Mich[l] Lee ..	0 2 8	
			0 10 7½
14	The Governors of the Poor of the town & parish of Wakefield for a close lyeing below the Nether Walk mills ..	0 5 4	
	And hath help of [*blank*] for a Barne & two closes Crofts in the Occupation of Thomas Allott	0 1 4	
	Elizabeth Briggs, wid[ow] for two Houses one in the market place in the Poss[ession] of Sam[l] Liversiedge & the other in her own poss[ession] ..	0 3 4	
	John Hawksworth for a House in the Church Yard in the Poss[ession] of Joseph Binnes	0 0 7	
			0 10 7
	Totall ..		7 7 9½

Wee The Jury Sworne for the Lord of the Mannor of Wakefield abovesaid doe upon our enquiry into the Old Rentalls & evidences concerning our said Graveship of Wakefield find & present that there are fourteen Graves within our said Graveship and that the persons abovesaid vnder their several Numbers ought to serve the office of Grave in their Respective turns for their Lands and tenem[en]ts there mentioned And have Helpers which are there set down vnder the same Number for their Lands and tenements there also mentioned, and that those Persons vnder the Number Two doe serve the Office for this present yeare beginning att Mich[ae]lmas Last and the rest successively as they follow in their Numbers, and that the respective rents vnder every Number are due and payable yearly to the Lord of the said Mannor

Tho: Birkhead
Tho: Wilson
Fr: Pitt
Tho: Pollard
Tho. Warberton
Sam[l] Vsher
Jn[o] Nevison

Benj Sigston
John Dawson
Anthony Bland
Robert Scott
James Braithwaite
John Pollard

THE GRAVESHIP OF SANDALL

The Graveship of Sandall is boundred by Heath to the North East by Okenshaw & Walton to the East by Chivit & Wooley which lye in the Parish of Royston, to the South by Bretton & Nether Shitlington to the West, by the River of Calder to the North, and hath within it The Freehold & Copyhold Tenn[en]ts following who pay Rents &c according to the Verdict taken out of The Court Rolls of the Mannor as followeth :—

Maner[ium] de Wakefield } Ad Magn[am] Cur[iam] Baron[em] Nobilissimi Thome Ducis de Leeds pr[ae]nobilis ordinis Garterij Militis D[omi]ni Manerij de Wakefield Tent[am] ib[ide]m p[er] adjournament[um] vicesimo die Maij Anno Regni D[omi]ne n[ost]re Anne Dei Gra[tia] nunc Regine Magne Brittanie &c octavo

The Verdict of John Grice,[1] Gervas Norton,[2] James Swallow, Henry Rayner,[3] John Webster, Robt Dickinson John Chapman John Hirst, Joseph Hirst, Thomas Hawksworth, George Fairburne, John Lambert, and Anthony Bedford being Freehold[e]rs & Copyhold[e]rs within the Graveship of Sandall of and concerning the Freehold & Copyhold Lands & Tenem[en]ts within the said Graveship which pay Rents & doe service to the Lord of the said mannor of Wakefield

		£	s.	d.			
1st	John Lambert for Laith Croft late Lawson's & formerly Fields lyeing in Sandall	0	0	4			
	Do for a Close in Castle Feild late Norfolks	0	0	6			
	And hath help of James Haigh, Gent: in the right of his wife for a house & Land at Milnthorp in poss[ession] of Jno Lamb[er]t	0	2	0			
	Sr Jno Daltson Baront for Roughley Hill in the poss[ession] of Thomas Marshall	0	3	4			
	Do for his Lands in the Old Feild late the Lady Mary Bolds & formerly Grice	0	4	0			
					0	10	2
2	Willm Webster in the right of his wife for a Mess[uage] & 7 acres of Land at Stanbrigg late Taylors in the poss[ession] of John Chapman	0	1	6			
	Do for severall Closes at Stanbrigg called Woolgraves late Rhodes' & heretofore Eliz: Saviles	0	1	9			
					0	3	3

[1] *H.P.*, 85. [2] *H.F.M.G.*, III, 911. [3] *H.P.*, 118.

	Dº for 1/3 p[ar]te of his Lands at Hollingthorp	0	4	4			
	Joseph Wood, Clerk for a close of Freehold late Taylors	0	0	6			
	And have help of Willm̃ Smith for a hous & Croft on Humbley side ..	0	1	0			
	John Chapman for a hous & Land in Chapelthorp	0	0	6			
	Richard Rayner for a Cottage ..	0	0	6			
					0	10	1
3d	Joseph Hirst for a hous & three Closes of Land in Chapel Thorp in his owne poss[ession] formerly Audsley Land	0	2	1			
	Dº for other three closes in Chapel Thorp..	0	1	8			
	John Hirst for a Mess[uage] a Boyne & Lands in Chapelthorp ..	0	5	10			
	And hath help of Wm Hanson for a Cott[age] & orchard on Hall Green	0	0	6			
					0	10	1
4	John Webster for one half of his Lands formerly Swifts & late Carters ..	0	9	5			
	And hath help of Joseph Prance for a messuage & Crofts late Blands at Newbiggin Hill	0	0	8			
					0	10	1
5	Samuel Burslum Gent for a Mess[uage] and Lands at Dawgreen late Woods & formerly Agnes Leeks.. ..	0	4	0			
	And hath help of The Heirs of Thomas Webster for a hous & Lands thereunto belonging, lyeing at Sandall Three houses	0	5	2			
	Joseph Oley for Fossardhous	0	0	2			
	Richd Healey for a hous & a Croft in his owne poss[ession] at Humley end	0	0	2			
	Richard Pearson for a Cottage in the poss[ession] of Joseph Booth ..	0	0	2			
	Robert Cook for a Cottage & Croft in Chapel Thorp	0	0	2			
	Eliz: Rayner & John Moor in the right of his wife for Three Cottages at Hall Green	0	0	3			
					0	10	1

No.	Description	£	s	d	£	s	d
6	Samuel Hide for a mess[uage] & Lands at Newbiggin Hill late Dickinsons	0	1	9			
	And hath help of Robert Dickinson for a Mess[uage] & Land at Newbiggin Hill	0	1	8			
	Do for a Kilne at Newmiller Damm ..	0	0	1			
	The Heirs of Wm Weightman for certain Closes of Land called Haslewells & Green Close	0	2	8			
	The Feofees of The Chapel for a Mess[uage] & Lands at Chapel Thorp in the poss[ession] of John Walker ..	0	0	4			
	Robert Dickinson for Two Closes called Long Tofts	0	0	7			
	Do for Burnit & Carter Lands	0	1	6			
	Do for Prince Land	0	1	6			
					0	10	1
7th	John Wood, Gent for half p[ar]te of his Mess[uage] & Lands at Woodthorp late Halls & formerly Roes ..	0	7	1½			
	Do for Six acres of Land late Huchinsons ..	0	2	0			
	And hath help of Samuel Oxley for a hous on Crigleston Cliff ..	0	1	0			
					0	10	1½
8th	John Grice, Gent. for all his Lands & Tenem[en]ts in Sandall ..	0	8	8			
	And hath help of Joseph Wood, Cl[erk] for Four acres of Field Land late Lawsons	0	1	4			
					0	10	0
9th	Willm Beau-mont, Gent for a Mess[uage] and Lands in Hollingthorp now in the poss[ession] of Rob: Elam	0	2	6			
	Do for Knowle Close & Clay Lands late Boines	0	3	4			
	Do for Riggs Land	0	0	4			
	Do for a Free Rent there	0	0	7			
	Do for Oxley Land	0	0	2			
	Do for a Free Rent	0	1	8			
	Do for Three Closes in Hollingthorp in Robert Elams poss[ession] late Marshalls	0	2	4			
	Do for a Rood of Land late Shillitoe ..	0	0	1			
					0	11	0

10th	John Wheelwright Gent: for Two Mess-[uage] a Croft a Kilne with Lands thereunto belonging in Sandall in the poss-[ession] of Michael Whelewright Gent.	0	0	9	
	And hath help of Michael Whelewright Gent for a hous & land in his own poss-[ession] and late in the poss[ession] of [*blank*] Mires	0	0	10	
	Do for a hous & Land in the poss[ession] of Jonas Barber & himself ..	0	0	3	
	Do for Oley Inge	0	1	0	
	Jonas Barber for an Acre & a half of Land in Woodthorp feild ..	0	0	6	
	Thomas Moor for his hous at Sandall Pinfold	0	0	6	
	Joseph Wood, Cl[erk] for Scoleys now in the poss[ession] of Tho: Shillitoe ..	0	1	4	
	James Haigh Cl[erk] for a close called Binns Close	0	1	0	
	Mr Lawson for certain Closes nere Sandall Moor in the poss[ession] of Thomas Marshall	0	1	2	
	Richard Norfolk, Gent for certain Closes in the poss[ession] of Saml. Robinson	0	2	7	
	Gervas Sedgworth for a Mess[uage] & Two Crofts & field Land ..	0	0	2	
					0 10 1
11th	Richard Shaw, Gent for Shooterhill & other Lands formerly Tho Grices	0	2	3	
	And hath help of Francis Pitt, Gent for Sugar Closes	0	2	0	
	Daniel Oley, Gent for Pugnall Land in the poss[ession] of Jno Clarkson	0	5	10	
					0 10 1
12th	Henry Raynor for Boyne Land ..	0	4	2	
	Do for Three Acres & a half of Land late Halls	0	2	0	
	Do for a Cott[age] on Crigleston Cliff ..	0	0	1	
	Do for a Close called Deanroyd late Fyefields	0	2	8	
	Do for a hous & Two Crofts late Milners ..	0	0	7	

No.	Tenant and holding	Rent	Total
	And hath help of Thomas Lee for a Cottage	0 0 6	
			0 10 0
13	John Elam for a mess[uage] & Lands & thereunto belonging now in the poss[ession] of Robert Elam ..	0 5 1	
	James Swallow for Lands late Elams and formerly Wades	0 0 5	
	Willm Webster for Joan Royd late Elams	0 0 8	
	And hath help of Elizabeth Walker for a Close of Land in Pignall and other Lands late Norfolks and formerly Halls	0 2 0	
	D^o^ for Barker Land	0 1 4	
	D^o^ for 2 acres of Land late Lamberts & formerly Norfolks	0 0 7	
			0 10 1
14	Edward Allot, Gent for a Close of Land called Meldroyd lyeing in Crigleston	0 1 4	
	D^o^ for Adam Roid being halfe of the Lands late John Allots of Bentley & a Close called Quarell close ..	0 5 7	
	And hath help of John Burnett for a mess[uage] & Lands att Dirtcarr & Certaine Field Lands ..	0 0 11	
	George Fairbarne for a mess[uage] & Lands to the same belong in the Slack in Criglestone	0 1 8	
	Samuel Firth for a Small Close lyeing in Many gates in the poss[ession] of Henry Sharp	0 0 4	
			0 9 10
15	John Smith, Gent for Lands late Boynes lyeing in Dirtcarr in the poss[ession] of Jonas Burnett & Richd Cusworth	0 3 4	
	D^o^ for two acres called Goits & one Close called Hassacks & a close called Riley Royds and another Close called Newsam Ing with other Lands late Saviles & all his other Lands late Johnsons, Blackers, & Saxtons	0 7 0	
			0 10 4

No.	Description						
16	Edward Allott, Gent: for four acres and a halfe of Land lyeing att the side of Crigleston Cliff late Johnson ..	0	1	6			
	Do for three acres there late Jepsons ..	0	0	6			
	And hath help of James Swallow, Gent for three acres of Land on the top of Crigleston Cliff late Barbers ..	0	1	0			
	Willm Webster in right of his wife for Carr Close adjoining on Woolley Moore	0	2	0			
	England & Fiffeild for a mess[uage] and Lands in Hollingthorpe ..	0	4	2			
	Joseph Cooke for Oxley Lands.. ..	0	0	4			
	Thomas Bolland for a House in the poss-[ession] of Geo: Cooke ..	0	0	2			
	Joseph Bedford for a Cott[age] att Chapel Thorpe	0	0	1			
	Thomas Ramsden for a House & Cott-[age] att Hill Top	0	0	1			
					0	9	10
17	John Webster for his Lands att Pledwick..	0	3	0			
	Anne Norton for her Lands att Pledwick..	0	6	3			
	And hath help of Thomas Shillitoe for Chappel Close	0	9	11			
	[*sic*]				0	9	11
18	Gervas Norton, Gent for one fourth parte of his Lands in Kettlethorp	0	7	0			
	Do for Johnsons house and Croft late Smiths	0	0	4			
	Do Feoffee for Thomas Norton for a mess[uage] & Land att Woodthorp	0	0	3			
	And hath help of John Norton[1] for Land late Barbers called Well Ing ..	0	1	1			
	Do for a House and Croft in the poss-[ession] of Francis Sannderson late Baxters	0	1	0			
	Do for an Inge and p[ar]te of Dentcliffe Oakes	0	0	7			
					0	10	3
19	John Webster for the other halfe of His Lands formerly Swifts and late Carters	0	9	5			

[1] *H.F.M.G.*, III, 911.

No.	Description	£	s	d	£	s	d
	D° for a close called Ridings late Crawshaws	0	0	7			
					0	10	0
20	Gervas Norton for the second fourth parte of his Lands att Kettlethorp	0	7	0			
	And hath help of John Norton, Gent. for a Mess[uage] & Lands late Robinsons & formerly Elams in the poss[ession] of John Wadsworth	0	3	3			
					0	10	3
21	William Webster for two third parts of his House & Land at Hollingthorpe formerly Rhodes	0	8	6			
	And hath help of Mrs Lawson for a close near Sandal Moore in Wm Brooksbanks poss[ession] called Many Gates	0	1	2			
	William Womack for House at Hill Top..	0	0	1			
	Thomas Savage for a House in the poss[ession] of Ad[a]m Ward ..	0	0	1			
	Stephen Atkinson for a House and Croft..	0	0	1			
	Barnard Jewitt for a Cottage	0	0	1			
					0	10	0
22	Mrs Burdett for a mess[uage] & Lands at Daw Green late Sr Thomas Beaumonts	0	2	8			
	D° for Land late Johnsons	0	1	2			
	And hath Help of Thomas Hawksworth for a house & Croft in his own Poss[ession]	0	0	6			
	D° for Carr closes late Fifields.. ..	0	3	5			
	Edward Beckett for severall Cottages att New milne Dam	0	1	0			
	Richard Haigh for a Cottage	0	1	0			
	Jeremy Milner for Land in the Pitt Close..	0	0	3			
					0	10	0
23	Ciril Arthington Esq[1] for one third parte of Milnethorpe Hall & his Lands thereunto belonging	0	8	9½			
	And Hath help of John Bedford for a Cott[age] in his own poss[ession]	0	0	4			

[1] *C.D.*, I, 239.

	The Heirs of Robert Melwood for Town Row	0 1 0	
			0 10 1½
24	John Nevile Esq & Geo: Empson, Gent: in the right of his wife for their first third parte of all their Lands & ten-[emen]ts in Sandall Graveshipp	0 9 2	
	The Heirs of John Kirke, Gent. for Hassacke & formerly Boynes ..	0 0 8	
	William Cooke for two closes called Rideings att Hill Top ..	0 0 3	
			0 10 1
25	Cerill Arthington Esq for his second third parte of Milnthorpe Hall & the Lands thereunto belonging ..	0 8 9¼	
	And hath Help of Sam[1] Dickinson for a House & 3 Closes	0 0 10	
	D° for Land late Grices	0 0 3	
	D° for Blacker House	0 0 2	
			0 10 0¼
26	John Wood, Gent. for the other Half parte of his Mess[uage] & Lands att Woodthorpe late Halls & formerly Roes	0 7 1½	
	And Hath help of Joseph Beevers Gent:[1] for a House	0 0 4	
	D° for Mess[uage] & Lands where he now dwelleth	0 0 8	
	D° for a House & two Closes att Humley formerly Stringers	0 1 10	
			0 9 11½
27	Ciril Arthington Esq[r] for his last third parte of Milnethorpe Hall & the Land thereunto belonging	0 8 9¼	
	And hath Help of Henry Bradley for two Closes called Black bancks ..	0 1 2½	
			0 9 11¾
28	Gervas Norton for the third fourth parte of his land att Kettlethorp ..	0 7 0	
	D° for Bottom Field..	0 0 3	
	D° for Thorntree Close & other Inclosure late Sam[l] Wadsworths..	0 2 2	
	D° for a close & a Mess[uage] late Thomas's	0 1 0	
			0 10 5

[1] *H.F.M.G.*, II, 748.

29	Robt Mouncton Esqr for Hoyle Farme late Midletons	0	3	0			
	And hath Help of the Hon[ora]ble the Lord Raby for his Lands called Bradfeyld Farme in the poss[ession] of Edward Allot, Gent	0	3	8			
	Peter Hirst for Field Closes in Chappelthorpe	0	2	0			
	The Governours of the Poor of Sandall for Boynefirth	0	2	0			
					0	10	8
30	The Governors of the Poor of Sandall for a mess[uage] in Dirtcarr & the Land thereunto belonging in the poss[ession] of Robert Cusworth	0	2	0			
	And hath Help of Mr Ward of Pontefract for Land late Grices	0	3	8			
	D^o for Land late Taylors	0	1	2			
	D^o for Land late Beatsons	0	0	3			
	D^o for Land late Wheelwrights ..	0	0	7			
	D^o for Land late Nortons	0	0	8			
	D^o for Land late Wades	0	2	4			
					0	10	8
31	James Swallow, Gent: for his Lands late Sprigonalls	0	1	2			
	Ditto for the rest of his Lands in Painthorp that were not charged before	0	2	7			
	D^o for Milners Land	0	0	4			
	D^o for Lands att Dawgreen late Blackers..	0	2	8			
	D^o for a Cottage on Hallgreen late Robinsons	0	0	1			
	And hath Help of John Rhodes of Flocton Gent. for Lands att Blacker Hall	0	3	0			
	Anthony Bedford for a house in Criglestone in his own possession ..	0	0	1½			
	John Saunderson for a Cottage.. ..	0	0	1½			
					0	10	1
32	John Wood, Gent in right of his wife for Lands late Moors & formerly Hutchinsons	0	5	3			
	D^o for land in Gallas Field late Browns..	0	0	4			

No.	Tenant	Rent	Total
	D^{o} for a close called Hazlewells & Land in Gallas Field late Weightmans	0 2 9	
	And hath Help of the Governo^{rs} of Wakefield free Schoole and almshouses for Kilne hill in the poss[ession] of Wm Brooksbanck	0 2 0	
	Willm Preston for his Lands in Dirtcarre..	0 0 4	
	Robert Hirst for a House in Dirtcarre..	0 0 2	
	James Burnett for a House in Dirtcarr ..	0 0 2	
			0 11 0
33	Nathaniel Johnson Gent[1] for his Lands in Painthorpe formerly John & Oliver Haighs	0 3 2	
	And hath Help of Nicholaus Fenay, Gent:[2] for Fenay Royd in the poss[ession] of John Hunt ..	0 3 4	
	Francis Leake for his House & Land ..	0 0 10	
	D^{o} for Long Close	0 1 4	
	D^{o} for a close in Carsam late Browns ..	0 0 4	
	Wm Norton for a Cott[age] on Dawgreen..	0 1 0	
			0 10 0
34	Brian Allot, Gent: for Lands late Rogers & all other his Lands except half of his Lands late Godfrey Copleys Esqre	0 13 2	
			0 13 2
35	Gervas Norton, Gent: for the last fourth parte of his Lands att Kettlethorp	0 7 0	
	And hath Help of John Lord for a House & Land in Milnethorp in the poss[ession] of Robt Himsworth ..	0 2 10	
	The Heirs of Robt Beckwith for a House in Milnethorpe ..	0 0 2	
	D^{o} for a House and Croft late...... Harrisons	0 0 5	
			0 10 5
36	John Nevile Esqr & George Empson, Gent in the right of his wife for their last third parte of all their Lands & ten[emen]ts in Sandall Graveshipp	0 9 2	
	And hath Help of the Governo^{rs} of the Poor of Sandall for Feather House in the poss[ession] of Wm Shaw ..	0 0 2	

[1] *C.D.*, III, 216.

[2] *H.F.M.G.*, II, 635.

No.	Tenant						
	Saml Dickinson for a House and Croft att Hill Top	0	0	3			
	Joseph Lee for a House & Croft att Hill Top	0	0	4			
	John Oxley for a House & Croft at Criglestone	0	0	2½			
					0	10	1½
37	John Copley[1] of Doncaster Esqr for his Mess[uage] & Lands in Dirtcarr in the Poss[ession] of Henry Raynor..	0	5	4			
	And hath Help of the Constable of Normanton for Normant[on] Boynes	0	3	4			
	The Heirs of Bartin Allott, Gent for a House & three Crofts att Woodmoore Side	0	1	2			
	Mary Hawksworth, widw for a Cott[age] & Croft on Woodmooreside ..	0	0	2			
	Anthony Boulton for a Mess[uage] & Land in Crigleston in the poss[ession] of Saml Oxley	0	0	8			
					0	10	8
38	John Nevile Esqr & George Empson, Gent: in the right of his wife for their last third parte of all their Lands and ten[emen]ts in Sandall ..	0	9	1			
	And hath Help of Francis Duckingfield for a House	0	0	6			
	John Oxley of Sheffield for a House & Land in the poss[ession] of John Saunderson	0	0	6			
					0	10	1
39	Edward Allott, Gent: for one half of his Lands bought of Godfrey Copley Esqr	0	5	7			
	And hath Help of Bretton Boynes (vizt) out of Sr Matthew Wentworth Farme	0	0	2			
	Out of Richard Waltons Farme ..	0	0	2			
	Out of Widw Walshaws Farme.. ..	0	0	2			
	Out of Joseph Robinson's Farme ..	0	0	2			
	Out of Timothy Rhodes Farme ..	0	0	2			
	Out of John Hall Farme	0	0	2			
	Out of Thomas Clarkson Farme ..	0	0	2			
	Out of Richard Sykes Farme	0	0	2			

[1] *C.D.*, I, 20.

Joseph Hall for a Messuage & Lands thereunto belonging	0	2	11				
Marmaduke Shepley for a House late Richard Walkers	0	0	1				
				0	9	11	
Totall ..				19	19	9	

Wee the Jury Sworne for the Lord of the Mannor of Wakefield abovesaid do vpon our Enquiry into the Old Rentalls & Evidences concerning our said Graveship of Sandall find & present that these Thirty nine Graves within our said Graveship & that the Persons abovesaid vnder their Severall numbers ought to serve the office of Graves in their respective turns for their Lands & ten[emen]ts there men[ti]oned & have the Helpers which are there set down vnder the same number for their Lands & ten[emen]ts there also mentioned And that those persons vnder the number six do serve the office for this present yeare beginning att Micha[e]l[mas] last and the rest successively as they follow in their numbers and that the respective rents vnder every number are due & payable yearly to the Lord of the said Mannor

John Grice	Robert Dickinson	Tho: Hawksworth
Ger: Norton	John Chapman	George Fairbarne
Ja: Swallow	John Hirst	John Lambert
John Webster	Joseph Hirst	Anthony Bedford

THE GRAVESHIP OF HORBURY

The Graveship of Horbury is bounder'd by The Graveship of Thornes to the East, The Graveship of Osset to the North, Southwood to the West and the River of Calder to the South & hath within it the Freehold & Copyhold Ten[an]ts following who pay Rents &c according to the Verdict taken out of the Court Rolls of the Mannor as followeth

Maner[ium] de Wakefeld } Ad magn[am] Cur[iam] Baron[em] Nobilissimi Thome Ducis de Leeds pr[ae]nobilis Ordinis Garterij militis D[omi]ni Man[er]ij de Wakefield tent[am] ib[ide]m p[er] adjournament[um] vicesimo die Maij Anno Regni D[omi]ne n[ost]re Anne Dei gra[tia] nunc R[egi]ne Magne Brittanie &c octavo

The Verdict of Francis Rhodes, John Hunt, John Haigh, Ralfe Walker, David Coope, Willm̃ Walker, Josias Peace, John Cawthorne, Richard Wormall, John Binns, Robert Walker, Jeremia Serjant & Daniel Thornes, being Freeholders being Copyholders within the Graveship of Horbury of and concerning the Freehold & Copyhold Lands & ten[emen]ts within the said Graveship which pay rents & doe service to the Lord of the said mannor of Wakefield

		£	s.	d.	£	s.	d.
1st	John Haigh for two Crofts in his own occ[upation]	0	0	2			
	Elkanah Coop for one Rood in Westfield one in Midlefield & another Rood in Stonebrigg field late Jn° Haigh's	0	0	3			
	And have Help of Richard Witton Esqr for Boat Ing, Tallard Royd, Vpper Stenard, Renald Inge, Medley Inge, East Royds, & the rest of Lupsit Lands which are within the Graveship of Horbury	0	5	6			
	Eliz: Carr for an acre & a halfe in Southfield	0	0	1½			
					0	6	0½
2d	John Hirst a House A Backside & orchard late Bollands	0	0	0½			
	And hath Help of Henry Halstead for a House bought of Jennett Land..	0	0	1½			
	Joseph Thornes for a Pighell & half an acre of field Land	0	0	7½			
	Robert Walker for certain Field Lands..	0	0	2			
	Thomas Richardson a Newhouse & Close att Streetside formerly Curtices	0	0	2			
	Wm Curtice for a House & Croft on Sowood Green	0	0	2			
	Saml Lee for a Croft	0	0	3			
	Thomas Pashley a house & Croft on Sowood Green	0	0	3½			
	The Heirs of Thomas Scorey for a house in Ossett	0	0	1			
	Mary Cunningham Widw for a house in Ossett	0	0	1			
	Josia Hepworth for two Sel[ions] of Land in the Westfield of Ossett	0	0	2			
	Samuel Land for Lands in Ossett ..	0	0	3			
	John Scott for Lands in the occ[upation] of Tho: Archer	0	0	11			
	D° in the occ[upation] of Wm Stephenson..	0	0	9			
	Wm Middlebrook for Lands in Ossett ..	0	0	3			
	John Milner for Lands in Ossett ..	0	1	2			

	James Cordingley for that parte of his farme in Ossett in the occ[upation] of Joseph Phillip which lyeth within the Graveship of Horbury.. ..	0 0 1½	
	The Heirs of Thomas Taylor for Lands in the occ[upation] of Tho: Wade	0 0 6	
			0 6 1½
3d	Josias Oates, Gent for his Lands in Ossett now in his own poss[ession] nere Pild ars Lane butting on a Close called Shoulder of Mutton	0 0 6	
	And hath Help of Jossua Wilson in right of his Wife for Forrest Lands	0 0 8	
	John Peace for a Close called Runting ..	0 0 9	
	John Sugden for Land in Ossett ..	0 0 4	
	Joseph Haigh of Whitley for his Lands in Ossett in the occ[upation] of Joshua Haigh	0 2 4	
	John Philips for a House in Ossett ..	0 0 2½	
	Robt Nettleton	0 0 4	
	Widw Sagar house in Ossett	0 0 1	
	Joshua Wilson Senr	0 0 3	
	Jennett Land for a Small Cott[age] in Horbury	0 0 1	
	Joshua Horner for certain Field Land ..	0 0 6	
			0 6 0½
4th	Tho: Leeke, Gent.[1] for ⅛ of Horbury Hall & the Lands thereunto belonging late Dr Leaks	0 5 5	
5th	Wm Wormall for Hawking Croft & Upper Croft & certain Field Land in all the Fields of Horbury ..	0 1 0	
	Widw Cawthorne for the halfe of two houses & a Croft in her own occupation	0 0 5	
	And have help of Mr James Haigh Cl[erk][2] for a house & Croft in the occ-[upation] of James Oakes & certain Field Land And also three Closes called Cassings & a Close called blunt Ing	0 1 5½	
	Joseph White in right of his wife for a house	0 0 2	

[1] *C.D.*, II, 133. [2] *ibid.*

	Tho: White for a House & Croft & Field Land	0	0	2			
	Wm Mansfield for a house	0	0	0½			
	James White for 2 Houses & certain Field Land	0	0	8			
	The Heirs of Wm Langfield for a house & field land	0	0	6			
	Richard Wormall for his House & Croft a Close & three Roods of field Land	0	1	2			
	Winifred Hoyle a House and Croft & Field Lands	0	0	7			
	The Church Wardens for the Vicarage house	0	0	1			
	The Cunstable for Bull Inge	0	0	1			
					0	6	4
6th	Elkanah Coop for one ⅓ of his house & orchard &c	0	0	0¼			
	Wm Copendal Gent: for ⅓ of Nether Hall formerly Binnes & late Horaxes	0	0	4			
	And have Help of Wm Issott for two houses & severall Closes & certain Field Land to the same belonging ..	0	3	11½			
	Wm Carr an House Orchard & Field Land	0	0	5			
	Mary Carr for Michel Close & ½ an acre of Field Land	0	0	6			
	The Heirs of Edw[ar]d Speight for an acre in Westfield	0	0	4			
	Joseph Oxley in right of his wife for his house & Croft	0	0	2½			
	Mary Thorns widw for his house & Croft att Thorne Cliff [Hall Cliffe?]	0	0	1½			
	Sarah Hoyle Widw for ½ an acre of Field Land	0	0	0½			
	Isabell Caslas for a house att Hall Cliffe ..	0	0	1			
					0	6	0¼
7th	Dr Davinson for ⅓ of his Lands in Ossett in the occ[upation] of John Bradford	0	4	6			
	And hath Help of Tho: Richardson for Long Lands late Wm Harrups ..	0	0	8			
	John Whitley for his Lands in Ossett ..	0	0	6			
					0	5	8

8th	Tho Leeke Genn for one half of Mr Robt Leeke's Lands formerly Medleys	0	3	0			
	And hath Help of Geo: Cockill for a house & Close & certain Field Land	0	0	7			
	John Whitley for his Lands in Ossett ..	0	2	9			
					0	6	4
9	Daniel Thornes for his first half parte of Hardshaw Lands	0	0	2			
	Wm Sunderland for certain field Lands att Hardshaws & Two Houses & Lands in Tho Hirst occ[upation] ..	0	1	1			
	And have Help of the Heirs of Laurence Cockill for two houses a Croft & ½ an acre of field Land, NC[1] ..	0	0	5			
	Dorothy Castlas widw for a House & Croft & field Land in all the fields	0	1	7			
	Dorothy Harrison Widw for a House & Garden-stead	0	0	4			
	John Wood for two Houses & certaine Field Lands in Milnefield & Stone brigg field	0	0	2½			
	Jer: Serjant for six Roods of Field Land &c	0	0	4½			
	Tho: Craven for two houses & certain Field Land	0	1	5			
	Tho: White two Houses	0	0	2			
					0	5	9
10th	Danl Oley, Gent. for certain Field Land, late Mitchels in the occ[upation] of Tim: Denison	0	1	6			
	Do for a Close called Ellis Stenard in the occ[upation] of Jno Hunt ..	0	3	0			
	And hath Help of the Governors of Batley Free Schoole for Houseing & Lands in the occ[upation] of John Armitage	0	0	6			
	James Goodinson for Shanking Castle ..	0	0	2			
	Chr[ist]ofer Gawthorpe a house at Hall Cliffe	0	0	1			
	Wm Craven for his House & certain Field Land	0	0	3			

[1] N.C.=not compounded.

	John Hunt for halfe an acre in Westfield & half an acre in Midlefield	0	0	6			
					0	6	0
11th	Tho: Leeke, Gent: for ⅙ of Horbury Hall & the Lands thereunto belonging	0	5	5			
					0	5	5
12	Thomas Leeke, Gent for the other half of Mr Robt Leeks Lands formerly Medleys	0	3	0			
	And hath Help of Francis Rhodes for a house and Croft & certain Field Land	0	1	9			
	Sarah Rhodes, Spinster for two Closes ..	0	0	7			
	Mary Stephenson for a House	0	0	1			
	Francis Stephenson for a house & ½ a rood of Land	0	0	1½			
					0	5	6½
13	Dr Davinson for ⅓ of his Lands in Ossett in the occ[upation] of John Bradford	0	4	6			
	And hath Help of Joseph Spurr for his Lands in Ossett	0	0	6			
	Mary Ingham Widw for a house and Croft on Ossett Lights ..	0	0	2			
	Charles Nettleton Cl[erk] for his Lands in Ossett	0	0	6			
					0	5	8
14	Tho: Leeke, Gent: for ⅙ of Horbury Hall & the Lands thereunto belonging	0	5	5			
					0	5	5
15th	George Bracebridge for a House & Croft in his own Occ[upation] late Norths and certain Field Land late Haighs, Speights, Walkers, & Dawsons.. ..	0	1	4½			
	And hath Help of Eady Carr Widw for her house & Croft & certain Field Land	0	0	7			
	Anne Walker Widw for an house an Orchard & certain Field Land ..	0	0	10			
	Tho. Goodall for two Closes	0	0	4			
	Benjamin Coop for his Lands in Horbury	0	1	10			
	Geo: Broadhead an house an Orchard & a rood of field Land ..	0	0	2			
	John Stringer for field Land	0	0	9			
					0	5	10½

No.							
16	James Sill, Gent: for a mess[uage] & the Lands thereunto belonging in the occ[upation] of Richard Norfolke, Gent.	0	1	0			
	And hath Help of Thomas Pearson for a house & a Close	0	0	3			
	Richard Thornton Esq[r] for ⅓ of a Mess[uage] & Lands thereunto belonging in the occ[upation] of Dan: Sill Cl[erk]	0	4	4			
					0	5	7
17th	The Heirs of John Wadsworth for a Mess[uage] & the Lands thereunto belonging now in the occ[upation] of his Wid[w]	0	3	10			
	D[o] for a House & two Crofts late Matershaws	0	4	1			
					0	7	11
18	Joseph Hirst for a house in Ossett late Geo. Naylors	0	0	4			
	And hath Help of James White for Raven royds	0	2	0			
	Sarah Wilson Wid[w] for Tho: White Lands	0	0	2			
	Tho: Beatson for a Farme Vnder Storshill in the occ[upation] of Francis Marsden	0	3	8			
					0	6	2
19	Tho: Leeke, Gent. for ⅕ parte of Horbury Hall & the Lands thereunto belonging	0	5	5			
	And hath Help of W[m] Pollard for ½ of his house three Crofts & certain field land	0	1	1½			
					0	6	6½
20	Deborah Cawthorne wid[w] for one half of her Two houses Crofts and orchard late Awdsleys and formerly Rob[t] Thornes	0	0	5			
	D[o] for certain fieldland bought of Langster	0	0	8			
	And hath Help of Thomas Carter p[er] a house	0	0	5½			
	W[m] Langster for a Croft & field Land ..	0	0	11			
	John Batty for a house & Croft & a rood of Land	0	0	2			
	Wid[w] Awdsley for ½ an acre	0	0	1			

		£	s	d	£	s	d
	John Cawthorne for certain field Land ..	0	0	9			
	John Binnes for a house & a Close ith Hodge Laine	0	0	6			
	Wm Pollard for field Land	0	0	9			
	Eliz: Batty for houseing & Garths ..	0	0	4½			
	Tho: Wood a house & Croft & half an acre of field Lands	0	0	1			
	Saml Hoyle for a House & certain field Land	0	0	7½			
					0	5	9½
21	Dr Davinson for one third of his Lands in Ossett in the poss[ession] of John Bradford	0	4	5			
	And hath help of Benjamin Briggs for a close called Town royd ..	0	0	9			
	Martha Heald wid^w^ for two acres of field land	0	0	4			
	Francis Marsdin for ½ an acre ith West-field	0	0	2			
					0	5	8
22	Elkanah Coope for halfe of his Lands late Haigh's & formerly Binns..	0	0	0½			
	Wm Copendale, Gent for ⅓ of Nether Hall & the Lands thereunto belonging	0	0	4			
	And have Help of Samuel Wadsworth for his house in the poss[ession] of M^r^ De Pree & certain Land thereto belonging	0	5	9			
					0	6	1½
23	Josias Pease for certain field Land bought of Speight	0	0	2			
	D^o^ for his House and Croft late Sara Woods	0	0	8			
	D^o^ for a Croft late Jaggars	0	0	4			
	D^o^ for the rest of Jaggar Land.. ..	0	0	5½			
	And hath Help of Edward Ramsden for a close	0	0	4			
	Joshua Coop for Batty & Sunderland Land	0	1	2			
	Mathew Gelder for an house Orchard & field Land	0	1	2			
	Ralph Walker for certain field Land ..	0	1	6			

	Wm Walker for a house & a rood of field Land	0	0	3			
	Rebecca Ambler for certain field Land in the poss[ession] of Jeremia Sarjant	0	0	8			
					0	6	3½
24	Wm Wormall for Jennet Walshaw's house & Orchard	0	0	6			
	And hath Help of Wm Denison for a house & Croft & severall Closes	0	4	10			
	Tho: Hunt for two Houses a Croft & certain f[iel]d Land	0	1	9			
					0	7	1
25	Josias Oates, Genn for Fletcher house & Lands now in the poss[ession] of John Cawthorne	0	3	2			
	And hath Help of Richard Thornton Esq for ⅓ of a mess[uage] & Lands thereunto belonging in the occ[upation] of Mr Dan: Sill Cl[erk] ..	0	4	3½			
					0	7	5½
26	Wm Dawson for his house and Lands to the same belonging in his own occ-[upation]	0	2	0			
	And hath Help of John Rhodes, Gent: for the Hall att Northgate Head & the Lands thereunto belonging ..	0	5	10			
					0	7	10
27	Thomas Leeke Gent. for ⅕ of Horbury Hall & the Lands thereunto belonging late Dr Leeks ..	0	5	4			
	And hath help of Wm Pollard for ½ of his House three crofts & certain field Land	0	1	2			
					0	6	6
28	Tho: Blacker for his Houseing Orchard & Croft to the same belonging with certain field Land	0	1	0			
	And hath help of Alice Carr widw for Houseing a Croft & certain field Land	0	2	4			
	Josias Wilson for an acre & ½ ith Mill-Field	0	0	9			
	Robert Thornes for a house, Croft & certain field Land	0	2	2			
					0	6	3

29	Daniel Thornes for his half parte of Hardshaw Land	0	0	2			
	D° for Certain field Land in his own occ[upation]	0	1	0			
	D° for a rood he bought of Elias Carr ..	0	0	1			
	And hath Help of Richard Thornton Esqr for ⅓ of his mess[uage] & Lands thereunto belonging in the occ[upation] of Mr Danl Sill Cl[erk] ..	0	4	4			
	Wm Thornes for a house & certain field Land	0	2	0			
					0	7	7
30	Elkanah Coop for ⅓ parte of his house & orchard late John Haigh's & formerly Binnes	0	0	0¼			
	Wm Copendall, Gen: for ⅓ parte of his Nether Hall & the Lands thereunto belonging	0	0	4			
	And have Help of Mich[ae]l Parker in right of his wife for Dawson Tomroyd	0	0	10			
	Tempest Pollard for his House, Orchard inclosures & certain field Land—p[ar]te N.C.	0	5	1½			
					0	6	3¾

Free Rents due out of Flockton & collectable by The Grave of Horbury vizt

A Farme in the occ[upation] of Geo: Eastwood	0	0	11			
One in the occ[upation] of Richard Bretton	0	1	5			
One in the occ[upation] of Tho: Bedford ..	0	1	0			
One in the occ[upation] of Wid^w Pease ..	0	0	6			
One in the occ[upation] of Dr Senior ..	0	0	5½			
One in the occ[upation] of Wid^w Hampshire	0	0	5½			
One in the occ[upation] of John Scafe ..	0	0	5			
One in the occ[upation] of Mr Rhodes ..	0	0	5½			
One in the occ[upation] of Joshua Dickinson	0	0	5½			
				0	6	1

Free Rents Due by Sir John Armytage out of Hartchstead & collectable by the Grave of Horbury (viz[t])

Out of Fearneley Inge	0	0	2	
Out of Jackson Farme	0	0	3½	
Jonas Drake's Farme	0	0	3½	
Abraham Woods	0	0	6	
Richard Poplewels	0	0	6	
John Hansons	0	1	0	
Tho: Dysons	0	0	3	
John Claphams	0	0	9	
W[m] Poplewells	0	0	8	
Moses Brooks	0	0	4	
Tho: Hirsts	0	1	2	
Edward Coopers	0	0	2	
Wid[w] Baldersons	0	1	2	
W[m] Fourneshaws	0	0	7	
				0 8 0
Totall ..				10 0 10

Wee the Jury sworne for the Lord of the Mannor of Wakefield abovesaid do vpon our Enquiry into the Old Rentalls & Evidences concerning our said Graveship of Horbury finde and present that there are Thirty Graves within our said Graveship And that the persons abovesaid Vnder their severall numbers ought to serve the Office of Graves in their respective Turns for their Lands & Ten[emen]ts there mentioned and have the Helpers which are there sett down under the same Numbers for their Lands and tenēmts there also mentioned And that those Persons Vnder the Number (30) do serve the Office for this present yeare beginning att Mich[ae]l[mas] Last And the rest successively as they follow in their Numbers And that the respective rents vnder every Number are due and payable yearly to the Lord of the said Mannor

Francis Rhodes	John Cawthorn	Jeremiah Sargant
John Hunt	Richard Wornall	Daniell Thornes
Ralph Walker	John Binns	David Coop
Josias Peace	Robert Walker	William Walker

THE GRAVESHIP OF ALVERTHORP

The Graveship of Alverthorp, is boundered by the Graveship of Stanley to the East The Graveships of Wakefield and Thornes to the South-East Ardsley to the West & Thorp to the North & hath within it The Freehold & Copyhold Rents & Ten[emen]ts following who pay Rents &c according to the Verdict taken out of the Court Rolls of The Mannor as followeth

Maner[ium] de Wakefield } Ad Magn[am] Cur[iam] Baron[em] Nobilissimi Thome Ducis de Leeds pr[ae]nobilis Ordimis Garterij Milit[is] D[omi]ni Man[er]ij de Wakefeld tent[am] ib[idem] p[er] Adiournament[um] vicesimo die Maij Anno Regni Domine n[ost]re Anne Dei gra[tia] nunc R[egi]ne Magne Brittanie &c Octavo

The Verdict of John Clarkson, John Denison, Robert Holden, John Lumble, John Scott, Samuel Smith, Samuel Jackson, Gersham Houldsworth, Samuel Oldroyd, James Firth, Joshua Creakill, Samuel Glover, and Robt Scott being freeholders & Copyholders within the Graveship of Alverthorp Of and concerning the Freehold & Copyhold Lands & Tenements within the said Graveship which pay rents and do service to the Lord of the said Mannor of Wakefield

		£	s.	d.			
1	Daniel Mawd Gen: for his two acres and an half of Land called Dog Croft & heretofore the Land of Richard Bonny and Wm Worman and the rest of his compounded Lands in Alverthorpe	1	1	2			
	Do for Brodefore Land N.C.	0	1	8			
	Do for Savil Land N.C.	0	0	4			
					1	3	2
2	The Governours of the Free School of Burnley in the County of Lancaster for a mes[suage] & Lands thereunto belonging in the occ[upation] of John Ross	0	1	6			
	And have help of John Batty Esqr[1] for Four Closes in Flanshaw in the occ[upation] of Samuel Oldroyd & for two Closes in the occ[upation] of Wm Holdsworth & for four other closes in the occ[upation] of John Scott & for two other closes in the occ[upation] of Joseph Nicholson & Matthew Glover & for two other closes in the occ[upation] of Joseph Clark	0	8	8			
					0	10	2

[1] *C.D.*, I, 264.

No.	Entry	£	s.	d.	Total
3	John Clarkson for a mess[uage] & Croft in Newton in his own poss[ession]	0	0	9	
	And hath help of John Lumbe for his p[ar]te of Silcoats	0	4	5½	
	The Heirs of John Smith for a mess-[uage] att Newton	0	0	2	
	Richard Shaw, Gent. for 5 Closes near Potovens Beck in the occ[upation] of Wm Fenay	0	1	10	
					0 7 2½
4	John Clarkson for three acres of field Land in St Johns field & Cliffe Field in his own poss[ession]	0	0	9	
	Do for a way through a Close he bought of Mr Brombley	0	0	4	
	And hath Help of Joseph Lumbe for his p[ar]te of Silkcoats	0	4	5½	
	James Wood for Narway Lane Close in the occ[upation] of Gersham Holdsworth	0	0	9	
	Ebanazar Holdsworth for a mess[uage] & orchard in Alverthorp ..	0	0	1½	
	Guersham Holdsworth for a mess[uage] & orchard there	0	0	1½	
					0 6 6½
5	Henry Robinson Cl[erk] for a Barne & Lands anciently called Bunny Hall now in the occ[upation] of Joseph Dyson	0	2	6	
	And hath Help of Robt Hopkinson, Gent: in right of his wife for 3 closes lying twixt Broad foard & Longgrave head in Jumble Field in the occ[upation] of Jacob Rhodes	0	4	8	
					0 7 2
6	Henry Robinson Cl[erk] for Lands on the South side of Bunny Hall in the occ-[upation] of Robt Naylor ..	0	2	0	
	Do for a close of Land in the occ[upation] of James Best	0	0	4	
	And hath Help of the Earl of Cardigan for Batty farme	0	2	3	
					0 4 7

7th	John Dennison for a mess[uage] & six Closes of Lands in Flanshaw in his own occ[upation]	0	2	9			
	And hath Help of Rachel Kirke, Widw for John Kirke Land	0	3	3			
	Do for Taylor Land, Houseing & Croft in the occ[upation] of John Scott..	0	1	0			
	Do for Houldsworths a Close called Laine Close in the occ[upation] of Guersham Holdsworth ..	0	0	9			
	Do for Pickles Land	0	0	10			
	Do for Glover Land	0	0	1			
					0	8	8
8th	Susannah Sill widw for two Closes of Land lying at Longrave head on both side Lain: one in the occ[upation] of John Scott & the other in the occ[upation] of Robt Gunson ..	0	5	6			
	And hath Help of Widw Heald for Houseing & Three Crofts att Wakefield Beck	0	0	11½			
					0	6	5½
9th	Wm Heward Esqr & Joseph Watkinson Gent. for Earleys now in the occ[upation] of John Scott of Wakefield ..	0	2	0			
	And have Help of John Batty Esqr for a Close called Stock Ing in the occ[upation] of Saml Batty & five closes in the occ[upation] of John Beaumont with several buildings vpon the same	0	4	6			
					0	6	6
10	Benjamin Smith for a house & two closes in Flancil Lane	0	0	6½			
	And hath help of Joshua Sagar for a close lately purchased of the said Benj.	0	0	3			
	Do for a mess[uage] & 2 Closes & a Pighell in Flancel bought of Mrs Idle now in the occ[upation] of himself & Jon Beaumont	0	0	9			
	Widw Fleeming for a House att Broad foard, Joyning on Cliffe field ..	0	0	10			
	Sam̃l Glover for a Cott[age]	0	0	2			
	John Scott for a mess[uage] & Croft in his own poss[ession]	0	0	4½			

	Mary Kirke for a Cott[age]	0	0	1			
	Richard Norfolke Gent: three Ten[emen]ts & 3 closes in the occ[upation] of Cornelius Clarke	0	1	6			
	John Nevile Esq for the vpper Mills on Wakefield Dam	0	2	0			
					0	6	7
11th	Joseph Wadsworth for Houndroyd al[ia]s Spring Close & Higging Close & Prome Close in his owne poss[ession]	0	4	0			
	And hath Help of Mrs Wheatley for her two thirds of two Closes att Humble Jumble Brigg	0	2	2			
	The Hon[ora]ble the Lord Raby for ⅙ of the same	0	0	7			
	Robt Munckton Esqr for the other ⅙ ..	0	0	7			
					0	7	4
12	The Heirs of Obadiah Lee Cl[erk] for certain Lands called the Hawks near Humble Jumble Bridge in the occ[upation] of Robt Gunson ..	0	1	7½			
	And have Help of the Heirs of Thomas Baskervile for severall Lands about the Cliffe Field	0	5	1			
					0	6	8½
13	Mr Browne in right of his wife one Close called Shortfield or Pale Close adjoyning on Fidling Close now in the occ[upation] of Rachel Kirke Widw ..	[*blank*]					
	N B The Lord Raby pays the rent being included in No 19th and what is short here in making vp a Grave is over in that Number 19	[*blank*]					
14	Samuel Smith for several ten[emen]ts & Lands att Spent in his own occ[upation]	0	3	2			
	And hath Help of Richard Fostard for two Closes one called Wheat Close & the other Little Close att Spent in the occ[upation] of Samuel Smith..	0	1	1			
	Peter Smith for one close called New Close in his own occ[upation] ..	0	0	5			
	Robt Holden a mess[uage] by Westgate Moor side in his own poss[ession]	0	0	3½			

	James Firth a House & Croft att Westgate moor side	0 0 3		
	The Governours of the Free School of Wakefield for Storys Land ..	0 1 6		
			0 6 8½	
15	The Heirs of Mr Wm Mawd for a mess[uage] in Alverthorpe & halfe an acre of Land now in the occ[upation] of Samuel Kirke & John Jackson Two Closes oth Back oth House in his Widw poss[ession] one mess[uage] and severall Closes of Land in Flanshaw now in Samuel Battys poss[ession] & one other mess[uage] & several Crofts now in the occ[upation] of Richard Burrall	0 7 10		
			0 7 10	
16	John Dawson for a Cottage lyeing neare the Broadfoard in his own poss[ession]	0 0 6		
	And hath Help of Wm Burrough for another close	0 0 4		
	Samuel Hide for another Close ..	0 0 4		
	Mrs Dawson for another Close there ..	0 0 0		
	Mr Jer: Spink a farm closes near Cliffe Hill Tree	0 2 10		
	Mr John Coope for his moyety of 5 Closes near Broadford ..	0 2 8		
			0 6 8	
17	The Heirs Mr Wm Horne for Lands in Moore Croft in the occ[upation] of Mr Robert Mills	0 1 4		
	Chr[ist]ofer Hewit for Moor Crofts now in the occ[upation] of Mr Hirst & [*blank*] Bracebridge for Little Hawks ..	0 3 8		
	And have Help of Francis Mawd, Gent: for a small Croft oth Back Laine side a close at Cliffe Hill & the Mill Damme Close	0 2 2		
	Do a small Close att Bradford side bought of John Kirk.. ..	0 1 0		
			0 8 2	
18	Willm Heward Esqr & Joseph Watkinson Gen: for a mess[uage] called Flanshaw Hall & the Lands thereunto belonging	0 8 1		
			0 8 1	

		£ s d	
19th	The Hon[ora]ble the Lord Raby for Middleton Fleeming & Brown Land now in the occ[upation] of Sam[l] Jackson & Sam[l] Clarke	0 15 6	
	D[o] for Birkhead Land	0 2 2	
			0 17 8
20	John Nevison for five closes of Land lyeing att Flanshawe one in the occ[upation] of Jer. Dixon & the other four in the occ[upation] of Jacob Rhodes	0 1 4	
	And hath Help of Daniel Oley, Gen: for a close near Broadforde in occ[upation] of Toby Sill ..	0 1 0	
	The Governours of The Poor for Wilfields in the occ[upation] of Jo[n] Bedford	0 1 4	
	Edward Batty for Fidling Croft ..	0 0 1	
	Joshua Creakill a mess[uage] in Alverthorpe Lane	0 0 2	
	Sam[l] Oldroyd p[er] 3 mess[uages] ..	0 0 2	
	Rob[t] Scott a mess[uage]	0 0 2	
	Rich[d] Loxley or M[rs] Kirke a mess[uage] N.C.	0 0 4	
	The Heirs of Geo: Lewis for 3 houses ..	0 0 3	
	Joseph Prance for 3 Crofts near Wakefield Bridge	0 0 10½	
	Sam[l] Jackson a Mess[uage]	0 0 5	
	John Crumbock a Mess[uage]	0 0 4	
	John Wormall a mess[uage] N.C. ..	0 0 1½	
	Ferdinand Smith a Mess[uage] ..	0 0 1	
	Gervas Roberts a Mess[uage]	0 0 1	
	John Kirke a mess[uage]	0 0 2	
			0 6 10
	Total ..		3 3 0½

Wee the Jury Sworne for the Lord of the Mannor of Wakefield abovesaid doe vpon Our Enquiring into the Old Rentalls & Evidences concerning our said Graveship of Alverthorp finde & present that there are 20 Graves within our said Graveship of Alverthorp And that the persons above named vnder their severall Numbers ought to serve the office of Grave in their respective Turns for their Lands & Tenem[en]ts there mentioned And have the Helpers which are there sett down vnder the same Number for their Lands & Tenem[en]ts there also mentioned And that those persons vnder the number four doe serve the office for this present yeare beginning att Mich[ae]l[mas] Last & the rest successively as they follow in their Numbers. And that the respective rents vnder every Number are due and payeable yearly to the L[or]d of the said mannor

John Clarkson	Samuel Smith	Joshua Creakill
John Denison	Gershom Houldsworth	Samuel Glover
Robert Houldin	Samuel Oldroyd	Robert Scott
John Lombe	James Firth	Samuel Jackson

THE GRAVESHIP OF STANLEY

The Graveship of Stanley is boundered on the East by Methley & The River of Caldar on the South by Wakefield on the West by Alverthorp & on the North by Lofthouse and hath within it the Freehold & Copyhold Ten[emen]ts following who pay Rents &c according to The Verdict taken out of the Court Rolls of The Mannor as followeth

Maner[ium] de Wakefield } Ad Magn[am] Cur[iam] Baron[em] Nobilissimi Thome Ducis de Leeds prenobilis ordinis Garterij milit[is] D[omi]ni Maner[ii] de Wakefeld tent[am] ib[ide]m adjournament[um] vicesimo die Maij Anno Regni D[omin]ne n[ost]re Anne Dei gra[tia] nunc R[egi]ne Magne Brittanie &c octavo

The Verdict of Oswold Hatfield, Thomas Graves, Richard Smirthwait, Richard Harrison, Thomas Smith, James Moxon, Samuel Birks, David Law, William Armitage, John Wilks, Richard Illingworth, Wm Fenay, & Richard Everingham being Freeholders, and Copyholders within the Graveship of Stanley of & concerning the Freehold & Copyhold Lands & Ten[emen]ts within the said Graveship which pay rents & doe service to the Lord of the said mannor of Wakefield

1st	Sr Lyon Pilkington Barr:[1] for ⅓ parte of all his Lands & Tenem[en]ts in Stanley of which there are three closes within the mannor of Midgley called old St Swithens, little St Swithens & Oxe close	0 15 2	
			0 15 2
2d	Robt Benson Esqr for Harrison & Cartmell Farme now in the occ[upation of Jno Lake	0 5 6	

[1] *C.D.*, II, 325.

	And hath Help of Mary Sugden, widw for Crombe Lands	0	0	9	
	John Heald in right of his wife for Hackin Hills & house & Croft in Stanley	0	2	5	
	Oswald Hatfield for Penny yard & Edd Croft	0	2	2	
					0 10 10
3d	The Hon[ora]ble Lord Raby for all his Lands in Stanley	0	19	0	
4th	Willm̃ Copandall Gent for half parte of his farme formerly Hills in the occ[upation] of Richard Harrison (vizt) the House & Croft adjoyning to't	0	1	0	
	And hath Help of Oswold Hatfield Gent for Laverack Hall & all the Lands thereunto belonging & the Doles in Lawfield	0	3	6	
	Richard Everingham for his Lands in Stanley formerly Harrisons ..	0	3	1	
	Mr John Clarkson of Silkstone Cl[erk] for a House & Land with certain field Land thereunto belonging in the occ[upation] of Arthur Clarkson & a house in the occ[upation] of Eliz: Clarkson & Alice Rhodes	0	2	4	
	Richard Marsden in right of his wife for his houseing & Lands att head of Ouchthorpe Laine	0	2	0	
					0 11 11
5	Robert Mounckton Esqr for Kelshaw house & Croft thereunto belonging and also for all his other Lands & Ten[eme]nts within the Graveship of Stanley	0	6	3	
	And hath Help of David Law for Land formerly Beckwiths lying in the Cross field N.C.	0	0	3	
	Do for Wallers Lands in Ouchthorpe Laine a House & Croft ..	0	0	0½	
	Do for a house & Croft in Stanley Towne in the occ[upation] of Richard Frubbisher	0	0	1	
	Danl Oley, Gent for a house & Lands att Newton in the occ[upation] of John Clarkson	0	0	10	

	Samuel Peaker for a house & Land in Stanley in the occ[upation] of John Sternwhite	0	1	7½			
	Sarah Robinson wid^{w} for a house & Land in Stanley	0	0	3			
	Tho: Smith for one acre of Land formerly Laws in Kirkefield ..	0	0	3½			
	Wid^{w} Walker for Paradice Closes ..	0	0	2			
					0	9	9½
6	The Trustees of Joseph Armitage late oth Woodside Gen: for ⅓ of his Lands in Ouchthorpe Laine formerly Roger Nowells Esqr	0	6	0			
	And have help of Sr Wm Benson Knt for 3 closes in the occ[upation] of Thomas Grave	0	2	8			
	Robt Beckwith Cl[erk] house & croft att Ouchthorpe Laine	0	0	4			
	Bridgett Kay for a Cott[age] in Ouchthorp Laine	0	0	1			
	Richard Nettleton for a house & Land in Newton Laine in the occ[upation] of James Robertson	0	1	7			
					0	10	8
7	Robert Wood Gent for Nockett house & Land late Mr Rogers ..	0	1	9			
	And have Help of The Heirs of Joseph Roper for Nockett Lands lyeing on the Woodside in the occ[upation] of Mathew Lindley & Tho: Lee	0	2	0			
	Wm Copendale, Gent a Close called the Peel	0	0	6			
	The Governours of the Free School of Wakefield for Royston Banck in the occ[upation] of John Sugden a house & Land adjoyning to Harwood field & Laine in the occ[upation] of Wm Traughton & other their Lands in Stanley	0	5	1			
	John Sugden for his house & Land thereunto belonging	0	2	4			
					0	11	8

8	Wm Copendale Gent for the other half parte of Hill Lands being a close above the house called the Flatt in ye occ-[upation] of Richard Harrison & a farme in the occ[upation] of Edw: Smith formerly Ed[ward] Horncastles ..	0	1	7			
	And hath help of himself for Kent house & the Lands thereunto belonging	0	1	5			
	Geo: Burnhill Gent for the great Intack & Gervas Naylor Farme ..	0	6	10			
	The Heirs of John Brettner for a Close & one acre of Field Land in the occ-[upation] of Joseph Beckwith..	0	0	10			
	Anne Clegg widw for her house & Land in Stanley	0	0	8			
					0	11	4
9	The Trustees of Joseph Armitage late of Outwood side Gent for another third parte of the Lands he bought of Roger Nowel Esqr	0	6	0			
	And have help of Robert Watson Gent in the right of his wife for lands & tenem[en]ts in Stanley late Mr Clarks in the occ[upation] of Mr Gill, Sarah Robinson &c	0	3	4½			
	John Sunderland a house & croft near the Lodge	0	0	4			
					0	9	8½
10	John Smith, Gent for his Lands & Ten-[emen]ts late Harrises & formerly Snydals & Challenors now in the occ[upation] of Tho: Grave ..	0	5	0			
	And hath help of Thomas Graves for a house & Croft near Lee Moor ..	0	0	4			
	The Governors of the Poor for a house & Land in Stanley in the occ[upation] of James Stocks	0	1	9			
	Elizabeth Meager widw for certain Lands Lyeing att Ouchthorpe Lane End in the occ[upation] of John Wood ..	0	0	7			
	James Moxon for a house & Land in Stanley	0	0	8			
					0	8	4

		£	s	d	£	s	d
11	Robert Benson Esq[r] for Lands late Hopkinson's & formerly Hobsons now a Farme in the occ[upation] of Jn[o] Rayner	0	1	8			
	And hath Help of Samuel Peaker for a Cott[age] & a Garden Stead in the occ[upation] of John Mills ..	0	0	2			
	Robert Shaw Gent for Northey 7[s] Pilkington Land 6[d] per Cottage 2 ..	0	7	8			
	Samuel Bargh for Field Lands & Michills	0	0	4¾			
					0	9	5¾
12	M[r] Gideon Mawd Cl[erk] for a Mess[uage] called Boxhall & The Lands thereunto belonging	0	0	7½			
	Tho: Denton Gent for his moyety of John Sugden Farme	0	1	3			
	Sam[l] Firth Gent for 2½ acres of Land in Pinderfield	0	0	10			
	Wid[w] Johnson for Bowling Green house	0	0	2			
	Margaret Clarke, Spinster, for Field Land late Oystons or M[rs] Greenwoods	0	1	4			
	John Wood of Woodthorp Gent in right of his wife for Longfield, Northfield Closes & certain Field Land in Stanley	0	5	5			
	The Heirs of Joseph Marsden for Broadhugaps	0	0	6			
	Tho: Lee in right of his wife certain Field Land in Stanley ..	0	0	10			
					0	10	11½
13	John Savile Esq[r] for Lands att Bottoms in the occ[upation] of Rich[ar]d Smirthwaite	0	1	3			
	And hath help of [*blank*] Milner for a Cott[age] oth West o'th Outwood in the occ[upation] of Jo[n] Hardwick N.C.	0	0	3			
	Margret Broadhead widw for Spinke Farme now in the occ[upation] of John Lake N.C.	0	6	9			
	Theophilus Calverley, Gent for Belhouse & Croft	0	0	6			

	Wm Denison of Althouse for a Cott[age] & Croft in the occ[upation] of Thomas Heptonstall	0	0	4			
	The Heirs of Peter Roper for a Cott[age] att Lee Moore Gate	0	0	2			
	Richard Smirthwaite for a Cott[age] att Bottoms	0	0	1			
	Mathew Smith for a house & Croft att Westhouse Yate	0	0	3			
					0	9	7
14	Sr Lyon Pilkington Ba[rrone]t for ⅓ parte of all his Lands & tenem[en]ts in Stanley of which there are Lands called Tom Croft & Lands lyeing in St Swithens formerly Grice's Lands ..	0	15	2			
					0	15	2
15	Joseph Armitage Gent for a mess[uage] called the Lodge & the Lands thereunto belonging now in his own occ[upation]	1	0	1			
					1	0	1
16	The Heirs of Buckley Wildfrid Gent for Beal Lands att Bottoms now in the occ[upation] of Richard Smirthwaite	0	1	3			
	And hath help of the heirs of Richard Cockill for two closes one by the water side & the other called Twitter Cliff	0	1	9			
	Mrs Lawson widw for a house att Stanley Laine end & Lands thereunto belonging now in the occ[upation] of Sam Birch	0	1	0			
	Wm Lee for a house & Croft att Lee Moore	0	0	3			
	Susannah Wright Widw for a house & Croft in the occ[upation] of Wm Hoyland	0	0	4			
	Tho. Smith for a house & Croft near Lee Moore	0	0	7½			
	Robert Wood Gent for Hanson Land (vizt) Marshall Croft & Little Inge Royd	0	1	2			
	John Wilks for 2 houses & Lands att Carr Yate	0	0	6			
	Anthony Abson for Wilks Land (vizt) for a house & 3½ acres of Land belonging it 1d ob[olus] N C	0	0	11½			

No.	Entry	£	s	d	£	s	d
	Oswold Hatfield Gent for Field Land late Burnhills	0	2	6			
					0	10	4
17	Mr Henry Robinson Cl[erk] for Lands att Bunnyhall oth Back oth Laith	0	0	3			
	And hath help of Tho: Birkhead for Willow Closes, Falkiner Closes, Colly hall Closes, & the rest of his Lands in Stanley	0	5	4			
	Sarah Sill widw: for a house & Lands thereunto belonging formerly Hatfields & Jacksons & now in the occ[upation of Matthew Lindley	0	5	8			
					0	11	3
18	The Trustees of Joseph Armitage late of the Outwood-side Gent for the last ⅓ parte of the Lands bought of Roger Nowil Esqr among w[hi]ch are Dewsy-royds	0	6	1			
	And have help of James Burrhouse for a house in Ouchthorp ..	0	0	1			
	Jno Harrison for Dodgson house in Ouchthorp Laine	0	0	3			
	Do for Land in the Lawfield near p[ar]ke pail	0	0	2			
	And for 2 acres more late Mr Robt Woods	0	0	7			
	Robt Sellers for a Cott[age] in Ouch-thorpe Laine	0	0	0½			
	Joshua Thornes for Lands att Brani-carrs in the occ[upation] of John Wormall	0	0	11			
	Anthony Milner for Ward Land (vizt) Two Farms att Snowhill & Woodside in the occ[upation] of Ger[vase] Naylor & John Thompson	0	2	4			
					0	10	5½
19	Robt Benson Esqr for his Lands att Wrenthorpe	0	2	4			
	And hath help of Mrs Wood Widw for the Waterside, North Fields & certain Field Land in Stanley	0	8	2			
					0	10	6

20	Wm Horton Esqr for ½ of his Mess[uage] & Lands thereunto belonging called Broom hall late Lowdens & formly Listers & now in the occ[upation] of James Wood	0	4	1			
	And hath help of Wm Armitage for a house & Croft oth side of the outwood F.	0	0	1			
	Willm Fenay for Andrews house & orchard att Potovens ..	0	0	6			
	Edward Brooke for a house & Land near Kirkhamgate	0	0	2			
	Geo: Teall for Browns Cottage.. ..	0	0	6			
	The Heirs of Richard Grave for a house near Lofthouse yate in the occ[upation] of Benj: Benton	0	2	2½			
	The Right Hon[ora]ble the Earle of Cardigan for a house oth West oth Outwood in the occ[upation] of Saml Bowling	0	0	5			
	Do for houseing & Land in the occ[upation] of James Bowling ..	0	0	5			
	Do for a Croft formerly in the occ[upation] of Sharp & Leake ..	0	0	2			
	Mrs Cooper Widw for two houses & a Croft oth West oth Outwood in the occ[upation] of Peter Smith & [*blank*] Wormall	0	0	6			
	Joseph Diekson for houseing & Crofts near Lofthouse yate	0	0	7			
	Widw Lee for Darbys in the occ: of Sarah Bell	0	0	3			
	Rachel Kirke Widw for a house & Lands att Snow-hill in the occ[upation] of Peter Hudson	0	2	3			
	Widw Lee for a house & Croft near Lingwell yate	0	0	2½			
					0	10	4
21	Willm Horton Esqr for a mess[uage] & Lands called Broom Hall late Lowdens & formerly Listers & now in the occ[upation] of James Wood ..	0	4	1			
	And hath help of Robert Firth for a house near the Lodge oth Outwood	0	0	1½			

		£	s	d			
	Benj: Bevit for a house at Potovens formerly Wm Fenays	0	0	1			
	Robt Glover for 2 Cott[ages] in his own occ[upation] one of them was late in his sonne Samuels	0	0	5			
	James Bowlin for a Cottage & Garth late Eliz: Green	0	0	3			
	Mary Hall, Spinster for a house & Croft att Kirkham Gate	0	0	6			
	The Heirs of Ralph Hick for a house & Lands att Potovens in the occupation of Danl Glover	0	1	4			
	Richard Illingworth for a house & Garth by Kirkham Gate	0	0	2			
	Thomas Illingworth for a house & Garth by Kirkham Gate	0	0	6			
	The Right Hon[orab]le The Earle of Cardigan for a house & Land in the occupation of Roberte Lumbe ..	0	0	6			
	James Nayler a Croft near Lofthouse yate	0	0	1			
	Timothy Bowling for a house & Croft at Brandicarr	0	0	3			
	The Heirs of Richard Shaw Gen: for Lands & houseing at Potovens in the occupation of Wm Fenay ..	0	1	3			
	Joseph Naylor for a house oth Woodside near Lingwell Yate formerly Westermans in the occupation of Wm Nettleton	0	0	2			
					0	10	1½
2	Robert Benson Esqr for a Farme called Turton Farme in the occupation of Jno Lake & formerly the Lands of Jno Hopkinson Esqr	0	4	0			
	And hath help of Matthew & Joshua Hanson for a house & Lands in Stanley	0	0	5			
	John Wilkinson of Greenhead Esqr for a house & Lands in the occupation of Peter Raith & another house & Lands in the occupation of George Carver ..	0	5	5			
					0	9	10

23	Sr Lyon Pilkington Barronett for ⅓ of all his Lands & Tenem[en]ts in Stanley of which are 14 acres wanting ½ a rood bought formerly by Mr Lyon Pilkington of John Bradford[1]	0 15 2	
			0 15 2
24	Robert Benson Esqr for the Long Closes & certain Field Land in the severall Towne fields of Stanley late Mr Hopkinsons & formerly, Robert Hobsons	0 12 6½	
	George Gibson for a Cott[age] & Backside in Ouchthorpe Laine to be helped vnder the number (18) ..	0 0 1	
			0 12 7½
	Totall of the yearly Rents collectable by the Grave of Stanley ..		14 4 3½

Wee The Jury Sworne for the Lord of the Mannor of Wakefield abovesaid doe Vpon our Enquiry into the Old Rentalls & Evidences concerning our said Graveship of Stanley finde & present that there are Twenty four Graves within our said Graveship and that the Persons abovesaid Vnder their several Numbers ought to serve the office of Graves in their respective Turns for Their Lands & Tenem[en]ts there mentioned & have the helpers which are there set down vnder the same Numbers for their Lands & Tene[me]ts there also mentioned and that those Persons vnder the same Number Five doe serve the office for this present yeare beginning att Mich[ae]l[mas] Last and the rest successively as they follow in their Numbers And that the respective rents vnder every Number are due & payable yearly to the Lord of the said Mannor

Oswold Hatfield	David Law
Tho: Graves	Wm Armitage
Richard Smarwhat	John Wilkes
Ri: Harrison	Richard Illingworth
Thomas Smith	Samuel Birkes
James Moxon	Will: Fenay

Richard Everingham

THE GRAVESHIP OF OSSET

The Graveship of Osset is boundered by the Graveship of Thornes to The East The Graveship of Horbury & The River of Calder to the South, Mirfield to the West & Heckmondwike Batley Soothill and Chidsill to the North And hath within it The Freeholders & Copyholders following who pay Rents &c according to The Verdict taken out of The Court Rolls of the Mannor as followeth—

[1] *C.D.*, I, 145.

Maner[ium] de Wakefield } Ad magn[am] cur[iam] Baron[em] Nobilissimi Thome Ducis de Leeds pr[ae]nobilis ordinis Garterij milit[is] D[omi]ni Manerij de Wakefield tent[am] ibidem p[er] adjournament[um] vicesimo die Maij Anno Regni Domine n[ost]re Anne Dei gra[tia] nunc Regine Magne Brittannie &c octavo

The Verdict of Marke Whiteakers, Josias Hepworth, Percival Terry, John Peace, Francis Marsdein, John Saxton, Joshua Haigh, Joseph Hirst, Timothy Kitson, Thomas Terry, John Graham, John Fletcher & John Scholefield being Freeholders & Copyholders within the Graveship of Ossett of and concerning the Freehold & Copyhold Lands & Tenem[en]ts within the said Graveship which pay rents & doe service to the Lord of the said Mannor of Wakefield

1[st]	Michael Parker for a mess[uage] & Lands thereunto belonging in Earles Heaton in the poss[ession] of Tho: Whiteakers & Jn[o] Marshal	0	1	7¼			
	And hath Help of W[m] Hall in right of his wife for Sunnigate Closes, Tungs acre & Lands in Great Syke Field formerly Hutchinson	0	2	0			
	Josias Oates Gent for Lands in Earles-heaton	0	4	6			
	Anthony Milner for a house & Land ..	0	1	6			
	Henry Hemingway for a house & a Croft ..	0	0	8			
					0	10	3¼
2[d]	Charles Nettleton, Clerk for all his Lands & Ten[emen]ts in Earles Heaton	0	15	9			
					0	15	9
3	Robert Bradford for all his Lands & Ten[emen]ts in Ossett ..	0	4	1			
	And hath help of Richard Armitage & Benj: Kighley for a house & Croft in Ossett	0	0	2			
	Wm̃ Hirst for Smith & Bradfoard Lands ..	0	2	1½			
	Anthony Milner for a house & croft ..	0	0	2½			
	John Milner Jun[r] for a mess[uage] & Lands	0	2	3			
	Thomas Gill for his Lands in Ossett ..	0	1	9			
					0	10	7
4	The Trustees of the Heirs of Thomas Taylor for a Mess[uage] & Lands in the poss[ession] of Thomas Wade ..	0	1	6			

No.	Item	£	s	d	£	s	d
	And hath help of Thomas Birkhead Gent for a house & Land att Streetside	0	0	3			
	Thomas Wilby for a Cott[age]	0	0	1			
	Roger Hirst for a Cott[age]	0	0	1½			
	Thomas Blackburne for a Cott[age] ..	0	0	1			
	Wm Hall in the right of his wife for a Mess[uage] & Lands att Streetside	0	8	6			
	Richard Terry	0	0	1			
					0	10	7½
5	Thomas Peace for a Mess[uage] & Lands thereunto belonging in Osset ..	0	1	0			
	Joshua Peace for a house and Croft in his owne poss[ession].. ..	0	0	4			
	And have help of Robert Shaw Gent: for a Mess[uage] & Lands lyeing in Osset	0	7	9			
	John Terry for Ratcliffe Land.. ..	0	1	9			
					0	10	10
6	John Smith Gent for Lands late Tho: Hodgsons now in the poss[ession] of John Grime	0	12	4			
					0	12	4
7	John Smith Gent for his Lands in Gawthorpe late Bradleys now in the poss[ession] of John Grime ..	0	1	4			
	Do for Lands in the Poss[ession] of John Terry	0	0	10			
	And hath help of John Curtice for a house & Land on Sowood Green in the poss[ession] of Michael Wheelwright & for Kirkbalks in Gawthorpe..	0	1	8			
	John Turner Gent for his Lands ..	0	6	3			
					0	10	1
8	John Speight for Lands late Fearnleys now in the poss[ession] of Nicholaus Gunson	0	0	4½			
	Do for Micklefield Close late Vshers ..	0	2	0			
	And hath help of John Nettleton Gent[1] for his Lands	0	1	3			
	The sd John Speight for all his Lands in Gawthorpe	0	6	8			
					0	10	3½

[1] *H.F.M.G.*, I, 127.

9	Richard Hemmingway for a mess[uage] & Lands in Earles Heaton now in his own possession	0	1	5			
	And hath Help of Tattersall Wid[w] for a Cott[age] & Garth	0	0	6			
	John Westerman for a house & Garth ..	0	1	0			
	Tho: Shepley for a Cottage	0	0	6			
	[*blank*] Wilson Wid[w] for a house & Garden	0	0	6			
	Abraham Firth for a house & Land vnder Earles Heaton Hill	0	0	5			
	W[m] Lee for a house & Croft vnder Earles Heaton Hill	0	0	4			
	Henry Heald for a Cott[age] & Garth Vnder Earles Heaton Hill ..	0	0	8			
	Richard Speight for a Cott[age] Vnder the Hill	0	0	6			
	Jeremie Cunningham for a House & Ground vnder the Hill ..	0	0	4			
	John Wheelwright Gent for a house & Land in the poss[ession] of Edw[ar]d Broadhead & James Askive ..	0	0	6			
	John & Thomas Whiteacre for their Houseing & Land oth Top of the Banck	0	0	4			
	Mich[l] Parker juñ in right of his wife for a house & Land att Battley Carr head	0	2	0			
	Thomas Fothergill for a Cottage ..	0	0	0½			
	John Gupwell for a house & Land ..	0	0	9			
	Joseph Jepson for a Close called James Close late Greenwoods ..	0	0	6			
					0	10	3½
10	Dr Davinson for soe much of his Lands as are within the Graveship of Ossett in the poss[ession] of John Bradford & Edward Thornes	0	5	0			
	And hath help of Robert Thornes for a house & croft in the poss[ession] of W[m] Wright	0	0	1			
	Joseph Hirst for his house & Lands soe much as are within the Graveshipp of Ossett	0	1	1			

	Entry				Total
	[*blank*] Dewce Widw for a Cottage in Ossett	0	0	2½	
	John Hirst for Carnel House	0	0	6	
	Samuel Land & Wm Nettleton in the right of their wifes for Lands in Osset	0	0	6	
	Joshua Ellis for a Cott[age] House & Garth in Sowood Green ..	0	0	1	
	Joshua Thompson for a Cott[age] House in Sowood Green	0	0	1	
	Robert Wright for a house & Land in his own poss[ession]	0	0	5	
	Wm Bramley for a house & Garth on Ossett Lights	0	0	4	
	George Pickard for a house & Garth on Ossett Lights	0	0	2	
	Richard Fostard for Liversiege.. ..	0	0	3	
	Joseph Naylor for a Cott[age] on Ossett Lights late Wades	0	0	4	
	John Townend for a house & Croft on Ossett Lights	0	0	6	
	Mary Ingham, Widw for house & Land ..	0	0	6	
					0 10 0½
11	Wm Ingham Jun for a Mess[uage] & Lands late Grices	0	2	11	
	Joshua Haigh for Lands late Grices ..	0	2	0	
	Wm Hirst & Richard Fostard for Lands late Grices	0	2	0	
	Josias Hepworth for Lands late Grices ..	0	1	0	
	And have Help of Robert Nettleton for Deyhouse	0	0	1	
	John Ingham for his Lands	0	0	3	
	John Scholefield for his Lands late John Ingham	0	0	3	
	Wm Ingham Senr for a Cott[age] late Williams	0	0	3	
	John Wade for a Cottage house ..	0	0	4	
	Wm Ingham Junr for a Cott[age] House & Peace Land.. ..	0	0	7	
	John Jagger for a house in the poss-[ession] of Rob: Jagger ..	0	0	5	
					0 10 1

12	The Heirs of Bartin Allott Gent for a Mess[uage] & Lands in Gawthorpe in the poss[ession] of Percivall Terry Junr	0	2	1½			
	Do for a house in Ossett late Ellis house ..	0	0	2			
	And hath help of John Murgatroyd Gent for Lands att Dewsbury late Bedfords	0	1	3			
	The Heirs of Mr Ramsden for Lands at Dewsbury	0	2	10			
	John Dawson for a House & Land att Bouthroyd	0	0	11			
	Joseph Awty for a house & Land att Batley Carr head	0	1	6			
	James Shepley for Woodman Carrs ..	0	1	3			
					0	10	0½
13	Joseph Haigh of Whitley for a Mess[uage] & Land in the poss[ession] of Joshua Haigh	0	0	9			
	And hath help of John Phillips for Gedham	0	0	8			
	William Harrop for his house & Lands ..	0	0	8			
	Mark Whiteakers for two houses & Lands in Ossett	0	0	5			
	Edward Megson for a Cott[age] att Streetside	0	0	6			
	Grace Radcliffe widw for a Cott[age] att Streetside	0	0	6			
	James Spurr for his house & Croft att Streetside	0	0	3			
	John Hirst Gent for Bolland Land ..	0	0	3			
	Jonas Thomas for Bouthroyd House & Land late Liversedges ..	0	4	1			
	Thomas Gill of Wakefield for Vpper Rye Croft	0	0	2			
	Do for Liversiedge Farme	0	1	8			
	John & Alice Hutton for a Cott[age] in Earles Heaton	0	0	1			
					0	10	0
14	The Lord Raby for a Mess[uage] & Lands thereunto belonging now in the poss[ession] of Widow Bargh formerly Saviles	0	4	4			
	And hath help of [*blank*] Wilson widow for Smith Lands	0	1	4			

	Wm Midlebrooke for a Mess[uage] & Lands in Ossett	0	1	2	
	Jonas Cordingley for a House & Land ..	0	0	8	
	Sr George Savile Bart for Lands & ten[emen]ts att Hanging Heaton in the poss[ession] of Charles Greenfield	0	0	4	
	Do in the poss[ession] of Wm Ridlesden & Benj Dey	0	0	2	
	Do in the poss[ession] of Wm Dernbrough	0	0	2	
	Do in the poss[ession] of Anthony Fearnley	0	0	2	
	Do in the poss[ession] of Mark Whiteakers	0	0	2	
	Do in the poss[ession] of Samuel Nettleton	0	0	2	
	Do in the poss[ession] of John Beyeiy ..	0	0	2	
	The Governours of the Free School of Wakefield for House & Land in the poss[ession] of John Jagger ..	0	1	9	
					0 10 7
15	John Scott of Wakefield Gent for a Mess[uage] & Lands thereunto belonging in the poss[ession] of Thomas Archer And a close in the poss[ession] of Wm Stephenson	0	1	0	
	And hath help of Joshua Thornes for a house & Lands on Ossett Lights	0	0	4	
	Richard Foster Senr for a house & Land on Ossett Lights side	0	1	10	
	Thomas Jagger for a Cottage on Ossett Lights	0	0	2	
	Wm Stephenson for a Cott[age] on Ossett Lights	0	0	4	
	Francis Marsdin for a Mess[uage] & Lands on Sowood Green ..	0	4	4	
	James White of Middlestowne for his Lands in Osset	0	0	5	
	Wm Curtice Sen: for a Cottage on Osset Lights	0	0	3	
	Joshua Thornes for Lands late Bradfords	0	0	5	

	Willm Langster or the heirs of Wm Bingley for a close called Dickinson Royd	0	0	9			
	Charles Howden for 2 Cottages in the poss[ession] of George Wood ..	0	0	3			
	James Firth for a Cottage	0	0	1			
	Widw Burnley for a Cottage	0	0	1			
					0	10	3
16	John Peace Senr for a Mess[uage] & Lands in Ossett in his own possession	0	2	1			
	And hath help of John Peace Junr for Lands late Gills & Hewits ..	0	2	3			
	John Wilson for Liversiedge Land & Maplewell	0	2	1			
	John Sugden for a Mess[uage] & Lands in Osset	0	0	6			
	Thomas Hunt for a house in [*blank*] Atocks poss[ession]	0	0	2			
	Judith Glover for two Cottages & Land ..	0	0	4			
	The Governors of the Poor for Elvage House	0	0	6			
	John Robinson for a house & Lands ..	0	2	10			
					0	10	9
17	Timothy Kitson for a mess[uage] & Lands thereunto belonging ..	0	0	4			
	D^o for five acres of Land late Tho: Peaces ..	0	0	4			
	And hath help of John Wood of Woodthorp Gent: for a house & Land	0	1	1			
	John Nettleton for two Cott[age] Houses	0	0	3			
	Willm Bingley for a Mess[uage] & Lands in the poss[ession] of Jno Nettleton	0	0	11			
	D^o for Lands in the Poss[ession] of Fossard	0	0	8			
	Wm Heron Gent: for [*blank*] Land Farme	0	3	0			
	Mary Land, widw, for Rye Royds ..	0	2	2			
	Richard White for house & Land ..	0	0	4			
	Joseph Phillips for two Cottages late Moses Greens	0	0	2			
	Wm Heron, Gent for a farme in the poss[ession] of Joshua Wilson ..	0	1	0			
					0	10	3

No.	Entry				Total
18	The heirs of John Oates for one half of all his Lands & Ten[emen]ts in Earles Heaton	0	5	7	
	And hath help of John Scholefield for a house & Lands vnder Earls Heaton Hill in the poss[ession] of James Speight	0	0	8	
	Widw Wadsworth of Horbury for her Lands in Gawthorp	0	4	3	
					0 10 6
19	Richard White for a mess[uage] & Lands in Earles-Heaton in the poss-[ession] of James Longley ..	0	2	0½	
	And hath help of Widw. Dawson for a Cottage	0	0	0½	
	Widw. Mitchell for a Cottage	0	0	1	
	Richard Wood & Sam[l] Mitchell for a Cottage	0	0	0½	
	Thomas Hallyley for a House & Lands..	0	7	5	
	John Saxton for a House	0	0	1¼	
	Abraham Saxton for a Cottage ..	0	0	0½	
	Thomas Hemingway for a house & two Lands	0	0	2	
					0 9 11¼
20	John Clapham of Hartchstead in the right of his wife for a mess[uage] & Lands in Ossett in the possess[ion] of Christopher Wilson	0	0	7	
	And hath help of Thomas Pashley for a Mess[uage] & Lands	0	4	2	
	Elizabeth & Mary Schory for a Mess-[uage] & Lands	0	2	2	
	Josias Hepworth for his Lands ..	0	3	0	
	Henry Heald for a Cottage	0	0	2	
					0 10 1
21	Thomas Terry for a Mess[uage] & Lands in Gawthorp in his own Possession	0	0	10	
	And hath help of Widow Fletcher for her House & Lands	0	0	11	
	John Fletcher for his house & Land in Gawthorpe	0	0	10	
	John Graham for his Lands in Gaw-thorpe	0	1	8	

Willm Naylor for his house & Lands ..	0	3	1			
Richard Graham for his house & Lands..	0	1	11			
Parcivel Terry Sen[r] for his house & Lands	0	1	2			
John Parkinson for a house & Ouelers Croft	0	0	2			
				0	10	7
The Heirs of John Oates for the other halfe of his Lands & Ten[emen]ts in Earles Heaton	0	5	7			
John Scholefield for his house & Lands..	0	4	11¼			
D[o] for Thomas Graves Land	0	1	0			
D[o] for a House & Land late Parcival Terrys	0	0	6			
				0	12	0¼
Totall of The yearly Rents collectable by the Grave of Osset ..				11	16	2¼

N.B. There appears to be the following mistakes in this Verdict viz:—

	s.	d.
No 5 John Terry overcharged ..	0 0	6
No. 6 John Smith Gent ..	0 2	0
No. 10 Robert Thornes	0 0	1
	0 2	7

Soe this Rentall apeares but to be £11 13 7¼

Wee The Jury sworne for the Lord of the Mannor abovesaid doe vpon our enquiry into the old Rentalls & evidences concerning our Said Graveship of Ossett find & present that there are Twenty two Graves within our said Graveship and that the Persons abovesaid vnder their several Numbers ought to serve the office of Graves in their respective Turns for their Lands & ten[emen]ts there mentioned & have the helpers which are there sett down vnder the same Numbers for their Lands & ten[emen]ts there also mentioned And that those Persons vnder the Number three doe serve the office for this present yeare beginning at Mich[ae]l[mas] last and the rest successively as they follow in their Numbers And that the respective rents vnder every Number are due & payable yearly to the Lord of the said Mannor

John Peace	Joseph Hirst	John Graham
Francis Marsdin	Timothy Kitson	John Fletcher
John Saxon	Thomas Terry	John Scholefield
Marke Whiteaker	Josiah Hepworth	Parcivall Terry

THORNES GRAVESHIP

The Graveship of Thornes

The Graveship of Thornes is bounded by the River of Calder to the East and South, by Horbury Graveship & Osset to the West & by Alverthorp & Wakefield to the North and hath within it the Freehold & Copyhold Tenants following being set down as the majority of The Jury that were sworne ordered & methodiz'd but sume disagreeing to the method & turne of serving the Office of Grave wo[ul]d not agree to a Verdict

1st	Richard Shaw, Gent for a mess[uage] & Lands in the occupa[tion] of John Bedford	0 4 0	
	Do for a Close joyning upon the Calder River in his owne possession ..	0 0 4	
	And hath help of James Swallow for a hous & Land in Thornes ..	0 0 6	
	James Harrison for 4 Closes Three in the occ[upation] of Willm Armitage and one in his owne..	0 2 8	
	Wm Dennison for his Lands adjoyning on Snapethorp	0 0 8	
		———	0 8 2
2d	Sr Charles Goreing for $\frac{1}{6}$ p[ar]te of all his Demesne Lands & Teneme[n]ts at Snapethorp		0 10 $9\frac{1}{2}$
3d	Joseph Smith for a Mess[uage] & Lands in his owne Occupation late Harrisons	0 1 6	
	And hath help of the heirs of John Kirke for a Close called Hale Inge in the occ-[upation] of Samuel Peaker ..	0 1 6	
	Mary Kirke Wid[ow] for Two Closes at Lawhill in the occ[upation] of Willm̃ Dickson	0 3 0	
	The heirs of Wm Lawson Gent: for Two Closes in the occ[upation] of Joseph Smith	0 1 5	
	John Wood of Woodthorp Gent in right of his Wife for a Close adjoyning upon the river Calder in the occ[upation] of Wm Copendall	0 1 5	
		———	0 8 2

4th	The Governors of the Poor of Wakefield for Two Closes called Crabtree Close & Wheat Close & 3 acres of feild Land	0	2	7			
	Do for inclosure at beck mouth.. ..	0	0	9			
	Do for Closes at Lawhill late Kays ..	0	1	9			
	And have help of Joseph Watkinson Gent: for his Lands at Lawfield Yate in his owne occ[upation] ..	0	3	6			
	The Governors of the Poor for Land in the occ[upation] of John Godley	0	0	2			
	Joseph Briggs Cl[erk] for a Close in the occ[upation] of Jonathan Bradley	0	0	7			
	Daniel Mawd Gent: Samuel Peaker & others being Trustees of Mr Fosters charity for a mess[uage] & Croft & 3 Roods of Land in the occ[upation] of Ben: Bedford	0	0	4½			
					0	9	2½
5th	Sr Charles Goreng Baront for another 6th p[ar]te of all his lands & Tennem[en]ts at Snapethorp ..				0	10	9¾
6th	Daniel Mawd Gent for Joseph Watkinson Gent & others being Trustees for Taylors Charity & their Land in Thornes	0	4	1			
	And have help of the heirs of Thomas Goodall for a hous & Croft at Streetside	0	0	2			
	Wm Hioward Esq: for 4 Closes at Whinny Moor	0	1	4½			
	Mrs Lee for a Close called Bunny close in the occ[upation] of John Ellis..	0	1	3			
	Saml Peaker for a hous & Land in his oune poss[ession] ..	0	1	3			
	John Ellis for his hous	0	0	0½			
					0	8	2
7th	The heirs of Willm Horne Gen: for a Mess[uage] & Lands called Pryorhous or Greenend hous in the occ[upation] of Jer Smith & all their other Lands & Tenem[en]ts in Thornes ..	0	4	10			
	And have help of Thomas Wilson Gent: for Nether law, the Ryecroft, & certain Lands in the Lawfeild ..	0	2	0			

	Fr: Pitt Gent: for a hous & Land in the occ[upation] of Wm Hall ..	0 1 0	
	Thomas Hawkins for certain feild Land in the Lawfield	0 0 4	
			0 8 2
8th	Sr Charles Goreing Baron^t for another ⅙ of all his Lands & Tennem[en]ts at Snapethorp		0 10 9¾
9th	Richd Witton Esq for one half of Lupsit hall Demesne bein formerly Saviles & Harrises		0 14 10
10th	Richd Witton Esq for the other half of all his Lands & Tennem[en]ts at Lupsitt		0 14 10
11th	Sr Charles Goreing Baron^t for another ⅙ of all his Lands & Tennem[en]ts at Snapethorp		0 10 9¾
12th	The Governors of the Free School of Wakefield for Lands in the occ[upation] of Samuel Batty & others ..	0 1 8	
	And have help of Mrs Sill for Lands late Mawds at Westgate moor side ..	0 4 10	
	D^o for Stocks Land	0 1 5	
	Francis Allen for a hous & Land in the occ[upation] of Geo: Fawsit & Jno Horner	0 0 10	
			0 8 9
13th	James Hebdin for a Messuage & Lands in his oune poss[ession] ..	0 0 4	
	And hath help of Edward Clarke, Cl[erk] for Kirkgate Lands, Stock Inge &c late Wilsons now in the occ[upation] of Joseph Watkinson Gent. ..	0 6 2	
	Abr[aha]m Beevor Gent for a Close in Thornes moor head in the occ[upation] of Benj: Bedford	0 1 9	
			0 8 3
14th	Sr Charles Goreing Baronet for another ⅙ of all his Lands & Tennem[en]ts at Snapethorp		0 10 9¾
15th	Joseph Richardson Cl[erk] for a Close called Stables Close in the occ[upation] of George Faweit NB. this Close Rent is paid by the Lord Raby in the 16th November below		

	And hath help of John Smith Gent: for a Close called Jack Inge in the occ[upation] of Samuel Peaker ..	0	2	6			
	D° for Thorns Mire	0	0	3			
	Grace Nayler widow for Lands in Lawfield	0	0	5			
	Wm Hall for a Mess[uage] & Lands ..	0	1	6			
	John Smith Gen: for his Land late Norfolks	0	1	0½			
	Ab^m Lee for a hous	0	0	1½			
	John Rhodes of Horbury for his Lands adjoyning on Snapethorp Lands	0	0	8			
	Phebe Wadsworth Widow for Lands in the occ[upation] of Joshua Raynor & John Dickson late Mattershaws	0	0	8			
	Wm Harrison for a Close at Westgate moor side in his owne occupation	0	1	0			
					0	8	2
16th	Francis Mawd Gent. for severall closes at Westgate moor head in the occ[upation] of Jer: Dickson & Saml Foxcroft late Grices	0	3	6			
	And hath help of the Hon[ora]ble The L[or]d Raby for his Lands in Thornes in the occ[upation] of John Scott, John Smith, Gent: & others ..	0	3	8½			
	Henry Bradley Gent: for a Close called Moorcroft in the occ[upation] of Wm Denton	0	1	0			
					0	8	2½
17th	Sr Charles Goreing for the last ⅛ p[ar]te of all his Lands & Tennem[en]ts at Snapethorp				0	10	9¾
	Totall of The Yearly Rents collectable by the Grave of Thorns				8	9	9

THE GRAVESHIP OF HOLME

The Graveship of Holme is boundered by Thurstonland, Burton, & Shepley, & Cumberworth, to the East, Denby, Karlicoats and the Mannor of Thurlston to the South, The County of Chester, Sadleworth, and Marstin to the West, and Melton, Honley & Thongue to the North, and hath wi[th]in it The Freehold &

Copyhold Tenements following who pay rents &c according to the Verdict taken out of the Court Rolls of The Mannor as followeth

Maner[ium] de Wakefeld } Ad magn[am] Cur[iam] Baron[em] Nobilissimi Thome Ducis de Leeds pr[ae]nobilis Ordinis Garterij militis D[omi]ni Manerij de Wakefeld tent[am] apud Newmill in Holmfirth p[er] adjournament[um] vicesimo quinto die Maij Anno Regni D[omin] n[ost]re Anne Dei gra[tia] nunc R[egi]ne magne Britannie &c octavo

The Verdict of Jonas Kay, James Earnshaw, Luke Wilson, John Newton, Philip Bray, Humphrey Roebuck, John Tincker, John Whitehead, Jerimie Kaye, Daniel Broadhead, Joshua Newton, George Hirst, Joshua Dixon, Richard Crosland & Henry Jackson being Freeholders & Copyholders within the Graveship of Holme of and concerning the Freehold & Copyhold Lands & Ten[emen]ts within the said Graveship which pay rents & doe service to the Lord of the said Mannor of Wakefield

1	Godfrey Crosland Gent for parte of Longley in Wooldale	0	11	4	
	Abraham Firth for his Mess[uage] & Lands at Longleys	0	4	7½	
	And have help of John Tyas for Long Ing	0	2	8	
	Mary Heckinbothom for Hade-Ing ..	0	1	5	
					1 0 0½
2d	Joshua Charlesworth for his Lands att Hollingreave in Fulstone ..	0	7	0	
	Humphrey Roebuck for his Lands att Hollingreave in Fulstone ..	0	4	0	
	Joshua Newton for his Lands att Hollingreave in Fulstone ..	0	1	7	
	And have help of James Hincliffe for 22½ acres of Land att Arunden in Cartworth	0	7	6	
					1 0 1
3	Joseph & Jonathan Swallow for their Lands in Townehead in Scholes..	0	6	2	
	And hath help of James Earnshaw for a Mess[uage] & 5 acres of Land ..	0	1	8	
	John Charlesworth Junr for Lands att Ryecroft & Jno: Tinker for his Lands there	0	5	2	
	[*blank*] Hamand Gent: for 9 acres of Land at Fair banck Knowe in Hepworth	0	3	0	

	David Haigh for 8 acres of Land in Bradshawe in Austonley ..	0	2	8			
	John Garlick Gent. for 2 acres in Hepworth Deane	0	0	8			
					0	19	4
4	John Whitehead for his Lands in Holme late Beardsells in his owne poss[ession]	0	2	11½			
	Arthur Beardsell for Royd	0	0	4½			
	Jonas Beardsell for his Land in Holme..	0	1	7			
	And have help of Luke Wilson for 30 acres of Land at Hades in Woldale	0	8	8			
	George Beardsell for his Land in Holme-woods	0	2	4			
	James Green for a Mess[uage] & Lands in Holme in the poss[ession] of George Beardsell	0	1	11			
	Abraham Earnshaw for 6½ acres of Land in Holme att Cliffe in the poss[ession] of Philip Earnshaw	0	2	2			
					1	0	0
5	Godfrey Cuttell for Lands att Sinder Hills & vnder Banck in Wooldale	0	5	8			
	Barth: & Tho: Bray for their Lands at Sinder Hills & Stock Lane ..	0	6	2			
	And have help of John Hirst for Couep[er] Flatt & Moorbrooke in Thong	0	0	8			
	John Garlick Gent: for Cowp[er] Flatt in Thong	0	0	8			
	Henry Jackson for Sandy Gate in Scholes..	0	0	5			
	The Heirs of Josias Newton for Lands in poss[ession] of Jonath: Eastwood in Scholes	0	0	9			
	Humphrey Hincliffe of Humberton his Lands there	0	1	3			
	Henry Jackson Senr for his parte of the Mount	0	3	1			
	The Heirs of Jno Hadfield for Ridle Pitt in Hepworth	0	1	1			
	Thomas Cuttell for a house & Browes in Wolldale	0	0	3			
					1	0	0

6	John Matthewman a[lia]s Copley for a mess[uage] & Lands in Cartworth called Kilne house banck	0	16	6½			
	And hath help of Joshua Earnshaw & George Sanderson in the right of his wife for 3 acres of Land in Awstonley late Broadhead	0	1	0			
	Thomas Noble in The right of his wife for 3 acres of land att Dickedge in Hepworth	0	1	0			
	John Cuttell for Cuttel Hey in Wooldale..	0	1	0			
	Jonas Kay Gent. for Farr field in Hepworth	0	0	6			
					1	0	0½
7	John Hirst for his Land att Cross lyeing in Thong in his owne possession	0	2	2			
	George Saunderson in right of his wife for Bothoms	0	1	2			
	D^o^ for Green Slack in the poss[ession] of John Halmshaw	0	1	0			
	John Littlewood for Nether Whickins in the poss[ession] of Timothy Mallinson	0	1	4			
	John Creswick for the Ings belonging Cross	0	0	6			
	Godfrey Hincliffe for Lands belonging Cross	0	0	10			
	And have help of Richard Marsh for his Lands att Flushouse in the poss[ession] of Daniel Heap in Austonley ..	0	1	6			
	John Green for his Lands att Flushouse..	0	1	6			
	Christopher Green for his Lands att Flushouse	0	0	9			
	Robert France for two Closes called Marsh & Charles Hey ..	0	0	8			
	Edward Bilcliffe for his Lands at Flush-house	0	0	5			
	James Earnshaw Gent: for Townend in Thonge	0	0	6			
	James Hincliffe for Good Greave ..	0	1	0			
	John Marsden in right of his wife for Lands in Bradshaw in the poss[ession] of John Roebuck late Haigh Land	0	3	4			

No.	Entry	£	s.	d.	Total
	George Hincliffe for his Land in Thonge..	0	1	0	
	John Taylor for Marke bothom ..	0	0	8	
	George Hirst for Heward Heys in Thonge..	0	0	5	
	James Mitchell for his Lands att Yew tree in Austonley in the poss[ession] of John Crosland	0	0	11	
	Thomas Hincliffe for Hick Bothom ..	0	0	4	
					1 0 0
8	James Earnshaw Gent: for his Lands in Holme in his owne possession ..	0	6	6½	
	D° for Newhouse Land called Mitchell Land	0	4	5	
	D° for Holme Woods in the poss[ession] of Joshua Hincliffe	0	4	0	
	D° for Lands in the poss[ession] of Arthur Beardsell	0	3	10½	
	D° for Lands in the poss[ession] of Jonas Beardsell called Fodder Lands	0	1	0	
					0 19 10
9	John Rowley for Mettem House & old mill in Foulstone	0	4	6½	
	Henry Jackson, Senr for his Lands in Wooldale	0	6	10	
	D° for Lands in his owne Joseph Earnshawes & Joshua Ellises possession	0	4	4	
	And have help of Jere: Kay for Lands at Cophirst	0	2	11¼	
	George Morehouse for his Lands att More Croft	0	1	5½	
					1 0 1¼
10	Jonas Kay Gent for Louk's house in Hepworth	0	7	7½	
	And hath help of Joshua Kay for Lands called Nabb & Rideing Ing in Hepworth	0	3	6	
	Jonas Kay Gent for Nabb in Hepworth..	0	5	10	
	George Lindley for Land att Nabb ..	0	3	2	
					1 0 1½
11	James Earnshaw Gent: for his Lands att Ramsden in Cartworth ..	0	13	9	
	D° for Bright Hill	0	0	6	
	And hath help of Jorden Chadwick in the right of his wife for 4 acres of Land formerly Castles	0	5	11	
					1 0 2

12	Benjamin Green for his Lands att Field End in Austonley	0	5	10			
	Thomas Hincliffe for his Lands att Field End	0	4	4			
	John Littlewood of Digleroyd in Austonley	0	1	6			
	The Heirs of Jonathan Hincliffe for Land in the poss[ession] of David Haigh	0	3	7			
	James Earnshaw for a Damm.. ..	0	0	0½			
	D^o^ for Hincliffe Milne in Cortworth ..	0	1	1½			
	And have help of Joshua Wortley for his Land att Hincliffe milne ..	0	0	4½			
	George Hirst for his Lands at Booth house	0	1	11½			
	Jonas Kaye for Roberts Land in Hepworth	0	1	0			
	The Heirs of Wm Rhodes for 2 acres of Land in Bradshaw, Knowle being part of 15 acres in the poss[ession] of Humphrey Woodhead & Abraham Taylor	0	0	8			
					1	0	5
13	Abraham Charlesworth & Joshua Charlesworth for their Lands att Hogley in Austonley	0	2	8½			
	John Wagstaff Gent: for his Lands att Hogley in the poss[ession] of Widow Wood	0	4	5			
	And have help of Thomas Hincliffe for Newfield in Bradshawe ..	0	1	4			
	Jonathan Eastwood for 2 Closes called Bankes	0	0	3			
	Geo: Hirst for 1 close called Crosland Inge in Austonley	0	0	6			
	D^o^ for his Land att Newland in Thwonge..	0	0	8½			
	John Roberts for a Close in Thonge called Gennit Hole	0	0	3			
	Henry Jackson for vpper woods in Austonley	0	1	0			
	Thomas Darby for Lands att Burnley in Thong	0	3	5			
	Joshua Dixon for Lands there.. ..	0	3	1			

	James Batty for a close & milne called Holme in Thong	0 0 4	
	Godf: Crosland for Land called Modwood in Cartworth	0 1 7½	
	Joshua Wilson for Great Fox Holme in Wooldale	0 0 3½	
	D^o for Little Fox Holme in Wooldale ..	0 0 3	
			1 0 2
14	Jonas Kaye Gent for Vpper & Neither Milnshaw & the Lands thereto belonging in Hepworth	0 19 5½	
	D^o for one of the Far Feilds in Hepworth..	0 0 6	
	D^o for ½ acre at Butterlee in Fulstone ..	0 0 2	
			1 0 1½
15	Richard Morton Jun: for the ½ parte of Dearshaw in Fulstone ..	0 3 2½	
	Richard Morton sen^r for the ¼ part of Dearshaw	0 2 1½	
	And have help of Humphrey Roebuck for his Land there at Dearshaw	0 1 9½	
	Henry Jackson Gent. for Nether Haddingley	0 1 5	
	Jonas Kaye Gent: for Hay Slacks ..	0 0 10	
	Richard Morton Senr for a Mess[uage] & Lands called Maythorn ..	0 7 11	
	Luke Wilson for parte of Little Hades ..	0 1 6	
	Joshua Butterworth for over Haddingley in Fulstone	0 0 9¼	
			0 19 6¾
16	John Green for Yate Holme for his Lands in Holme in the poss[ession] of David Haigh Christopher Green John Beever, Will. Hincliff, & George Hepenstall	0 11 3	
	And hath help of James Earnshaw Gent. for 3½ acres of Land late Wagstaffs	0 1 2	
	D^o for 2 acres of Land called Broadwell..	0 0 8	
	James Earnshaw & Philip Earnshaw for 1½ acres	0 0 6	
	Abr: Earnshaw for 4 acres of Land att Cliff in Holme	0 1 4	
	Geo: Beardsell for his Lands att Meal Hill in Holme	0 1 8	

	Dº for Over Close in his own possession..	0	2	0			
	James Earnshaw for Land in the poss-[ession] of Jno Hatfield ..	0	1	0			
	Thomas Peace for Nab Hey in the poss-[ession] of George Hepenstall in Holme	0	0	4			
	John Horsfield for Haigh Croft in Wool-dale	0	0	2			
					1	0	1
17	James Hincliffe for his Lands att Maw-kin House in Cartworth ..	0	10	2½			
	And hath help of John Hincliffe for his Lands called Dunsley ..	0	4	10			
	The Heirs of Bartin Allot Gent for a Close called Walkers Bothom	0	0	6			
	Thomas Cuttell for his Lands called Vpper & Nether Lane ..	0	1	10			
	Dº for his Land in the poss[ession] of Jonathan Ellis	0	0	3½			
	James Batty for 3 Closes called Lath Croft, Ryding, & Henpickel ..	0	1	1½			
	John Hoyle for Stable Croft & Dunsley Bothom	0	0	4¼			
	The Heirs of Robert Wagstaff Gent for a House & Croft & 3 closes called Shalleys in Thong	0	0	9½			
	Godfr: Crosland for his houses Gardens & Croft at Overbrigg	0	0	3			
	Thomas Mitchill for house & Croft there..	0	0	1½			
					1	0	3¾
18	Luke Wilson in the right of his wife for a mess[uage] & Lands att New Milne in Fulstone	0	0	8			
	Joshua Newton for Lands att New Milne in the poss[ession] of Henry Wilson formerly Hepworths ..	0	1	1			
	Dº in the poss[ession] [*blank*] Byram ..	0	0	10½			
	Dº in the poss[ession] of Jnº Bray ..	0	0	8			
	Jnº Clarkson for Land in the poss-[ession] of Edward Barraclough	0	0	5			
	The Heirs of Wm Rhodes for Lands in the poss[ession] of Jno Newton..	0	1	9½			

	Francis Matthewman for Witt bothom & a Close at New Mill ..	0 3 4	
	Thomas Darby Gent for Ellis Holme & Land at New Mill	0 1 7¼	
	The Lord of the Mannor for a house in the poss[ession] of Jnº Lockwood	0 0 0½	
	The Heirs of Bartin Allott Gent for a Water Course	0 0 4	
	And have Help of Abraham Taylor or his Heirs for 3 closes called Great Cliffe & 3 closes called Sisters Oakes..	0 0 9	
	The Heirs of Joseph Turton for Land called Bank House	0 0 5½	
	John Hoyle for Cliffe Closes	0 0 8	
	John Beaumont for a House & Close at Lidgate	0 0 2½	
	Humphrey Hincliffe for a messuage att Bawshaw in Wooldale ..	0 0 8	
	John Hincliffe for Land att Lydgate ..	0 0 7½	
	Henry Jackson Junʳ for a Mess[uage] & Land in Fulstone in the poss[ession] of Jnº Taylor	0 6 0	
			1 0 2¼
19	Willm Morehouse for Lands att Snowgate head in Fulstone.. ..	0 7 10	
	And hath Help of Godfrey Crosland for Lands at Chopherd in Wooldale	0 8 11	
	The Heirs of Wᵐ Hirst for Lands in Foulstone	0 3 1	
			0 19 10
20	Richard Matthewman Gent for Lands in Foulstone in the poss[ession] of Ed: Langley	0 3 5¼	
	Dº for Lands in the poss[ession] of Joseph Haigh	0 4 0¼	
	Thomas Morehouse for Lands in Foulston	0 5 7½	
	Joshua Newton for his Land in Foulston..	0 4 3½	
	Thomas Littlewood of Damhouse for 8a. 3r.	0 2 11	
			1 0 3½
21	Richard Matthewman Gent. for Lands att Snowgate head	0 4 2½	

	Francis Matthewman for Lands att Snowgate head & 2 Closes called Marshaw & Nabb Cliffe	0	2	4½			
	John Tyas for 4 acres of Land in Foulston	0	1	4			
	John Tincker for 4½ acres of Land ..	0	1	6			
	Henry Jackson for Matson Inge ..	0	0	2			
	Joseph & Jonathan Swallow for 1 acre of Land formerly Ayres ..	0	0	4			
	And have help of Thomas Jackson in the right of his wife for 1 acre of Land in Scholes in the poss[ession] of Jonathan Eastwood	0	0	4			
	John Tincker for Land att Snowgate head late Hugh Annises ..	0	2	3			
	Francis Matthewman for his Lands in Foulstone	0	4	10			
	John Tyas for 6 acres of Land att Stedbrooke in Hepworth	0	2	0			
	Henry Jackson Jun[r] for Broomfield in Wooldale	0	0	6			
					0	19	10
22	Jonas Kay Gent for a Mess[uage] & Lands called Butts Lee in Foulstone	1	1	10½			
					1	1	10½
23	Jonas Kaye Gent for Lands att Foster place in the poss[ession] of George Tincker	0	5	4			
	D° for Lands in his own possession ..	0	2	0			
	D° for Hey Slacks in the poss[ession] of Matthew Booth	0	4	3			
	D° for Field Head in the poss[ession] of John Lees	0	2	2			
	D° for Lands in the poss[ession] of John Jagger	0	0	6			
	D° for Lands in the poss[ession] of Joshua Booth at Foster place ..	0	1	8			
	D° for ½ acre of Land belonging to a Mess[uage] called Butter Lee in Foulstone	0	0	2			
	D° for 12 acres of Land att Barneside ..	0	4	0			
					1	0	1

No.	Item						
24	The Heirs of Joshua Tincker for Lands lyeing att Hoowood in the poss[ession] of John Dewsnop in Austonley late Armitages	0	8	8½			
	Godfr: Littlewood for Lands in the poss[ession] of Tho: Blackburn & Isaac Whiteley	0	5	2			
	And have help of John Littlewood for Whitewalls	0	1	9½			
	James Hincliffe for a Close called Doxon Shaw in Austenley	0	1	0			
	Nicholas Fenay Gent: for his Lands att Hogleys Green in the poss[ession] of Widow Gleadhill	0	3	9			
					1	0	5
25	Joshua Charlesworth for his Lands att Mossedge in Cartworth ..	0	7	0½			
	And hath help of Thomas Haigh for his Land there	0	2	3½			
	John Creswick for his Lands att Whitegate in Cartworth	0	6	6			
	Tho: Hincliffe for 2 closes called Marsh & Hollinbrigg	0	0	9			
	John Hincliffe for Hattersleys House ..	0	0	0½			
	John Cuttell for a close called Round Inge	0	0	6			
	John Tyas for 9 acres of Land lyeing in Hepshaw Edge	0	3	0			
					1	0	1½
26	Henry Jackson sen[r] for Land att Meal Hill in Hepworth in the poss[ession] of Thomas Hobson, Richard Midleton, & William Wagstaffe	0	12	3			
	And hath help of John Micklethwaite, & Edward Kenyon for parte of their Lands att Mathorne ..	0	7	9			
					1	0	0
27	Richard Crosland & Joshua Wortley for their Lands att Stubing in Austonley	0	8	5½			
	And hath help of John Dearneley for his Lands at Nether Stubing ..	0	4	2			
	James Hincliffe for his Land in Bradshaw	0	2	0			

	The Heirs of Jonathan Hincliffe for their Lands in Bradshaw in the poss[ession] of David Haigh called Bartin ..	0 1 0	
	The Heirs of Willm Rodes for 13 acres of Land in Bradshaw Knowle in the poss-[ession] of Humphrey Woodhead & Abraham Tayler	0 4 6	
			1 0 1½
28	John Creswick for his Lands in Thwonge in the poss[ession] of Joshua Broadhead, John Oldham, & Jonas Winpenny	0 9 5	
	And hath help of George Castle for his Land att Brigg in Wooldale ..	0 5 6½	
	Do for his Land att Ellen head in the poss[ession] of James Morton ..	0 3 4	
	James & Joseph Hincliffe for 5 acres of Land att Arunden in Cartworth	0 1 8	
			0 19 11½
29	Christopher Kay for his Lands in Hepworth	0 9 7	
	Philip Bray for his Lands att Dean head in Hepworth	0 2 8	
	Jonas Kaye Gent. for Booth Land in Hepworth	0 3 8½	
	Robert Beever for Marsh Land in Hepworth	0 4 2	
			1 0 1½
30	John Newton for his Lands & ten-[emen]ts belonging to Stackwood hill & Biggin	0 10 5	
	Do for Land att Wooldale	0 2 7	
	And hath help of Godfrey Crosland for Land late Hamby Land ..	0 1 8	
	Joseph Hincliffe of Arunden for Hamby-Land	0 0 6	
	John Morehouse for 3 acres of Land in Foulstone	0 1 0	
	Tho. Morton in the right of his wife for 12 acres of Land att Wilberclough	0 4 0	
			1 0 2
31	Samuel Wagstaffe Gent: for his Land in Cartworth att Vpper & Nether-hill-house in the poss[ession] of Joseph Kirke & Abraham Green ..	0 5 0	

No.	Entry	£	s	d	£	s	d
	And hath help of Godfrey Crosland for a house & a Croft	0	0	10			
	James Hincliffe for his Land att Hill House & a Close called Brearlee	0	2	8			
	John Hincliffe of Waterside for Bray Woods	0	0	6			
	Joshua Roberts for his Land att Hill house	0	3	5			
	Daniel Roberts for a house att Hillhouse ..	0	0	1			
	Daniel Broadhead for his Land att Lane head in Cartworth	0	2	2			
	Joseph Hincliffe for 16 acres of his Land at Arunden	0	5	4			
					1	0	0
32	Samuel Wagstaffe Gent. for his Lands in Holme lately Hattersley's in the poss[ession] of John Green, & John Wagstaffe & for Lands in the poss[ession of John Hadfield	0	3	4			
	Joseph Haigh for his Lands att Holmwoods in his own & George Hewards possession	0	3	9½			
	And have help of John Green for his house at Lydgate in Holme ..	0	0	1			
	James Earnshaw Gent for his Lands att Lane except Brodewell ..	0	6	11½			
	Philip Earnshaw for his Land in Holme ..	0	3	0			
	James Earnshaw for 2 acres of Land late Wagstaff's	0	0	8			
	Do for Lands in the poss[ession] of John Oldham	0	2	7½			
					1	0	5½
33	Daniel Broadhead for Lands in Thonge in his owne possession ..	0	6	8			
	Do for Lands in the poss[ession] of Joshua Hirst	0	3	0			
	Do for Lands in the poss[ession] of James Batty	0	0	8			
	And hath help of Chris[topher] Green in the right of his wife for Lands in the poss[ession] of Jonas Winpenny, & Widw Dixon	0	2	0			

	John Garlick, Clerk for his Lands att Hillack in Thonge	0	1	1			
	Widw Radcliffe for her Lands att Yew-tree in Austonley in the poss[ession] of Wid-Charlesworth	0	4	1			
	John Crosland for his Lands att Yewtree..	0	2	7			
					1	0	1
34	Abraham Radcliffe Gent for his Lands att Hepshaw	0	11	0½			
	And hath help of Joshua Rodes for Lands in Hepworth	0	4	3½			
	John Tyas for 4 acres of Land att Oxlee in Hepworth	0	1	4			
	[*blank*] Hamand, Gent. for 3 acres of Land att Fairbanck Knowl in Hep-worth	0	1	0			
	Joseph Fisher for a house in Cartworth ..	0	0	0½			
	Richard Hirst for 2 Closes of Land in Foulston called Moore lands ..	0	1	0			
					0	18	8½
35	Luke Wilson for Lands att Wooldale Town end & Stone banck ..	0	12	3			
	And hath help of Amos Bower for Land at Town End	0	3	6			
	James Bower for Land att Town End ..	0	3	0			
	Abraham Roberts of Fearnley for Land at Town End	0	1	4			
					1	0	1
36	Jonas Kaye, Gent. for Land att Barnside	0	12	9			
	Joshua Kay for Land att Barnside ..	0	8	6			
					1	1	3
37	Luke Wilson for Lands & ten[emen]ts in Wooldale late Ramsdens & ffenays	0	7	2			
	Do for a Mess[uage] & Land in Fulstone in the poss[ession] of James Bramfield	0	2	2½			
	Do for Linches	0	0	9			
	Do for his Lands att Hades in Wooldale late Hollingworths	0	0	9			
	And hath help of the heirs of Richard Ellis for Land late Fenays in Wooldale	0	0	10			
	Martha Morehouse for Coldall Ing ..	0	0	5			
	Michael Eastwood for Bradshaw Edge ..	0	1	0			

No.	Entry						
	Luke Wilson & Janes Bower for Hey end . .	0	1	6½			
	Luke Wilson for parte of Parkin Ing & Moor Croft	0	0	5			
	The Heirs of Richard Ellis for the other part	0	0	5			
	John Wilson for Land att Wooldale Town End	0	1	10			
	Joshua Wilson for Land att Town End . .	0	1	0			
	George Castle of Brigg for Rockle Royds . .	0	1	0			
	Philip Bray for Shaley Ing in Wooldale . .	0	0	10			
					1	0	2
38	Thomas Jackson in the right of his wife for Land att Scholes formerly Newtons	0	2	10			
	And hath help of Henry Booth for his Land att Hawckscarr in Scholes	0	1	3			
	D^{o} for Field Ing	0	0	10			
	Michael Eastwood for Bradshaw Inge . .	0	0	4½			
	Godfrey Horne in the right of his wife for Lands called Lee in Scholes . .	0	4	3			
	Luke Wilson for Westfield Inge in Scholes	0	0	8			
	John Tincker for Moorebanck in Scholes . .	0	0	4			
	Richard Morton for a Wood called Milne Haigh wood	0	1	0			
	John Green of Dale Lee for his Mess-[uage] & Land there in Scholes . .	0	7	6¾			
	Thomas Morton for Wilberclough in the poss[ession] of Adam Hirst in Scholes	0	0	11¾			
					1	0	1
39	Henry Taylor for his Land att Hill in Thonge	0	2	1½			
	John Taylor for his Land att Hill . .	0	2	0			
	Henry Booth for his Land att Hill in the poss[ession] of Josua Charlesworth, W^{m} & Richard Almond	0	6	10			
	The Heirs of Saml Dearnley, & Godfr: Crosland, for Lands att Hill in the poss-[ession] of Josua Wimpenny . .	0	4	5			
	The Heirs of Saml Dearnley for Land in the poss[ession] of Wid^{w} Dixon	0	2	0			
	And have help of Joseph Hincliffe for 7½ acres of Land att Arunden in Cart-worth	0	2	6			

	The Heirs of Henry Kay for Dobroyd Hills in Cartworth	0	0	1	
	David Dixon for a house in his own poss[ession] in Thonge ..	0	0	0½	
					1 0 0
40	Philip Bray for a Mess[uage] & Lands in Hepworth late Roebucks ..	0	5	8	
	Robert Beevor in the right of his wife for Lands late Roebucks ..	0	2	4	
	D° for Land in Hepworth	0	0	3	
	And have help of Thomas Hincliffe of Cross for his Land att Cross ..	0	5	8	
	Philip Bray for his part of Mount ..	0	3	7	
	Jonas Kay Gent. for his Land att Law late in the poss[ession] of George Tincker	0	2	7½	
					1 0 1½
41	Joshua & Caleb Broadhead for their Lands in Wooldale	0	4	8	
	Richard Ellis for his Land being ⅓ p[ar]te of a farm in Wooldale & for 3 acres of Land late Roebucks	0	3	4	
	Josua & Jonathan Gaunt for their Lands in Wooldale	0	3	11	
	Henry Jackson Senr for p[ar]te of a Mess[uage] late Roebucks farme	0	2	0	
	D° for Paddock Yate Farme	0	0	3½	
	John Pickard Gent for Lands late Saviles	0	2	10	
	And have help of Dorothy Ellis for a Cott[age] & Land called Whinbanck	0	0	10	
	Henry Jackson Senr for Priest Close, Stelhouse & garden	0	0	6	
	Luke Wilson for Mithambrigg & milne ..	0	0	4	
	Josua & Jonathan Gaunt for Roebuck Ing in the poss[ession] of George Morehouse	0	0	4	
	George Hollingworth for his Land & Cott[age] at Sow	0	0	7	
	Robt Merry for a House & croft in Cartworth	0	0	1	
	Jonas Kay Gent: for one acre of Land at Barnside	0	0	4	
					1 0 0½

No.	Entry	£	s	d	£	s	d
42	Josua Rhodes for his Land att Woodhouse in Cartworth	0	6	6			
	John Creswick for his Land there ..	0	3	2½			
	And have help of John Hincliffe of Waterside for his Land there ..	0	9	10½			
	John Crosland for Debroyd Hill & Watergreen	0	0	10			
					1	0	5
43	Richard Brooke for his lands att Nabb in Cartworth in the poss[ession] of David Dixon	0	7	8			
	Thomas Cuttell for his House	0	0	1			
	And have help of Luke Firth for his lands in Thonge in his owne & Abraham Morehouse possession ..	0	3	8			
	Christopher Green & Joshua Beaumont in the right of their wifes for Land in Thonge in the poss[ession] of Widow Dixon	0	2	0			
	John Creswick for his Lands in the poss[ession] of Godfrey Charlsworth	0	2	10½			
	James Earnshaw for his lands in the poss[ession] of Michl Midgley ..	0	1	8			
	Godfr: Crosland for his Lands in the poss[ession] of Wm Godard ..	0	0	7¾			
	Thomas Cuttell for his Land called Over Binfield	0	0	4			
	Robert France for his Land att Wheelsbrooke	0	0	8			
	John Haigh for his Land lately belonging to Wheelsbrooke.. ..	0	0	4			
	George Hirst & Danl Broadhead for one acre of Land	0	0	4			
					1	0	3¼
44	George Hirst for Jno Dearneley, Jno Kenworthy, Henry Booth, Joshua Butterworth, Adam Meller, & Edward Bilcliffe for one whole Mess[uage] & Lands to the same belonging called Callwell	0	18	4			
	And have help of George Saunderson in the right of his wife & Joshua Earnshaw for 4½ acres of Land att Huberum hill in Austonley..	0	1	6			

No.	Tenant and holding	£	s	d	£	s	d
	John Crossland for a house in the poss[ession] of Joshua Barber in Austonley	0	0	1			
	Nicholas Fenay Gent: for a house in the poss[ession] of Jn° Lawton ..	0	0	1			
					1	0	0
45	The Heirs of Matthew Morehous for a mess[uage] & Land called the Hall in Fulstone	0	15	8			
	John Tincker for Lands called Hey formerly belonging to the Hall..	0	0	4			
	And have help of Henry Jackson Senr for a house & Land att Foster Place in the poss[ession] of George Dyson	0	2	8			
	John Morehouse for a Mess[uage] & 5½ acres of Land in Fulstone ..	0	1	11			
					1	0	7
46	Christopher & Mary Green for a Mess[uage] called Green hous	0	12	8			
	And have help of John & Chris[topher] Green for 4 acres of Land lyeing in Great Wedderley	0	1	4			
	Godfrey Crosland for Brandow Flatts ..	0	1	9			
	Jeremy Kay for his Land at Little Copthirst	0	1	2			
	Wm Littlewood for his Land att Longley..	0	2	0			
	Godfr: Crosland for 5 acres p[ar]te of Lamawells	0	1	8			
					1	0	7
47	Godfrey Crosland Gent. for his Lands att Cartworth	0	16	2			
	And hath help of James Littlewood for his Land there	0	1	8			
	Joseph Hincliffe of Arunden for his Land called Old Royde ..	0	1	0			
	George Castle of Brigg for a close called Fletcher Ing	0	0	8			
	Luke Wilson for a close called Law Ing ..	0	0	8			
					1	0	2
48	Jonas Kaye, Gent. for p[ar]te of his Land in Hepworth late Lindleys	0	7	2½			
	Luke Wilson for his Land att Green Hill Banck in the poss[ession] of Daniel Cartwright	0	3	8			

No.	Entry						
	And have help of Mich[ae]l Eastwood for his Land att Field head in Hepworth	0	1	5			
	Jonas Kay, Gent. for Land belonging School in Hepworth	0	1	1			
	Jnº Tincker for Lands called Greenall banck in Wooldall in the poss[ession] of Jnº Brooke	0	2	3			
	James Taylor for one half of Banckhous in Hepworth	0	1	8			
	George Morehous of Stonebanck for the other p[ar]te of Banckhouse ..	0	1	8			
	Thomas Derby, Gent. for 2 acres of Land in Wooldale in the poss[ession] of Jnº Castle	0	0	8			
	Thomas Cuttell for Houses in Holmefirth towne in Wooldale	0	0	4½			
					1	0	0
49	Christopher & Mary Green for their Lands att Austonley	0	5	10			
	John Green att Yateholme for all the the ancient Lands belonging to the same in his own possession	0	6	6			
	And have help of Nicholas Fenay Gent for a Mess[uage] & Land called Town End in Austonley in the poss[ession] widw Charlesworth	0	4	0			
	George Saunderson in the right of his wife & Joshua Earnshaw for their Lands att Town End in the poss[ession] of Jos[ep]h Charlesworth ..	0	2	4			
	The Heirs of Jonathan Hincliffe for his Lands att Bradshaw late Eastwoods in the poss[ession] of David Haigh	0	0	10			
					0	19	6
50	John Roberts & Jnº Wagstaffe, Gent: for their Lands att Nether House in Thonge	0	2	9			
	Jnº Wagstaffe, Gent: for other Lands there in the poss[ession] of Jnº Oldham & David Dixon	0	1	9			
	Jnº & Abraham Greene for their Houses in Thonge	0	0	4			

	And have help of George Hirst for his Lands att Liphill in Thonge ..	0	2	0			
	Robert France for his Lands lying in Austonley in Thonge ..	0	4	5½			
	Jonathan Eastwood for his Land att Lane in Austonley	0	0	8			
	Jn° Rhodes for his Lands in Bradshaw in the poss[ession] of Josua Charlesworth	0	1	2			
	Wm Moreshouse for his Lands in Bradshaw late Shaws	0	2	8			
	John Haigh for 3 acres att Greengate ..	0	1	0			
	Thomas Morton for three acres of Land att Yelke Edge formerly Matthew Brays	0	1	0			
	Mr Garlick for 2½ acres in Hepworth Dean	0	0	10			
	Jonas Kay, Gent, for Lands att Hore Law in Hepworth	0	1	7			
					1	0	2½
51	Thomas Peace of Flocton for his Land att Brownhill in Cartworth in the poss[ession] of Abraham Earnshaw	0	5	8			
	Jn° Green for his Land there	0	5	8			
	And have help of Wm Wadsworth for his Land late Hugh Taylors in Hepworth	0	1	4			
	Mr Leggate for his Land Thushenholes in Hepworth	0	2	8			
	Jn° Green of Yate holm for Rack & Broad Ing in Holme	0	2	10			
	Godfr: Crosland, Gent. for 6 acres p[ar]te of Lamawells in Cartworth ..	0	2	0			
					1	0	2
52	John Tyas for a Mess[uage] & Lands att Oxlee	0	14	11½			
	And hath help of Humphrey Bray being in his minority for Lands called Speights Land in the poss[ession] of Joseph Marsh	0	0	8			
	Jn° Rooley for two closes called Staley Royds	0	1	0			

No.	Entry	£	s.	d.	Total
	Samuel Beevor for a mess[uage] & Lands called Foster Place ..	0	3	0	
	Philip Bray for Lands in Hepworth late Humphrey Brays his father ..	0	1	4¾	
					1 1 0¼
53	Joseph Haigh of Whitley for his Lands att Wardplace in Cartworth in the poss[ession] of James Batty ..	0	5	2	
	Thomas Hincliffe for his Land att Ward-place	0	4	8	
	Thomas Littlewood of Damhouse for his Land belonging Wardplace ..	0	2	8	
	D° for more Land there	0	0	8	
	Samuel Wagstaff for his Land there ..	0	1	3	
	Jonas Kay, Gent. for Caring	0	0	9	
	And have help of Luke Wilson for 7 acres of Land called Little Hades in Wooldale	0	2	4	
	Joshua Newton for one house called Great house & 3 closes called Modwoods in the poss[ession] of Joshua Smith	0	0	5½	
	Abraham Roberts of Farneley for Land att Lidgate in Wooldale in the poss-[ession] of Wid^w Dearneley ..	0	1	0½	
	John Marsden for a Mess[uage] att Ing-head in Wooldall	0	0	8½	
	Joshua Roades for a house in Hepworth..	0	0	3	
					1 0 0½
54	Jonas Kay, Gent. for Lands att Ebson House in the poss[ession] of George Tyas, Joseph Hudson, & John Brown, & Eliz: Turton in her own possession	0	8	1	
	Thomas Morton for Gate foot belonging to Ebson House	0	1	4	
	And have help of Henry Jackson Junr for Lands att Tottys.. ..	0	4	8	
	Luke Wilson for Land att Tottys in the poss[ession] of Joseph Kay ..	0	4	8¾	
	John & Joshua Newton for Land att Tottys in the poss[ession] of Joshua Earnshaw	0	0	7	
	John Roebuck for one close called Long Carr belonging to Ebson House	0	0	4	

No.	Entry	£	s.	d.	£	s.	d.
	Jonas Kay for 1 acre of Land being p[ar]te of Butt^{r} Lee	0	0	4			
					1	0	$0\frac{3}{4}$
55	John Tincker for $11\frac{1}{2}$ acres of Land in Scholes & Marshbanck & the rest of his Land in Scholes	0	4	5			
	Godfr. Crosland for Hade Ing	0	1	0			
	Jno Tyas for 4 acres of Land in Scholes ..	0	1	4			
	Luke Wilson or James Beever for 9 acres of Land in Scholes in the poss[ession] of Joshua Heap	0	3	0			
	Barbara Batty Wid^{w} for 2 acres of Land in Scholes in the poss[ession] of Joshua Batty	0	3	$4\frac{1}{2}$			
	And have help of Thomas Littlewood of Damhouse for 18 acres of Land	0	6	0			
	Jonas Kay, Gent: for one house & Farr field in Hepworth	0	0	$8\frac{1}{4}$			
	Philip Bray for Marsh Land in Hepworth ..	0	0	4			
					1	0	$1\frac{3}{4}$
56	Henry Jackson sen^{r} for a mess[uage] & Land called Hullock in his own possession	0	6	8			
	And hath help of Henry Jackson Junr for a mess[uage] called Stalyroid in the poss[ession] of Joseph Hobson ..	0	2	$2\frac{1}{2}$			
	John Roebuck for a close of Land called Nether house field now made into 3 closes	0	1	$1\frac{1}{2}$			
	Joel Morehouse for 17 acres of Land in Wooldale in the poss[ession] of Jonathan Hobson	0	5	2			
	John Micklthwaite & Edward Kenyon for 10 acres of Land at Mathorne	0	3	4			
	Jonas Kay, Gent. for his Lands att Mirey Lane in the poss[ession] of George Charlsworth	0	0	$10\frac{3}{4}$			
	Henry Jackson Senr for Land in his own poss[ession] & Henry Jackson Junr for Lands in the poss[ession] of Francis Beevor late Toulsons ..	0	0	$10\frac{1}{2}$			
					1	0	3

No.	Entry	£	s.	d.	£	s.	d.
57	John Roebuck for a mess[uage] called Holling House in Foulstone ..	0	8	11½			
	Do for Lands in Hepworth	0	1	7			
	And hath help of Luke Wilson & James Beever for Lands att Bearistall head in Hepworth	0	3	3½			
	Joseph Haigh for 1½ acres of Land in Holmwood Heys	0	0	6			
	Thomas Morton in the right of his wife for 2 acres of Land att Wilberclough	0	0	8			
	James Batty for 5 acres of Land called Prickmere banck in Thonge ..	0	1	8			
	John Woodhead Gent: for 3 acres of Land Lying att Snowgatehead in Fulstone	0	1	0			
	Jno Charlesworth senr for 3 acres of Land lying att Lathes in Wooldale	0	1	1¾			
	Jno & Christopher Green for 4 acres of Land lying in Great Nedderley ..	0	1	4			
					1	0	1¾
58	Henry Jackson Senr for a Mess[uage] called Holm house	0	7	3½			
	Do for Vpper Holm house	0	4	0			
	And hath help of Jno Haigh for 8 acres of Land lying att Greengate in Austonley	0	2	8			
	Abraham Firth for 4 acres of Land lying at Over longley	0	1	4			
	Jonas Kay, Gent for Standbanck Hill in Wooldale	0	0	9½			
	Henry Jackson senr for Land att Farbanck Knowl called Foxhouses	0	2	5½			
	Do for 1 close called Over Lease in Hepworth	0	0	6			
	Do for a mess[uage] & Land att Mount in the poss[ession] of Joseph Swallow in Fulstone	0	1	1			
					1	0	1½
59	Barbara Batty for a mess[uage] & 24 acres of land lying in Hepworth late Jacksons	0	8	0			
	And hath help of James Earnshaw for 10 acres of Land in Holme ..	0	3	4			

	Do for Drake hoult	0	0	8			
	Joshua Earnshaw for Land in Holme called Shawbanck & Schole croft	0	1	4			
	John Hollingworth of Meadow banck for 3 acres of Land in Holme in the poss[ession] of Jno Hinclife ..	0	1	0			
	John Green for 1 acre of Land late Hincliffes	0	0	4			
	Wm Hincliffe for 2 acres of Land in Holme	0	0	8			
	Henry Jackson Senr for a mess[uage] & Land called Woderhill & Burnedge in Hepworth	0	2	9			
	Do for Holms in Wooldale in his own poss[ession]	0	0	9			
	Henry Jackson Junr for Holms in Wooldale in the possession of Francis Beever	0	1	1			
	Mary Hincliffe for her houses in Wooldale	0	0	2½			
					1	0	1½
60	Henry Jackson Junr for his Lands att Booth house in Austonley in the poss[ession] of Joshua Brooke ..	0	2	10½			
	Do for Lands in the poss[ession] of Joshua Eastwood in Austonley ..	0	3	6½			
	Widw Radcliffe for Lands in the poss[ession] of George Collier, & Jno Charlsworth	0	4	8			
	John Wagstaffe, Gent: for his Lands att Booth house called Haggs in the poss[ession] of Joshua Charlesworth	0	0	9			
	James Hincliffe for Lands att Knowle & Achars	0	5	10			
	Dorothy Bingley for Lands att Achars ..	0	2	4			
					1	0	0
	The heirs of Jno Hadfield for Lands in Scholes in the poss[ession] of Wm Littlewood	0	3	11			
	The Heirs of Joshua Tincker for Lands in the poss[ession] of John Booth	0	2	8½			
	And have Help of Abraham Wood for for Whichfield in Scholes ..	0	6	10			
	Thomas Wood for Vpper Whichfeld in [*blank*]	0	2	0			

Philip Bray for Hawckscar Close ..	0	0	4			
Luke Wilson for a Green Slade in Wooldale	0	0	4			
Josias Wadsworth for a mess[uage] & Land in Hepworth in the poss[ession] of Francis Tincker .. .. (*sic*)	0	2	18			
Henry Jackson Junr for a mess[uage] & Land in the poss[ession] of Josua Haigh in Wooldale	0	1	0			
D^o for half of Matson Ing	0	0	2			
				0	19	11½
Shepley Rent for Turverrey				0	3	4
Lightings Moor				0	4	0
Totall of the yearly rents Collectable by the Grave of Holme				61	15	5¾

Wee the Jury sworne for the Lord of the Mannor of Wakefeld abovesaid doe vpon our Enquiry into the old Rentalls & Evidences concerning our said Graveship of Holme find & present that there are Sixty one Graves within our said Graveshipp and that the Persons aboves[ai]d vnder their several Numbers ought to serve the office of Grave in their respective turns for their Lands & Ten[emen]ts there mentioned and have helpers which are there sett down Vnder the same Number for their Lands & ten[emen]ts there also mentioned and that those persons vnder the Number One doe serve the Office for this present Yeare beginning att Michaelmas last and the rest successively as they follow in their Numbers and that the Respective Rents vnder Every Number are due and payable yearly to the Lord of the said Mannor

Jonas Kaye, Philip Bray, Joshua Newton, Hen: Jackson, Humphrey Roebuck, George Hirst, James Earnshaw, John Tincker, Jno Whitehead, Luke Wilson, Jeremie Kaye Jno Newton, Daniel Broadhead, Richd Crosland

SOWERBY GRAVESHIP

The Graveship of Sowerby is bounded by the River of Ryeburne to the East, Rushworth to the South, Lancaster Shire to the West, Heptonstall, Haworth, & Skircoat to the North and hath within it the Freehold & Copiehold Ten[an]ts following who pay rents &c according to the Verdict taken out of the Court Rolls of The Mannor as followeth

Maner[ium] de Wakefeld } Ad Magn[am] cur[iam] Baron[em] Nobilissimi Thome Ducis de Leeds pr[ae]nobilis Ordinis Garterij Milit[is] D[omin]i Man[er]ij de Wakefeld tent[am] apud Sowerby brigg p[er] adjournament[um] vicesimo die Maij Anno Regni D[omi]ne n[ost]re Anne Dei gra[tia] nunc R[egi]ne Magne Brittanie &c octavo

The Verdict of Thomas Oldfield, Jno Dearden, John Greenwood James Stansfield, Robert Brigg, John Gawkeroger, Jno Murgatroyd, Richard Holdroyd, John Farrer, Henry Whitworth, John Dixon, John Normanton, & John Sutcliffe being Freeholders & copyholders within the Graveship of Sowerby of & concerning the Freehold & Copyhold Lands & Ten[emen]ts within the said Graveship which pay rents and doe service to the Lord of the said mannor of Wakefield

Warley 1st The heirs of Mr James Oates for Murgatroyd a[lia]s The Hollins	0	5	0			
D^o^ for White burch	0	1	9			
D^o^ for Cawsey	0	2	8½			
D^o^ for Wadsworth Lands	0	1	8			
D^o^ for Booth stead	0	2	8			
D^o^ for Haigh hous	0	2	0			
D^o^ for Edge End	0	2	3			
D^o^ for Hill End	0	1	0			
And hath help of The Heirs of Abm̃ Wadsworth for a Messuage at Coldedge called the Hoyle	0	1	8			
The heirs of James Murgatroyd for Lyonel hous	0	0	4			
Thomas Longbottom for a Messuage in the Coldedge in the poss[ession] of John Greenwood formerly Murgatroyd Land	0	1	1			
				1	2	1½
Soyland 2d Jeramia Crosley for Hoyle Land at Light Hazles	0	11	8½			
And hath help of Jonathan & John Grimroyd for a mess[uage] and Lands at Quick Stavers	0	8	6			
John Walker for a Close bought off Quick Stavers	0	0	2			
Robert Thomas for a Mess[uage] called Quickin Hall	0	0	6			
The heirs of Joshua Horton Esq for a Cott[age] & close at the Mill Banck	0	0	5			

	Entry	£	s	d	£	s	d
	The Governors of the Free School of Littlebrook for a Mess[uage] & Lands at Crowelshaye in the poss[ession] of of Joseph Makrill	0	1	4			
					1	2	7½
Sowerby 3d	Willm Greenwood for all his Lands called Mythomroyd formerly Drapers & Haighs	0	14	8			
	And hath help of Wm Thomas for Hus-hill	0	0	6			
	Samuel Stansfield for a Mess[uage] in Crowel Shays	0	2	6			
	John Allinson for a Mess[uage] called the Trees	0	0	11½			
	Mr John Cockcroft for ground called the Washous	0	0	4			
	Mr Henry Cockcroft for a Mill Damm near Mayroyd	0	0	4			
	John Smith for a Mess[uage] at Quarril Hill called Bank hous.. ..	0	0	7½			
	John Hoyl for a Cott[age] called Ladstones	0	0	2			
	John Ellis for a Cottage in the mill banck	0	0	1			
	Richard Sterne Geñ[1] for Lands lyeing at Scout late Naylors.. ..	0	1	5			
					1	1	7
Warley 4th	John Midgley for 2 messuages called the old Rideing & Kilnhurst	0	4	10			
	The heirs of Abrm̃ Wadsworth for 3 messuages called Reaphirst ..	0	4	7½			
	And have help of Benjamin Wade for a Mess[uage] called Peel hous & 11 other messuages & Cottages thereunto belonging	0	11	3			
	The heirs of Mr James Oates for p[ar]te of Rydeinghead	0	1	0			
					1	1	8½
5th	The heirs of Madm Thornhill for 2 mess[uages] called Thorp hous & Hoyle banckhead	0	3	6			
	John Cockcroft Gen: for 2 messuages called Wheatley Royd & blindelaine	0	10	0			

1 *H.F.M.G.*, II, 516.

		£	s	d	£	s	d
	And have help of Henry Hellewell for 2 Thirds of a Mess[uage] called Inge head	0	1	4			
	Richard Sterne Gent for a mess[uage] in Blackwood	0	3	1			
	Anne Brooksbanck for Lands at Bryerley Brigg called Milnhill	0	0	4			
	The heirs of Samuel Wilson for Hann-carr & Stubbingholme ..	0	3	0			
	Tymothy Wadsworth for one field formerly Holgates	0	0	9			
	Sarah Sutcliff for ⅓ p[ar]te of Ingehead ..	0	0	7½			
					1	2	7½
6th	Willm̃ Sutcliffe for a mess[uage] called Hylegley	0	2	5½			
	James Allinson for Clunters	0	2	8			
	John Greenwood for a Close called Brockhoyles	0	0	2			
	Matthew Scott for a mess[uage] called Acker	0	1	4			
	Josias Norminton for a Mess[uage] called Dearstone Slack	0	3	8			
	The Coeheirs of Mrs Barcroft for a mess[uage] called Bent now Henry Bradshaws Esq	0	1	6			
	And have help of the heirs of Mich[ae]l Oldfeild for Nab end.. ..	0	4	5			
	The heirs of Joseph Lord for Brownhill..	0	1	6½			
	Thomas Sagar in the right of his wife for Rawend	0	2	4			
	Josias Norminton for p[ar]te of Brownhill	0	0	1½			
					1	0	2½
Warley 7th	The heirs of Joshua Wade for a mess[uage] at High Saltonstall..	0	19	2			
	The heirs of Jonas Wood for p[ar]te of High Saltonstall Land ..	0	4	0			
	Joseph Holme for p[ar]te of High Saltonstall called Vpper hey ..	0	1	0			
	And have help of Paul Greenwood for a Mess[uage] near Deep Clough ..	0	2	8			
	Paul Greenwood for Sumerbooth ..	0	0	2			
					1	7	0

Sowerby 8th William Horton Esq for 3 mess[uages] & Lands thereunto belonging called Baiteings, Upper Baitings, & Baiting Yate & 2 other mess[uage] in Manshead				1	4	7½
Sowerby 9th Thomas Dobson for 3 messuages called Stonegreen Lain & Rattan rowe	0	8	0			
Thomas Sunderland for a Mess[uage] called Laverack hall	0	1	4			
Henry Sydall for a Messuage in Sowerby Deyne	0	1	0			
John Sugden for a Messuage called feild end	0	0	8			
John Patchet for a Messuage called Jack Hey	0	1	6			
John Dearden Gent for 3 Cott[ages] in Sowerby & 2 closes called Butcher Carr & Parrock	0	0	6			
Elkana Hoyl for 2 closes called the Intack & Holme	0	0	5			
Richard Holdroyd for a messuage in Sowerby	0	3	6			
John Normanton for a close late Firths..	0	0	6			
Do for an Inge late Haighs	0	0	4			
Mathew Wadsworth for Haven	0	3	0			
				1	0	9
Warley 10th John Boocksbanck for a messuage in Warley Towne late Oldfields	0	2	4			
And hath help of Thomas Oldfield for a Messuage in the Laine called Stock Laine & a Mess[uage] called Brode Tree & another called Puding Hall & 3 Cottages near Harwood Well	0	5	0			
Joseph Bryer for a Messuage called Rusting Stone	0	0	6½			
John Ecles for a Mess[uage] called The Edge	0	0	11			
Richard Tattersall for a mess[uage] called The Hollings near Sowerby Bridge	0	4	10			
Tho: Oldfield for another Cott[age] called Harwood well	0	0	2			

	£	s	d	Total
Robert Towne for 2 mess[uages] in Warley Towne	0	5	8	
Jno Trueman for a Close called Ashley ..	0	0	5	
				0 19 10½
Soyland 11th Robert Parker Esq for a Mess[uage] in Sowerby Deane ..	0	4	8	
John Smith for his Lands in Pikehill Street	0	5	2	
Jonathan Fairbanck for Two Messuages at Sowerby Brigg	0	5	3½	
And have help of James Ryley for Lands called Waterstawles Freehold ..	0	1	0	
Richard Tattersall for 2 holmes & a wood	0	1	8	
Jonas Thomas for a Mess[uage] called Pitt Freehold	0	0	10	
Jer: Crosley for a mess[uage] in Turwin..	0	2	4½	
				1 1 0
Sowerby 12th Elkana Hoyl for a mess[uage] in Staningden called Vpper Swift place	0	3	6	
James Ogden for a Mess[uage] called Lower Swift place	0	3	0	
And have help of Geo: Clegg for a Mess[uage] called Smithy Clough ..	0	2	0	
Allen Whiteley for a mess[uage] & Cottage above the Smithy Clough	0	4	4	
John Kenworthy for a Mess[uage] adjoyneing the Smithy Clough ..	0	1	6	
James Ogden for a Mess[uage] near Lower Swift Place	0	1	6	
Elkana Hoyl for 2 Mess[uages] at Shaw..	0	2	8	
John Wheelwright for a Fulling Mill & Mess[uage] near Brograns ..	0	1	5	
Willm Thomas for half of a Mess[uage] called Burnd Moor	0	1	6	
John Shaw for a Mess[uage] at West Swift Cross	0	0	5	
Dr Ryley for a Cott[age] near Clay Clough	0	0	4	
George Hoyl for a hous & Land & Whitegate head	0	0	4	
Ely Gleadhill for a Mess[uage] at Soyland Mills	0	0	4	
				1 2 10

Warley 13th	John Farrer for a Mess[uage] called Cliff hill & 2 other mess[uages] in Warley Towne	0	12	4	
	And hath help of Richard Smith for 2 Closes called Ashleys ..	0	2	5	
	James Murgatroyd for a Mess[uage] called Westfield head.. ..	0	0	7	
	Willm̃ Deane for a Mess[uage] in the Clough late Kings	0	0	7	
	Tho: Oldfield for p[ar]te of Stock Laine..	0	0	6	
	John Wadsworth for p[ar]te of Stock Laine	0	1	0½	
	James Chadwick for p[ar]te of Stock Laine	0	0	5½	
	John Bryercliff for Daysey banck & Holme	0	1	4	
	The Coeheirs of Mrs Barcroft for 2 messuages in the Edge now Willm̃ Leigh Esq	0	2	4	
					1 1 7
14th	The heirs of Thomas Rayner for 2 Mess-[uages] in Soyland	0	4	0	
	Richard Firth for Two Messuages in the Wood	0	1	0	
	John Foxcroft for lower Kebroyd ..	0	2	6	
	Richard Firth for 2 mess[uages] called Kebroyd & Highfield.. ..	0	5	7	
	And have help of John Ryley for a Mess[uage] called Hanging Lee	0	2	3	
	The heirs of Joshua Horton Esq for 2 mess[uages] & a Cottage near Soyland Mill	0	3	6	
	James Hill for a Mess[uage] called Hoyle-banck & Severhills	0	2	1	
	The heirs of John Wilkinson for another p[ar]te of Severhills	0	0	4	
	Michael Firth for a Mill Dam at Ripponden	0	0	2	
	James Hill for a mess[uage] called Vpper Burntmoor	0	1	8	
	The coeheirs of Mrs Firth for one Goyt & 2 Mill Dams at Soyland Mill ..	0	0	5	
					1 3 6
15th	John Hoile for a messuage called upper Lumbe	0	7	7	

John Kenworthy for a mess[uage] called Lower Lumbe	0	2	9	
And have help of John Smith for a mess[uage] called Dearplay ..	0	6	0	
The heirs of Joshua Horton Esqr for a mess[uage] near Crawell Shaws	0	1	6	
The heirs of Thomas Thornhill for ½ of the Scout	0	2	2	
Jeremia Crosley for a mess[uage] called Tootill	0	1	6	
				1 1 6
Warley 16th John Crosley, Gent for a Mess[uage] called Ludendein royd with all the Lands thereto belonging ..	0	2	6	
And hath help of Timothy Crowther for a Mess[uage] called Shepherd house	0	1	10	
Wm Blaymires for a Mess[uage] & a Cott[age] at Sheperd hous ..	0	2	4	
Nathan Wood for a Mess[uage] called Wainstalls	0	0	8	
Jno Beanland for Sutcliff Farme ..	0	0	8	
Do for his owne Farme	0	2	8	
Do for 2 farmes at Coldedge	0	2	3	
Ambrose Patchit for a Farme at Coldedge	0	1	3½	
John Helliwel for Land at Coldedge ..	0	1	8	
Ambrose Patchit for Haigh Quoit ..	0	1	0	
Richard Holgate for p[ar]te of Westroyd..	0	1	4	
Abrm̃ Patchit for a Farme at Coldedge ..	0	1	3½	
				0 19 6
Soyland 17th John Preistley for a mess[uage] called White Windows ..	0	1	8	
The heirs of Joshua Horton Esqr for a mess[uage] called Hangend ..	0	4	0	
Richd Dearden for 4 closes bought off Hangend	0	1	0	
The heirs of Joshua Horton Esqr for a Mess[uage] called Normanton Farme	0	1	6	
And have help of Mr Bradshaw for a Mess[uage] called Gaukeroger..	0	1	7	
The heirs of Joshua Horton Esqr for another Mess[uage] called Gaukeroger	0	1	9	

Michael Sydall for a Mess[uage] called the Buck	0	2	6			
Jonathan Hanson for a Mess[uage] called the Delfes near Bower Slack ..	0	3	4			
Jer: Crosley for 2 closes bought off Delfes Farme	0	0	8			
Wm Byrom for a Mess[uage] called Yokeing Clough	0	1	2			
Henry Sunderland for a Mess[uage] called Burnhous	0	2	3			
				1	1	5
Sowerby 18th The heirs of Mr Barcroft for a mess[uage] called Booth hous now Mrs Anne Brockholes	0	3	0			
Thomas Towneley for a mess[uage] called Milner place	0	4	10			
Mr Bradshaw for a Mess[uage] in Wood laine	0	3	11			
Do for a Mess[uage] called Winehaven ..	0	1	9			
Do for a Mess[uage] in Blackwood ..	0	2	1			
And have help of Jer: Crosley for a Mess[uage] called Bent ..	0	2	0			
Robt Scales for a mess[uage] called Deanhey	0	2	0			
Jer: Crosley for a mess[uage] in Crowill shaws late Greenwoods ..	0	1	7			
Josias Norminton for a mess[uage] called Myric Hall	0	0	8			
				1	1	10
Warley 19th Robert Midgley for a Mess[uage] called Magson house	0	6	0			
Thomas Barker for a mess[uage] & Lands called Roebucks	0	6	0			
And have help of Josias Stansfield for a mess[uage] called Gravestones..	0	3	0			
John Sugden for a mess[uage] called Holling Hall	0	1	8½			
John Hanson for a mess[uage] o'th bottom of Coldedge	0	1	8			
Abrm Patchit for a Mess[uage] in the Cold Edge called upper hous p[ar]te of it Freehold	0	2	0			
				1	0	4½

Entry						
Soyland 20th Richard Holdroyd for a mess-[uage] called Brigroyd ..	0	8	4			
And hath help of Jonathan Hanson for a Mess[uage] called Redyshaw ..	0	2	7			
Jeramia Crosley for a Mess[uage] called Hoyle heads	0	1	8			
James Ryley for a Mess[uage] in Soyland formerly Turner Land ..	0	2	8			
The coeheirs of Mrs Barcroft for a Mess-[uage] at Tootill End now Mrs Anne Brockholes	0	4	2			
Isaac Crowder for a mess[uage] near Goodgrave	0	0	6			
Richd Holdroyd for a mess[uage] called (Pirson) [Prison ?]	0	0	2			
Henry Fielding for a mess[uage] called Clay Clough	0	2	0			
John Gaukroger for 3 closes & a Cott-[age] on Soyland Moor ..	0	1	6			
Do for a Barn at Flathead	0	0	1			
				1	3	8
Sowerby 21 Mr Bradshaw for a Mess[uage] called the Hollins	0	4	0			
The heirs of Mr Barcroft for a mess[uage] called the Hollins now Wm Leighs Esq	0	2	6			
Joshua Marcer for a mess[uage] called Sties	0	6	1			
John Norminton for a Mess[uage] in Wood Laine..	0	1	6			
And have help of Josia Norminton for a Mess[uage] called Higgin Chamber	0	5	1			
Ester Wadsw[or]th for a Mess[uage] called Long pipe	0	2	1			
				1	1	3
Warley 22d Richard Tattersall for a mess-[uage] called Aplehous ..	0	2	4			
Paul Greenwood for a mess[uage] called Slack	0	2	5			
Joshua Farrar for a Mess[uage] called Homleton hill	0	1	0			
David Greenwood for a Mess[uage] ad-joyning to the Slack	0	2	2			

Tho: Holdsworth for a mess[uage] called Sandsfore	0	1	10			
Ely Greenwood for a mess[uage] adjoyning the said Slack ..	0	1	0			
And have help of Mich[ael] Ingham for a Mess[uage] called Batch ..	0	3	1			
Thomas Oldfield for a mess[uage] called the Windill royd	0	1	3			
George Oldfield for a Mess[uage] lyeing above Sowerby Brigg called Brode Inge	0	1	5			
John Walker for a Mess[uage] lyeing above Deep Clough in Ludenden Deinehead called Upp[er] hous ..	0	2	4			
Thomas Midgley for a mess[uage] near the Deep Clough called lowerhous	0	2	4			
Abrm̃ Ashworth for a Cott[age] in the Clough	0	0	0½			
				1	1	2½
Soyland 23d The Heirs of John Wilkinson for a Mess[uage] called Brownehill	0	2	2			
James Ryley for 4 closes near Bankhous head	0	1	5			
John Kenworthy for a Mess[uage] called Hingon Bancks or Dowery ..	0	1	4¾			
Michl Crosley for a Mess[uage] called Soyland Moor	0	2	3			
And have help of Jeramia Crosley for a mess[uage] called Lower Hoyl heads & certain Lands called Bryonbanck	0	3	0			
John Ryley for a Mess[uage] called Maden Stones	0	1	11			
Robert Halstead for a mess[uage] called Callis in Errinden	0	2	9			
The Coeheirs of John Bentley for ½ of Menebent	0	5	7			
The heirs of Joshua Horton Esq called the Nook in the Shaws ..	0	1	0			
				1	1	5¾
Sowerby 24th John Sutcliff for a mess[uage] called Stubleing	0	3	7			
Henry Cockcroft for a mess[uage] called Crownest	0	3	2			

Entry	£ s d	Total
Wm Sutcliffe for a Mess[uage] called Scout Mill	0 1 9½	
Elkana Horton, Gent for a Mess[uage] called Stannereyend	0 3 2	
John Greenwood for a mess[uage] called Elsabrough Hall	0 8 8	
Robert Halstead for p[ar]te of Callis in Eringden	0 0 8	
John Horsfold for a Mill Damm ..	0 0 6	
		1 1 6½
Warley 25th John Murgatroyd for a Mess[uage] called Newland & for 2 mess[uages in Warley Towne & for 2 messuages called Clough head & a Close near Ludenden	0 14 9½	
And hath help of John Bryce for a mess[uage] called Litle Moor ..	0 2 2	
Wm Leigh Esq for a mess[uage] called Westfield head	0 3 0	
Abrm̃ Bolton for a mess[uage] in the Edge above Warley Towne ..	0 1 3	
		1 1 2½
Soyland 26th Jer: Crosley for Land at Light hazles late Naylors & Brigs ..	0 9 11¾	
John Blackburne for a mess[uage] at Light hazles	0 2 0	
The heirs of Joshua Horton Esq for a Mess[uage] at Light hazles ..	0 3 10	
The heirs of Joshua Whiteley for a mess[uage] called Clay pit.. ..	0 2 11	
The heirs of Mr Ramsden for a mess[uage] called Hursthous ..	0 3 0	
Jer: Crosley for a mess[uage] at Hoylehead	0 1 7	
John Ryley for a Mess[uage] called Forge hous	0 1 2	
		1 4 5¾
Sowerby 27th Wm Sutcliffe for a mess[uage] called Banck Top	0 9 0	
Widw Normanton for a Mess[uage] called Bent close	0 3 0	
And have help of Wm Sutcliff for 2 mess[uages] called Dickson hill & Hulot Hill	0 8 4	

John Ramsden for 2 mess[uages] called Annabutlee	0	3	10			
				1	4	2
Warley 28th John Trueman for a mess-[uage] called the Steps ..	0	5	9			
Willm Hollingworth for a Mess[uage] called the Hangreen	0	3	9			
And have help of Stephen Carr for a mess[uage] called Causey head..	0	0	3			
John Dearden, Gent for a mess[uage] called the March	0	1	5			
John Trueman for a Mess[uage] called litle March	0	1	1			
Richard Dearden for a Mess[uage] called Duel Laine	0	2	6			
John Wainhous for p[ar]te of Causey ..	0	1	4			
Richd Wainhous for his p[ar]te of Causey..	0	0	4			
Widw Moore for a holme at Causey ..	0	0	6			
Richd Smith for a mess[uage] called black Wall	0	2	5			
John Apleyeard for a Mess[uage] in Ludenden Deinhead	0	1	8			
				1	1	0
Soyland 29th John Crosley, Gent for a mess-[uage] called the Royd ..	0	3	1			
And hath help of James Ryley for ½ of the Storth	0	0	6			
Do for a mess[uage] near the Royd ..	0	0	6			
John Wordsworth for a mess[uage] at Riponden near above the Spout	0	1	10			
John Gaukeroger for a mess[uage] at Flatt late Wilsons ..	0	2	1			
Do for a Mess[uage] at Flatt late Dysons..	0	1	7			
John Ryley for a mess[uage] at Flatt ..	0	0	4			
Richard Firth for a mess[uage] called Spout	0	0	4			
Abrm Firth for a mess[uage] called Laine head	0	2	8			
John Smith, Gent for 3 mess[uages] called Wren nest, Hardknot & Jackson Land	0	3	8			

Do for Another Mess[uage] at Hardknott	0	0	9			
Gilbert Holden for a mess[uage] called Wutherhill Freehold	0	1	3			
Robert Thornes for ½ of Burnt Moor	0	1	6			
Elkana Hoyl for a Mess[uage] in Soyland late Preistleys Freehold	0	1	6			
John Marsden for a mess[uage] at Hardknott	0	0	6			
James Whiteley for a mess[uage] at Ripenden	0	0	4			
Michl Firth for Tattersall Land	0	1	2			
Do for Townend Land	0	0	3			
				1	3	10
Sowerby 30th James Stansfield for a mess[uage] called lowefeild hous	0	5	0			
Thomas Oldfield for mess[uages] called the litle breck	0	2	10			
Jeramia Crosley for 2 Mess[uage] called upper field hous	0	6	7			
And have help of Susanna Thomas for a mess[uage] in Turvin	0	3	7			
Widw Moor for a mess[uage] called Brockwell	0	2	0			
The Heirs of Joshua Horton Esqr for a Mess[uage] called the Raw	0	1	5			
				1	1	5
Warley 31st Isaac Farrar for a mess[uage] on Warley Towne	0	3	4			
Do for Gregson Land	0	1	6			
James Chadwick for a mess[uage] called the Hill	0	2	6			
John Brooksbanck for a close called Goodheye	0	0	6			
Michl Firth for Sheep Coat Royds & Coat Hill	0	0	9			
John Tattersall for Litle Towne alias Slack	0	2	6			
Do for a Close called Pepperholme	0	0	2			
Benjamin Nicholson for a mess[uage] called Vpper bens	0	1	7			
Joseph Nicholson for a mess[uage] under the Ive Delfes	0	3	10			

Joshua Farrar for a Cott[age] & Land at Stonebrigg end	0	0	4			
D^o for a Farme called Stones	0	1	0			
				0	18	0
Soyland 32^d The heirs of John Crowder for a mess[uage] in Sowerby Towne	0	4	7			
John Normanton for 2 closes	0	0	8			
D^o for a Water Course	0	0	1			
Wid^w Moor for a Close	0	0	5			
And have help of the heirs of Joshua Horton Esq for Mess[uage] Sowerby Towne & 2 closes called Cross Stones & another lying near Gate Lands..	0	1	9			
D^o for another Mess[uage] in Sowerby Towne called Lister Lands ..	0	1	3½			
John Wadsworth for a mess[uage] in Finkil Street	0	1	4½			
Richard Dearden for Quarril Hill ..	0	0	7			
Benjamin Wade for a mess[uage] in Sowerby Towne	0	5	0			
The heirs of John Horton Esq for a mess[uage] & Cottage in Sowerby Towne	0	6	4			
				1	2	1
Sowerby 33^d Thomas Sunderland for a mess[uage] called Hattershelf ..	0	1	9			
Thomas Swaine for a Mess[uage] called Newhous	0	2	11			
Mr Francis Allinson for a Mess[uage] called Hollingbarro	0	2	4			
Mathew Wadsworth for a mess[uage] called Sand	0	1	1			
Thomas Swain for another Mess[uage] called Upper Hathershelf ..	0	1	9			
And have help of Jeremia Crosley for a Mess[uage] called Slake ..	0	3	6			
Wm Cockcroft for a Mess[uage] called Plain	0	2	3½			
Richard Thomas for a Mess[uage] called Pallas hous	0	1	11½			
Wm Greenwood for a Mess[uage] called Pallas Holme	0	2	9			

	£	s	d	£	s	d
Jonathan Sutcliffe for a hous & Croft called Litthouse	0	0	1			
				1	0	5
Warley 34th Anthony Naylor for a mess[uage] called Longbottom ..	0	5	6			
John Patchit for a mess[uage] called Little Longbottom	0	3	0			
Eleazar Tetlow for a Mess[uage] called Couperhous	0	3	0			
And have help of Anthony Naylor for a Mess[uage] called upper Long bottom	0	0	10			
George Carter or his heirs for a Mess[uage] called Warley Wood ..	0	1	6			
Matthew Smith for a mess[uage] above Warley Town	0	3	4			
Joseph Brice for Turner Land.. ..	0	1	8			
Do for Greenwood Land	0	0	7			
Eleazar Tetlow for Low holme.. ..	0	2	0			
				1	1	5
Soyland 35 Jo[natha]n Walker for a mess[uage] called Stocks in Sowerby	0	2	11			
Jno Preistley for a Close late Ryley Land	0	0	8			
The heirs at Joshua Horton for a mess[uage] called Chapil Yates ..	0	1	2			
Nathan Whiteley for a Cottage ..	0	0	2			
The heirs of Joshua Horton for another mess[uage] & a Cottage in Sowerby Towne	0	4	2			
Do another Cottage & Croft in Sowerby Towne	0	0	1			
John Dearden Gent for a Close called Lynn Croft	0	0	4			
Jonas Stansfield for a mess[uage] in Crowell Shaws	0	1	2			
Do for a Mess[uage] call lower Redd brinch & Wilkin Green ..	0	1	8			
Jno Walker for a mess[uage] called Pykelaw Freehold	0	1	8			
Wm Sutcliff for a mess[uage] called Pyklaw Freehold	0	1	8			

Wm Normanton for a mess[uage] called Oakeing Clough	0	0	10	
Saml Wood for a Cottage in Sowerby Street	0	0	1½	
Jno Dearden, Gent for 2 closes called Royds	0	0	4	
Jno Wood for a Cott[age] in Sowerby Street	0	0	1	
Jno Bentley for a Mess[uage] in Sowerby Dene	0	2	0	
The heirs of Mr Ramsden for a mess[uage] at Ratenrow..	0	1	0	
Wm Deane for a mess[uage] called Marrhill	0	0	4	
				1 0 4½
Sowerby 36th the heirs of Joshua Horton Esq for a messuage in Sowerby Towne & mess[uage] called Sheen hall	0	9	3	
And hath help of Izrael Wilde for Ballgreen	0	3	4	
The heirs of Joshua Horton Esq for a mess[uage] in Sowerby Townehead	0	2	8	
Abrm Hitchin for a mess[uage] near Ratton Row..	0	1	6	
The heirs of Joshua Horton Esq for a Mess[uage] in Turvin called Birch Land	0	2	6	
John Bentley for a mess[uage] called Steel	0	0	3	
Richard Dearden for a mess[uage] called Sowerby Deine	0	0	10	
				1 0 4
Warley 37th Nathaniel Murgatroyd for Hartley royd	0	5	4	
David Buckley for Eves hous	0	3	10	
James Murgatroyd for Stubbing hous ..	0	1	8	
Henry Mitchill for a mess[uage] called Marehill	0	1	8	
And have help of the Coeheirs of Mr Oates for 2 Cottages called Rydeinghead	0	0	5	
Do for a close called Catlopp	0	0	1	
Nathaniel Murgatroyd for a mess[uage] called Poplewells	0	3	2	

John Murgatroyd for a Cott[age] at Ludenden	0	0	1			
Wm Murgatroyd for a mess[uage] called Clough head	0	2	4			
Jonas Sladen for a Mess[uage] called Bend	0	1	1			
Eleazar Tetlow for a mess[uage] called Clough	0	1	1			
Henry Mitchell for a Mess[uage] near Marehill	0	0	5			
				1	1	2
Soyland 38th The heirs of Joshua Horton Esq for a Mess[uage] called Laine ends	0	2	2			
John Sydall for a Mess[uage] called Stubbin	0	1	9			
And have help of John Foxcroft for a mess[uage] called Sawhill ..	0	2	9½			
Jno Shaw for a mess[uage] called Coathill	0	0	8			
Do for a Messuage in the Millbanck ..	0	1	8			
Joseph Holdroyd for a mess[uage] in Sowerby Deine	0	1	10½			
Susanna Bentley for a mess[uage] called Rowley	0	3	8			
Samuel Platts for Sweet Oake.. ..	0	1	3			
The heirs of Joshua Horton Esq for a mess[uage] called Banks near the Oake	0	1	1			
Do for Coall Myne	0	5	0			
James Stansfield for a Mess[uage] called Laine Ends	0	1	0			
John Normanton for a Mess[uage] & one croft in Sowerby Towne ..	0	0	6			
John Walker for a Mess[uage] above Quick Stavers	0	0	8			
The heirs of Joshua Horton Esq for Rowley Inge	0	0	4			
				1	4	5
Sowerby 39th Elkana Hoyl for a Mess[uage] called Stones	0	7	2			
Henry Dyson for a mess[uage] called Stones	0	2	8			
Jno Whiteley for a mess[uage] called Ladywell	0	3	4			

The coheirs of Jo. Firth for a mess[uage] near Good Greave	0	2	0			
James Hill for a mess[uage] called Burnd moor	0	1	8			
John Feilden for a mess[uage] called Bowerslack	0	2	3½			
Jer. Crosley for 2 Mess[uage] called Clough banke & Tootill ..	0	1	5			
Wm Normanton for a mess[uage] near Bower Slack	0	1	0			
Elkana Hoyl for a mess[uage] called Stansfeild Heye	0	1	2			
Abrm̃ Ryley for Shaws Freehold ..	0	0	10			
Henry Ryley for Tootill Clough ..	0	0	7½			
				1	4	2
Warley 40th Robert Brigg for a Mess[uage] & a Cottage called Westfield & Litle moor	0	9	0			
Eleazar Tetlow for a Mess[uage] called Stoops	0	1	0			
And have help of Edmund Tattersall for Throstle nest	0	3	0			
Richd Holgate for a mess[uage] called Westroyd	0	2	0			
Willm̃ Emmott & Thomas Lister for a mess[uage] in the Edge above Warley Towne Joshua Scholefield occupier	0	2	0			
John Murgatroyd for 2 Closes called Nabbend	0	0	6			
Do for 2 Cott[ages] called Funtons ..	0	0	2			
Anthony Walker for 2 Cott[ages] called Funtons	0	0	2			
Abraham Shakleton for a mess[uage] called Oulnook	0	1	1			
John Clay for a mess[uage] called Oulnook	0	1	1			
John Ryley for a mess[uage] called Withingap	0	0	4			
				1	0	4
Soyland 41 John Walker for a mess[uage] called Wethersgreen ..	0	7	0			
Widw Brooksbanck for a mess[uage] called Swatt	0	0	1			

	And have help of John Sutcliff for a mess[uage] in Turvin ..	0	4	9	
	Henry Sutcliff Junr for a Mess[uage] called Withins Freehold ..	0	4	5	
	Henry Sutcliff Senr for a mess[uage] in the Withins Freehold ..	0	4	5	
					1 0 8
42^{d}	Josias Norminton for a mess[uage] called Snape	0	3	4	
	Henry Sydall for a mess[uage] called Hey end	0	1	5	
	Saml Stansfield for a mess[uage] called Lane	0	1	7	
	And have help of John Radcliffe for a mess[uage] called Long Edge ..	0	1	7	
	Joseph Clapham for a mess[uage] called Long Edge	0	1	7	
	The heirs of Joshua Horton Esq for a mess[uage] called Scout ..	0	6	0	
	D^{o} for a mess[uage] in Crowwell Shaws ..	0	2	4	
	Thomas Sutcliffe for a mess[uage] called Strait hey Freehold	0	1	0	
	Josias Stansfield for a Close late Hellewell Land	0	0	5	
	Mathew Wadsworth for a Close late Hellewell Land	0	0	5	
	Mrs Anne Brockholes for a mess[uage] called Mirewall	0	2	2	
					1 1 10
Warley 43	Joseph Holme for a mess[uage] called Peacock hous	0	4	4	
	Benj Wade for a Mess[uage] called Shaw Booth	0	2	0	
	The Coeheirs of Ab: Wadsworth for upper Shaw Booth	0	0	11	
	Geo: Beanland for a Mess[uage] above Peacock hous	0	2	6	
	And have help of ye heirs of Abr: Wadsworth for a Mess[uage] called Turpithill	0	1	4	
	The heirs of Mr Ramsden for 2 mess[uages] in Ludenden dein head..	0	2	11	

John Brigg for the rest of Turpit hill ..	0	0	4			
John Ryley for a mess[uage] at Cold Edge heretofore Stansfields ..	0	4	4½			
Ambrose Patchit for Lowkie Slade ..	0	1	4			
D^o^ for Top of Cold Edge	0	0	7			
				1	0	7½
Soyland 44 Elkana Hoyl for a mess[uage] called Wood Laine	0	6	6			
And hath help of Jno Dearden, Gent for a Mess[uage] at Sowerby Chapel Steel	0	2	5			
The heirs of Joseph Lord for a mess[uage] at Standing Stone ..	0	3	10			
Toby Ryley for a mess[uage] called Higham	0	2	6			
John Dearden, Gent for a mess[uage] called College Land	0	1	6			
The heirs of Samuel Wilson for a Mess[uage] called The Clough ..	0	2	8			
Mary Thomas for a mess[uage] in Turvin called the Cobcastle	0	1	8			
Mathew Wadsworth for a mess[uage] called Theaker Yate	0	1	0			
				1	2	1
Sowerby 45th Francis Allinson for 2 mess[uages] in Turvin	0	6	8			
The heirs of Mrs Barcroft for a mess[uage] in Turvin	0	2	7			
John Barraclough for a mess[uage] called Smithy Steads	0	2	0			
And have help of Jno Sutcliffe for ¼ of the Withens	0	4	5			
John Greenwood for anoth^r^ ¼ of the Wythins	0	4	5			
				1	0	1
Warley 46th Robert Brigg for a mess[uage] called Bank hous	0	4	0			
The heirs of David Smith for a mess[uage] called Pearscoot ..	0	2	6			
Wid^w^ Lockwood for a mess[uage] called Royd grave	0	2	4			
Thomas Oldfield for a Mess[uage] called Holmehous	0	1	6			

	£	s	d	£	s	d
And have help of Thomas Yorke Esq for 2 mess[uages] at Lower End of Cold Edge	0	2	10			
Abrm̃ Patchit for a mess[uages] called Holmehouse	0	2	0			
Nathan Wood for a mess[uage] called Hockcliffe	0	1	8			
The heirs of Abrm̃ Farrow for a mess-[uage] called The Slode ..	0	2	4			
Benjamin Wade for a Mess[uage] called Poplewells	0	0	3			
Abrm̃ Skelton for a mess[uage] called Squiril Kell	0	0	7			
Joshua Laycock for a mill Damme ..	0	0	2			
				1	0	2
Soyland 47th John Dickson for a Mess[uage] called Lower Bentley Royd ..	0	4	3½			
John Waterhous for upper Bentley Royd	0	3	4			
And have help of The Coeheirs of Edwd Tattersall, & John Tattersall of Hollings	0	3	0			
John Dearden, Gent for Ellen holme ..	0	1	6			
Thomas Oldfield for a mess[uage] called Clough hous	0	1	4			
Mathew Wadsworth for a mess[uage] near the Short-riggin.. ..	0	2	0			
Henry Hellewell for ⅔ of a mess[uage] called Bramton	0	1	4			
The heirs of Joshua Horton Esq for a mess[uage] called the Pinfold ..	0	1	0			
Susanna Bentley for a Close called Wellhead	0	1	0			
John Preistly for a Close late Hortons ..	0	0	3			
Thomas Oldfield for Turnlee	0	2	2			
Sarah Sutcliff Widw for ⅓ p[ar]te of Bramton	0	0	7½			
John Crosley, Gent for p[ar]te of Ellen-holme	0	0	3			
				1	2	1
Sowerby 48th The heirs of John Michill for a mess[uage] called The longroyd	0	7	10			
The heirs of Edward Farrar for a mess-[uage] called Gate Lands ..	0	2	4			

The heirs of Jacob Farrar for a Close & wood called Nether-ends ..	0	0	10			
And have help of Willm̃ Horton, Gent for 2 mess[uage] in Crowel Shaws ..	0	5	0			
Saml Pollard for a mess[uage] in Crowel Shaws	0	1	9			
The heirs of John Crowder for a mess-[uage] in Short riggin.. ..	0	1	0			
The heirs of Mrs Barcroft for a mess-[uage] near Short Riggin now Wm Leigh Esq	0	1	0			
John Bentley for a mess[uage] at Long Edge end	0	0	7½			
The heirs of Thomas Ryley for a mess-[uage] called Barton	0	2	0			
				1	2	4½
Warley 49th Arthur Mawd for 2 mess[uages] called Ivehouse & Jay nest ..	0	4	9½			
Anthony Nayler for a mess[uage] called High oldfield	0	6	1			
Edmund Starky for a mess[uage] called Ivehouse	0	3	9½			
And have help of John Crosley for a holme p[ar]te of the Ivehous ..	0	0	6			
John Brooksbanck for a mess[uage] called Towneley Land ..	0	1	4			
John Bryercliff for a mess[uage] called Daisy banck	0	2	8			
John Nutter for a mess[uage] called Bends	0	1	10			
				1	1	0
Soyland 50th Thomas Mitton & Nicholas Dawson for a mess[uage] called Birks	0	2	0			
Mr Michl Firth for Thomas Land ..	0	0	4			
Mrs Mary Firth for a mess[uage] at Soyland Yate	0	0	8			
Thomas Mitton & Nicholas Dawson for a mess[uage] at Flatt	0	0	8			
James Ryley for Townend Land ..	0	0	6			
Thomas Mitton for Townend Land ..	0	0	5			
John Gaukroger for 2 Cott[age] at Flatt-head	0	0	8			

And have help of the heirs of Joshua Whiteley for a mess[uage] in Soyland wood	0	1	4			
Richard Firth for a mess[uage] called Crosswells	0	1	6			
Jeramia Crosley for a mess[uage] called Shawedge	0	1	6			
James Ryley for a Mess[uage] called Soyland Moore & a Cott[age] called Bankhous Head	0	2	10			
Jeremia Ryley for a mess[uage] called Law Close & for Freehold ..	0	2	4			
Ely Gledhill for a mess[uage] called Barrathill	0	1	4			
The heirs of John Shaw for a mess[uage] at Dyson Laine end	0	1	10			
John Ryley for a mess[uage] called Swift Cross	0	1	5			
Tho: Fearnley, Gent for a Mess[uage] called Jackson Inge	0	2	0			
Geo: Rawnsley for p[ar]te of Smith Laine	0	1	7½			
				1	2	11½
Sowerby 51st Jeramia Ryley for 2 mess[uages] called the Holme & Spoutfield	0	8	5			
James Stansfield for 2 Mess[uages] called Boewood & Rattonrow ..	0	8	4			
And have help of Jerimia Crosley for a mess[uage] called Thunerton Delves	0	2	0			
Benjamin Brambley for a mess[uage] called Carr	0	2	4			
				1	1	1
Warley 52nd Mathew Wade for a Mess[uage] at High Saltonstall	0	5	0½			
David Crosley for a mess[uage] at Saltonstall p[ar]te of Mr Deane Land	0	2	6			
James Murgatroyd for a Mess[uage] at Saltonstall	0	3	0			
Jonathan Whitehead for a mess[uage] at Saltonstall	0	2	6			
And have help of John Halstead for a mess[uage] at Height	0	2	10			

James Murgatroyd for a Cott[age] called Lamhill End	0	0	2			
Wid[w] Walker for a mess[uage] at the Height	0	3	6			
Dan[l] Skelton for a mess[uage] at Lower end of Saltonstall Moore	0	1	4			
Henry Butterfield for a mess[uage] called Knowle	0	3	8			
				1	4	6½
Soyland 53[d] John Crosley for 2 mess[uages] called Smalees	0	7	10			
Elkana Hoyl for a Mess[uage] called Hollins	0	2	6			
And have help of Jeremia Crosley for a Mess[uage] near Blackshaw Clough	0	1	8			
James Ogden for a mess[uage] called Poke	0	0	4½			
Rich[d] Firth for a Messuage near Croswels	0	3	0			
John Ryley for a mess[uage] called Stansfield heye	0	2	4			
The heirs of Jn[o] Ramsden for a messuage called Greenholes ..	0	2	0			
Ely Gleadhill for a Cottage & Kilne at the Millbanck	0	0	1			
John Crosley for 3 Cottages near Shawell..	0	0	2			
Henry Sunderland for a Cottage & a close occupied with burnthous ..	0	0	6			
Joseph Lister for a Cottage	0	0	1			
John Fletcher for a Cottage at Dowery Yate	0	0	1½			
The heirs of Joshua Whiteley for a messuage in the Wood near Birks ..	0	0	8			
				1	1	4
Sowerby 54th Samuel Hill for a messuage called Meakin place in Soyland Towne	0	3	4			
And hath help of Henry Whitworth for a messuage called Shawell ..	0	4	0			
The heirs of M[r] Oates for a Messuage called Plain near Hoylheads ..	0	4	0			
Nathan Whitley for ½ of the Money Bent..	0	5	3			
John Hellawell for a Messuage called Four Laine ends	0	1	6			

The coeheirs of Joseph Firth for a Messuage called Watergreen ..	0	0	10			
John Marsden for 2 Messuage in Soyland Wood called Denton Ings ..	0	3	4			
John Ryley for a messuage called Blackhous	0	1	1			
The heirs of John Wilkinson for a messuage called the laine ends ..	0	0	10			
				1	4	2
Warley 55 The heirs of Jonas Wood for 2 Mess[uages] at Lower Saltonstall	0	10	6			
Mary Hezledine for a Mess[uage] called Hullothill	0	3	7½			
James Murgatroyd for 2 Cottages in Savile Hey	0	3	7½			
John Greenwood for a Mess[uage] at Lower Saltonstall	0	5	0			
And have help of Jonathan Whitehead for a mess[uage] called Lower Law	0	0	5			
Joseph Clapham for a Mess[uage] called Vpper Law	0	0	10			
				1	4	0
Soyland 56th Richard Royde for a Mess[uage] called Bestinghirst	0	3	6			
John Shaw for a Mess[uage] called Bestinghirst	0	3	6			
John Ryley for 2 Mess[uages] adjoyning to the said Bestinghirst ..	0	7	11			
And have help of John Ryley for a Mess[uage] called the Clough ..	0	3	0			
John Ryley for Farra Height	0	0	2			
John Kenworthy for a Mess[uage] called Brode holling	0	0	10			
The heirs of John Smith for a Mess[uage] above the Brodeholling ..	0	1	4			
Izrael Wilde for a mess[uage] called Hoyle	0	1	3			
James Adkinson for a Cott[age] at Broad holling	0	0	1			
Robt Butterfield for a Mess[uage] in Smith Laine	0	1	7½			
				1	3	2½

Sowerby 57 The heirs of John Whittakers for a Mess[uage] called Mythamroyd	0	3	3	
Richd Stearne Gent for Culpin Wood near Mythomroyd	0	1	5	
Wm Sutcliff for a hous & a close at Mythomroyd Brigg	0	0	10	
And have help of John Greenwood for a mess[uage] called Hollin hey	0	10	11	
Wm Sutcliff for p[ar]te of Hollin hey ..	0	0	5	
Henry Sunderland for a mess[uage] called Hanckclough	0	1	2	
The heirs of Thomas Thornhill, Gent for one half of Scout	0	2	2	
Isaac Farrar for a Wood above his hous..	0	0	4	
Henry Wilson for a Farme in Milnebanck	0	1	9	
				1 2 3
Warley 58 The heirs of Joshua Horton Esq for a mess[uage] called the Hoylhous	0	4	0½	
The heirs of John Kirke for Waterhill ..	0	1	6	
Jonathan Baumford for a Mess[uage] called Rawpighel	0	1	8	
And have help of the heirs of Richard Wainhous for ½ of a mess[uage] called Highroyd	0	3	1	
Jonathan Tattersall for the other half of High royd	0	3	1	
Tho: Turner for a mess[uage] called Roylshead	0	1	11	
Mathew Smith for Trough & Long Croft..	0	1	11	
Tho: Oldfield for a Close at Sandbedd ..	0	0	1	
Richd Tattersall for a Cottage & Close above the Old Mill	0	0	3	
The heirs of Joshua Horton Esq for Land above Hoylhous ..	0	0	1	
Geo: Oldfield for a Mess[uage] above Sowerby brigg Chapel ..	0	1	0	
John Murgatroyd for 2 Cott[age] at Ludenden	0	0	4	
The heirs of Mr Oates for Sargenfeild & a Cott[age]	0	0	5	
				0 19 4½

Sowerby 59th Timothy Stansfield for a Mess[uage] in Stansfield Clough ..	0 3 0	
And hath help of John Shaw for a Mess[uage] called Sowterhous ..	0 4 0	
The heirs of Jeramia Ryley for a Mess[uage] called Otter Lee ..	0 3 0	
Geo: Normanton for a Mess[uage] near Annabutlee	0 3 6	
Tho: Sunderland for a Mess[uage] near Joyning	0 1 3	
Wm Greenwood Junior for a Mess[uage] called Higgin Chamber ..	0 4 1	
Minister at Sowerby for a mess[uage] called Cold-Hindley	0 1 2	
James Stansfield for a Mill & Goyt called Stansfield Mill	0 1 0	
		1 1 0
Sowerby 60th The heirs of Joshua Horton Esq for a Mess[uage] called Gudgrave & for Minister house at Riponden	0 7 5	
Richard Stearn, Gent for a mess[uage] called Priestley Ing	0 6 8	
And have help of Josias Stansfield for a mess[uage] called Redbrinck ..	0 3 3	
Jonas Ingham for a Mess[uage] in Crowell Shaws	0 1 10	
Jno Gawkroger for a mess[uage] at Flathead late Wilsons ..	0 0 4	
James Ryley for 2 Closes called Seaven Roods	0 0 5	
Elkana Hoyl for a mess[uage] called Lainehead	0 1 5	
Wm Normanton for a Farme in Crowel Shaws & Two closes near Bowood Slack	0 2 8	
		1 4 0
Totall of the yearly Rents collectable by the Grave of Sowerby.. ..		65 13 5½

We the Jury sworne for the Lord of the Mannor of Wakefield abovesaid doe upon o[ur] Enquiry into the Old Rentalls & Evidences concerning o[u]r said Graveship of Sowerby finde &

pr[e]sent that there are 60 Graves w[i]thin o[u]r said Graves[hi]p & that the p[er]sons above under their severall Numbers ought to serve the Office of Grave in their respective turns for their Lands & Tennem[en]ts there mentioned & have helpers w[hi]ch are there set downe under the same Number for their Lands & Tennem[en]ts there also mentioned And that those Persons under the Number 25 doe serve the Office for this pr[e]sent year begining at Mich[aelmas] last & the rest successively as they follow in their Numbers and that the respective Rents under every Number are due & payable yearly to the L[or]d of the said Mannor And also we doe finde that every helper is to pay to the head Grave 4[d] for every penny rent & soe after that Rate for a greater or Lesser Sume

Thomas Oldfield	John Murgatroyd	Henry Whitworth
Jno Greenwood	Richard Holdroyd	John Sutcliffe
James Stansfield	John Farrar	
Robert Briggs	John Dickson	
John Gawkroger	John Normanton	

HIP[PER]HOLME GRAVESH[I]P

Manerium de Wakefield } **The Graveship** of Hip[per]holme is bounded by North Byerley, Wike, & Scholes to the East, Hartchshead Brighous, & Southowrom, to the South, Hallifax, Booths Towne, & Hauworth to the West, & Thornton & Clayton to the North and hath within it The Freehold[rs] & Copieholders following who pay Rents &c according to the Verdict taken out of the Court Rolls of the Mannor as followeth

Maner[ium] de Wakefield } Ad magnam Cur[iam] Baron[em] nobilissimi Thome Ducis de Leeds pr[ae]nobilis ordinis Garterij Militis D[omin]i Manerij de Wakefield tent[am] apud Lightcliffe p[er] adjournament[um] vicesimo quarto die Maij Anno R[e]gni D[omin]e Anne Dei Gratia nunc Regine Magne Brittanie &c Octavo

The Verdict of Joseph Crowther, Willm̃ Richardson, William Walker, James Lister, Thomas Holdsworth, Joseph Wood, Jonathon Preistley, Joshua Wright, Thomas Kitson, John Preistley, Jeremia Baxter, John Clay, Robert Ramsden, John Bargh, Samuel Crowder, & Samuel Ridlesden being Freehold[rs] & Copiehold[rs] w[i]thin the Graveship of Hip[per]holme of & concerning the Freehold & Copiehold Lands & Tenem[en]ts within the said Gravesh[i]p w[hi]ch pay rents & doe service to the Lord of the said Mannor of Wakefield

1[st]	Willm̃ Richardson Gent for Cliffhous & Lands	0	3	1½
	D[o] for 3 closes late Kershaws	0	2	5

		£	s	d	
	And hath help of Thomas Kitson for Cliff hill	0	0	7	
	Wm Walker, Gent for Knowle Top ..	0	0	7	
	Do for Street Farme	0	3	1½	
	Wm Walker Senr for Shibden head ..	0	3	11	
	Wm Cockcroft for a Farme in Hip[per]-holme	0	1	1	
	Wm Green, Gent for Bottom hall ..	0	1	6½	
	Nathaniel Souwood for Preistley hill ..	0	0	4	
					0 16 8½
2d	Nathaniel Priestley, Gent for Wester-Croft	0	3	2½	
	Joseph Gargrave in right of his wife & Mary Preistley for another p[ar]te of Westercroft	0	4	3½	
	And have help of Jno Clay for a messuage & Lands in North Owrom	0	4	4	
	John Gumersall & Jno Brogden for a Farme late Jonas Northens ..	0	1	3	
	Jonathan Priestley, Gent for Meylings Croft	0	0	2	
	The heirs of John Crowther for Stamps..	0	1	8	
	Do for Hall Farme	0	0	8	
	Joseph Wood, Gent for Fold	0	0	8	
					0 16 3
3d	Robert Ramsden for Quarlors.. ..	0	3	8	
	Do for Iveingcarr	0	0	4	
	Do for Heyward	0	3	6	
	Do for Northen Lands	0	1	4½	
	And hath help of the heirs of Richd Hoyle for Drake Lands ..	0	3	0	
	Do for Kirshaw Farme	0	3	1½	
	Edward Hanson for Only hous.. ..	0	1	4	
	Do for Salter Lee	0	0	7	
					0 16 11
4th	Michael Woodhead for Longshaw &c ..	0	3	1½	
	Do for Hazel Hirst	0	2	10	
	Do for Hill Top late Listers	0	0	4	
	Do for Francklin	0	1	8	
	Do for Horwithins or Roe	0	1	0	

		£	s	d	£	s	d
	And hath help of Jno: Holdsworth for Cawsey End	0	1	4½			
	John Sutcliff for Black Myres	0	2	10			
	Jer: Barstow for Green Sike	0	2	5			
	The heirs of Isaac Woodhead for Haire Clough	0	1	1			
					0	16	8
5th	John Bryercliff, Gent for Damm head ..	0	2	8			
	Do for Mutton Pitts	0	1	4			
	Do for Addersgate	0	2	2			
	Do for Driver Farme	0	1	11			
	And hath help of Mr Dawson for Damm head	0	2	10			
	Miles Ingham for Blakehill	0	2	9			
	John Wilman for Booth-banck ..	0	3	3			
					0	16	11
6th	John Fournace, Gent for uper Shipden hall Freehold 3s Copiehold 6d ..	0	3	6			
	Do for Holgate Farme	0	2	6			
	Do for Katherin Koyt	0	0	6			
	Do for Lee Single	0	2	0			
	Do for Naylor Farme	0	1	0			
	Do for Scott Farme	0	1	3			
	Do for Slingden head	0	3	8			
	Do for Royd Manks	0	2	3			
	And hath help of Isaac Wilson for a Cottage on the Wast above Pule	0	0	6			
					0	17	2
7th	Thomas Thornhill Esq for Brighous Mills	0	16	1			
	And hath help of Mr Coats for Nalson Farme	0	0	6			
					0	16	7
8th	The heirs of Joshua Horton Esq for High Sunderland	0	3	7			
	Do for Barker Farme	0	4	8			
	Do for Hagues Stocks	0	2	6			
	Do for Townend Farme	0	3	0			
	Do for a Cottage	0	0	6			
	And hath help of John Staincliff p[er] Scout	0	1	10			

		£	s	d	Total
	Joseph Wilkinson for North brigg ..	0	0	10	
					0 16 11
9th	William Drake Esqr[1] for Hall house ..	0	5	0	
	Do for Harley Green	0	1	8	
	Do for Crowroids	0	1	6	
	And hath help of Thomas Holdsworth, Gent for banck top	0	5	6½	
	Do for his Lands in Hip[per]holme ..	0	1	7	
	The heirs of [*blank*] Blackit for Banks ..	0	1	4	
	Jonathan Longbothom for Fooler Lands ..	0	0	2	
					0 16 9½
10th	The heirs of Tymothy Pollard for Rands ..	0	5	6	
	Mary Wainhous, Widow for banks ..	0	4	0	
	Do for Tilsons Lands	0	0	4	
	Do for Moor Close	0	0	4	
	And have help of John Ryley, Gent for Bancks	0	4	5	
	James Scholefield for Hoyl Land ..	0	0	6½	
	Do for Bowlin Dyke	0	0	7½	
	Do for Banck	0	1	0	
					0 16 9
11th	The heirs of Abrm̃ Hall Gent[2] for Booths Towne	0	1	10	
	Do for Jonathan Hall Land	0	5	10½	
	Do for Baracloughs	0	1	6	
	Do for Pearson Land	0	1	3	
	Do for Mr Joseph Hall Land	0	2	2	
	Do for John Wilson Farme	0	1	0	
	Do for Blakehill	0	3	5	
					0 17 0½
12th	Joseph Crowther, Gent for Old Land ..	0	9	0	
	Do for Whiteley Land	0	0	7	
	Do for Fore	0	0	3	
	Do for Hanson Land	0	1	6	
	Do for Rushworth Farme	0	1	1	
	Do for Bairstows Land	0	0	9	
	Do for Sym Carr	0	2	1	
	Do for Longbottoms	0	0	4	
					0 15 7

[1] *H.F.M.G.*, II, 507.

[2] *C.D.*, I, 117.

		£	s	d			
13th	John Smith, Gent for Scout Hall ..	0	16	6			
	Do for Wilton Lands	0	0	2½			
					0	16	8½
14th	The heirs of Robt Cowlin for Folly Hall ..	0	5	5½			
	Do for Knight Royd	0	5	1½			
	And hath help of Robert Northend for Knight Royd	0	5	2			
	Tho: Fearnley for Lands at Thorntree ..	0	1	1			
					0	16	10
15th	The heirs of Mr Oates for ancient Land ..	0	13	7			
	Do for Jno Holdsworth Farme ..	0	3	6			
					0	17	1
16th	Mr Heald for Synderhills	0	2	4			
	Do for Sowoodhous	0	3	8½			
	Do for Bryon Scholes	0	0	6			
	And hath help of Timothy Wadsworthe for Coall Mynes	0	5	0			
	Thomas Beatson for his Land	0	3	4			
	Mr Stanhop for Foor	0	1	8			
	Saml Whiteley for Foor	0	0	4			
					0	16	10½
17th	James Lister, Gent for a Messuage & Land at Shibden Mill	0	4	4			
	Do for Lower bryce	0	3	8			
	Do for Mytham	0	0	2			
	Do for Bowling Dyke	0	0	1			
	Do for a Fourth p[ar]t of Shibden Mill ..	0	2	0			
	Do for Southages	0	0	9			
	Do for Royds Lands	0	0	5			
	Do for one half pte of Peartrees.. ..	0	0	9			
	And hath help of Thomas Lister, Gent for a Mess[uage] in the poss[ession] of James Greave formerly Hopkins	0	2	7½			
	Do for Robert Gregory	0	0	5			
	John Smith, Gent for a Farme in Green-Laine in the poss[ession] of Abrm Hanson	0	1	3			
					0	16	10½
18th	Willm Horton Esqr for Coley Hall ..	0	4	4			
	Do for Smith Farme	0	1	8			

		£	s.	d.	Total
	And hath help of Jonathan Preistley for Winter Edge	0	2	2½	
	[*blank*] York Esq for Hazlehurst ..	0	4	6	
	Dr Prescot for Ryall Land	0	1	0	
	Do for upper Haslehirst	0	1	4	
	Do for Shitleton Hill	0	2	0	
					0 17 0½
19th	Mrs Fournes or Mrs Livesey for Hagstocks	0	6	3	
	Do for another p[ar]te	0	1	8	
	And hath help of John Bargh for Shugden Hall	0	3	4	
	Samuel Crowther for Lands head ..	0	1	5	
	Thomas Mawd in the right of his wife for Bryon Scoles	0	1	8	
	Do for Quarlors	0	0	6	
	Mary Booth & Eliz: Lightowlers for Richd Hayley Land at Leebrigg	0	1	9	
					0 16 7
20th	The heirs of Abm̃ Hall, Gent for Upper Bryer	0	1	11½	
	Do for Brig Land	0	4	7½	
	Do for Crowther Mill	0	1	4	
	And hath help of Sam̃l Lister of Horton for his Lands	0	1	2½	
	The heirs of James Cawbert & the heirs of James Hill for Howshroggs ..	0	2	11	
	The heirs of James Cawbert for Mrs Wood Farme	0	1	8	
	Do for Wilbys	0	1	0	
	The Governors of the Free School at Hallifax for Tymothy Stocks Farme	0	2	0	
					0 16 8½
21st	The heirs of Edwd Langley, Gent for Quarlers & Allan Royd ..	0	0	10½	
	Do for Bryon Scholes	0	2	2	
	Do for Laverhead	0	1	6	
	Do for Quarlers	0	0	6	
	Do for Land late John Langleys ..	0	0	1	
	Do for Bentley Land	0	2	11	
	Do for Thomas Flatters	0	3	6	

	Dº for Lidgate late Cockcrofts	0	1	0	
	Dº for Land late Godleys	0	1	11	
	Dº for Michael Ramsdens	0	1	6½	
	And hath help of John Priestley for Freehold Land	0	0	9½	
					0 16 9½
22d	The heirs of Mr Rosendall for Waterhous..	0	2	6	
	Dº for Tanhous	0	3	10	
	Dº for Colier Sike	0	1	6	
	Dº for Stephenhead	0	2	0½	
	Dº for Thomas Kitson	0	2	11½	
	And hath help of Mrs Mary Langley for Hip[per]holme	0	2	7	
	Sam̃l Ridlesden, Gent for Brookhous Ing..	0	1	6	
					0 16 11
23d	Joseph Crowther, gent for White hill ..	0	3	11	
	Dº for Laycock	0	1	3	
	Dº for Jer: Rhodes Farme	0	5	0	
	Dº for Brigland Strines	0	1	8½	
	Dº for Dañl Scott	0	2	7	
	Dº for Gregson Land	0	1	2	
	Dº for Bunny	0	1	4	
	Judeth Haldsworth for Land belonging Whitehill	0	0	3	
					0 17 2½
24th	Sarah Ramsden, Widow for Mythom ..	0	3	3	
	And hath help of [*blank*] for the 4 Laine Ends late George Ramsdens ..	0	3	0	
	Dr Richardson for Speight Land ..	0	0	4	
	Joseph Crowther for Lower limed hous ..	0	3	0	
	Dº for p[ar]te of Mr Halls	0	0	1	
	Dº for barehead	0	0	5	
	The heirs of Edwd Langley, Gent for Whiteley Ing head	0	3	0	
	Widw Bairstow for upper limed hous ..	0	2	2	
	The heirs of Jonathan Threapland for Windleroyd	0	1	6	
					0 16 9
25	The heirs of Charles Best for Laudymear..	0	0	9¾	
	Dº for a Cottage	0	0	6	

	D° for wall'd Close	0	2	2	
	D° for Wallis Farme	0	1	6	
	D° for Colier Syke	0	2	5	
	D° for Bolshaw	0	2	4	
	D° for Batlay's	0	0	9	
	D° for Woodend	0	0	3	
	D° for John Northends Bryonscholes ..	0	2	2	
	And hath help of Joshua Ingham for Colier Syke	0	2	5	
	John Wells for Huddhill	0	0	11	
	Benj: Wilkinson for Nobleholmes ..	0	0	8	
					0 16 10½
26	The heirs of M[r] Oates for Scullcoat brow ..	0	4	5	
	D° for Jagger Farme	0	2	6½	
	D° for Deans	0	1	0	
	D° for Milns's	0	0	4½	
	And hath help of Joseph Philips for Holkins	0	3	8	
	Richard Thomas for hanging royd ..	0	3	10	
	Richard Scarbrough for Parracks ..	0	0	7	
	Henry Gream for Hayley hill ..	0	0	4	
					0 16 9
27th	Joshua Wright of Hipperholme ..	0	1	9	
	D° for Browne Lands	0	1	2	
	Jer: Baxter for Noefeildyate	0	2	9½	
	And have help of John Morrice Jun[r] for his Lands	0	1	1	
	Dan[l] Oldfield for Moorclose	0	1	4	
	The L[d] Irwin for his Lands	0	1	1½	
	John Bargh for Blackmires Freehold ..	0	1	2	
	Joshua Laycock for Otes royd 2[s] 2[d] D[r] Crowbrough 2[s] 0½[d]	0	4	2½	
	Jno Fearnside for browside	0	1	4	
	[*blank*] Gleadhill for Blackmires ..	0	0	8	
					0 16 7½
	Totall of The yearly rents collectable by the Grave of Hipperholme				22 12 11½

We the Jury sworne for the Lord of the Mannor of Wakefeld abovesaid doe upon our enquiry into the old Rentalls & Evidences concerning the said Graveshp̄ of Hip[per]holme finde & present that there are Twenty seaven Graves within o[u]r said Graveship And that the p[er]sons abovesaid under their severall Numbers ought to serve the Office of Grave in their respective turns for their Lands & Tenne[men]ts there mentioned and have helpers which are there set downe under the same Number for their Lands & Tennem[en]ts there also mentioned and that those p[er]sons under the Number 9 doe serve the Office for this present year beginning at Mich[aelma]s last & the rest successively as they follow in their Numbers And that the respective Rents under every Number are due and payable yearly to the Lord of the said Mannor

Joseph Crowther, Wm Richardson, Wm Walker, James Lister, Jo: Wood, Jonathan Preistley, Joshua Wright, Thomas Kitson, John Preistley, John Clay, John Barke, Samuel Riddlesdein.

THE GRAVESHIP OF RASTRICK

The Graveship of Rastrick is bounded by Bradley & Dighton to the East, Huthersfield & Lindley to the South, Elland to the West, & the River of Calder to the North, w[hi]ch being small & noe Differances ariseing among the Copieholders relating to the Office of Grave and there not being resident Tenn[en]ts enough to make a Jury (soe much of the Copiehold Lands of that Graveship being ingross't into the hands of Thomas Thornhill Esq) The Survey was made only by such feow as were Resident who examined into the old Rentalls & evidences of the same w[hi]ch apeared to be as follow (vizt) 16

1st	John Nichols for a Farme in Tootill called Armitage Farme in the poss[ession] of Richard Brook ..	0	3	9			
	And hath help of Thomas Thornhill Esq for Mallinson Lands now a Farme in Tootill in the poss[ession] of Saml Cheetam	0	2	7½			
					0	6	5
2d	Sarah Gill, Spinster for a mess[uage] & Lands in Tootill in the poss[ession] of Joseph Fox & late in Richard Chapels				0	3	6
3d	Sarah Gill, Spinster, for a mess[uage] & Lands in Tootill in the occ[upation] of Joseph Fox & late of Tho Fox..				0	3	6
4th	Thomas Hanson, Gent[1] for ⅓ of a mess[uage] & Lands thereunto belonging called Boothroyd				0	6	8

[1] *H.F.M.G.*, IV, 121.

5th	Thomas Thornhill Esq for Brigroyd in the poss[ession] of Thomas Hirst	0	1	8¼			
	Thomas Pollard, Gent for his ½ p[ar]t of Brigroyd in the poss[ession] of Thomas & John Michel	0	2	6½			
					0	4	2¾
6th	Thomas Thornhill Esq for a Farme at Otes Green in the poss[ession] of Willm̃ Garlick				0	4	0½
7th	Thomas Thornhill Esq for Hanson Lands being half a farme in the poss[ession] of Jonas Preston ..				0	3	3
8th	John Nichols for Nether Woodhous & the Lands thereunto belonging				0	5	0
9th	Tho: Pollard, Gent for his other half p[ar]te of Brigroyd in the poss[ession] of Thomas & Jno Michill ..	0	2	6¾			
	And hath help of Mrs Law for Lands late Hansons in the occ[upation] of Jno: Bothomley	0	1	0			
					0	3	6¾
10th	John Murgatroyd, Gent for ⅖ of his Lands at Crowtrees	0	3	0			
	Thomas Thornhill Esq for ⅘ of his Lands at Crowtrees..	0	6	3½			
					0	9	3½
11th	Thomas Hanson, Gent for ⅓ of Bouthroyd	0	3	4			
	John Murgatroyd, Gent for ⅕ of his Lands at Crowtrees	0	1	6¼			
	Tho: Thornhill Esq for ⅕ of his Lands at Crowtrees..	0	3	1¼			
					0	7	11½
12th	Tho. Thornhill Esq for his Lands at Vpper Woodh[ouse] in the occ[upation] of Mathew Berry				0	9	6½
13th	Thomas Holme for a Farme late in the occ[upation] of Wm Garlick formerly Heys				0	4	0½
14th	Thomas Thornhill Esq for the other half of his Lands in the poss[ession] of Jonas Preston				0	3	3
15th	Thomas Thornhill Esq for Edwd Hanson Lands a farme now in the poss[ession] of John Swift ..				0	6	3

		£	s	d	£	s	d
16	John Murgatroyd, Gent for 2/5 of his Lands at Crowtrees	0	3	0			
	Thomas Thornhill Esq 2/5 of his Lands there	0	6	3½			
					0	9	3½
	Thomas Thornhill Esq for all his Lands at Fixby in his owne possession	1	8	4			
	Do for Tootill Hall	0	8	0			
	Do for Lands formerly Apleyards & late Bakers & Mawds	0	0	4½			
	Do for Lands bought of Mrs Law formerly Fletchers	0	0	9			
	Do for a Farme in the poss[ession] of John Hirst Junr	0	4	0			
	Do for Smaylees in the occ[upation] of Jno Nichols	0	0	9			
	Do for Midle Inge in the occ[upation] of Jno Cooper	0	0	4			
	Do for a Cottage called Spawforth in the occ[upation] of Wm Stake ..	0	0	2			
	Do for a Farme in the poss[ession] of Abrm̃ Dyson	0	0	4			
	Do for a Farme in the occ[upation] of James Syke	0	0	2½			
	Do for a Helme at Brigend	0	0	6			
	Do for Lands called Strangstie & Osburns in the occ[upation] of Tho: Holme	0	4	0			
	For Salmon Croft	0	0	4			
	Do for New Close in the occ[upation] of Pearson Laycock	0	0	3			
	Do for a Farme in the occ[upation] of John Bates	0	0	6			
	Do for a Farme called Lighteredge in the occ[upation] of Emanl Roulston	0	0	3½			
	Do for a Farme called Knowles in Fixby in the occ[upation] of Jo: Drake & Edwd Thomson	0	0	4			
	Do for a Farme called Wood in the occ[upation] of Thomas Oldfield	0	1	1			
	Thomas Pollard, Gent for a Farme called Laine head in the occ[upation] of John & Thomas Marsden	0	2	10			

	£	s	d
D° for a Close called Arnald Royd in the occ[upation] of Jno Marsden ..	0	0	6
The Heirs of Joshua Horton Esq for a Farme called Vpper Woodhous in the poss[ession] of Mathew Berry ..	0	6	10
Willm̃ Dawson for a Close called Snake-head in the poss[ession] of John Rush-worth	0	0	4
D° for Mill Cliffs	0	0	8
John Mallinson of Sct Ives for a Farme called Newil-ryding in the occ[upation] of Jn° Marsden	0	1	0
John Green, Gen for Closes called Leyland royds	0	1	0
Thomas Denton for 2 Cottages in the occ[upation] of Jn° Richardson & James Pearson	0	0	1
Sr John Armitage Baront for Shepley Lands in the occ[upation] of Joshua Rayner &c	0	3	9
D° for the attachm[en]t of the Mill Damm	0	0	4
John Nichols for Bentley Farme in the occ[upation] of Jno Brook ..	0	1	4
D° for New inclosure..	0	0	2
D° for Scholes	0	0	8
Joseph Buthroyd for a Cottage house called Madgelaghton	0	0	1
James Lister, Gent for Sutcliffe Wood in Hip[per]holme	0	1	1
Henry Gill for his lands in Brighous ..	0	0	8
John Wilton for a hous & Land in Brighous	0	0	6
John Smith, Gent for Lands at Slead Syke	0	0	4
The Inhabitants of Barkisland for their Twelve places	0	5	0
The Inhabitants of Stainland for their Twelve places	0	4	0
N B And for every Draught & Plow in Stainland & Barkisland 4d			
Totall of the yearly Rents collectable by the Grave of Rastrick ..	£8	11	5¾

SCAMONDEN GRAVESHIP

The Graveship of Scamonden is bounded by Stainland & Quarmby to the East, Slaghwit to the South, Marstin to the West, & Rushworth & Barkisland to the North. Upon the Survey the Rentall apears to be as followeth

Places							
1st	John Crosley, Gent for Egerton ..	0	8	10			
&	And Willm̄ Denton for Hay crofts ..	0	4	6			
2nd	John Hudson for a Cott[age] & one acre of Land	0	1	0			
					0	14	4
3d &	John Crosley for Leyfield	0	8	9			
4th	Thomas Denton, Gent for Crofthous ..	0	3	6			
	George Fairbanck the other p[ar]te of Crofthous	0	3	3			
					0	15	6
5th	John Crosley, Gent for his p[ar]te of Hanhead	0	2	4			
	Michael Hoyl for Heylands	0	3	0			
	Do for ½ of Hanhead	0	2	4			
	Mrs Ann Horton for the Mill hill ..	0	1	1			
					0	8	9
6th	Willm̄ Brooksbanck for Turner hous ..	0	4	3			
&	Susanna Denton for the Banks ..	0	2	6			
7th	Sarah Walker widw for Whiteley Lands	0	2	6			
	John Hoyl for Euse & Turner house ..	0	1	7½			
	Michael Hoyl for Euse & Turnerhous ..	0	1	7½			
	John Jessup & Thomas Shaw for Edwd Denton p[ar]te of Whitelees ..	0	2	6			
					0	15	0
8th	Michael Godley for broad Lee	0	1	6			
&	Willm Denton for his p[ar]te of Brode-Lee	0	1	6			
9th	John Godley for his p[ar]te late Bothom-leys	0	7	1			
	Wm Barraclough for his p[ar]te ..	0	1	6			
	John Walker for ye old hous p[ar]te of Broad Lee	0	2	11			
	Thomas Denton, Gent for Broad Lee called Scarr	0	0	6			

Do for that parte called Steelhous ..	0 0 10	
		0 15 10
Totall of the yearly rents collectable by the Grave of Scammonden		£3 9 5

INCLOSURES

There have bene severall Inclosures & Intacks made off the Wasts of the Mannor as allsoe Cottages erected on the Wasts and a great p[ar]te of them made Copyhold and some by Deed when the Crowne made Comissions for that purpose Freehold And the rest are holden of the Lorde either by Lease or at Will w[hi]ch are as follows

Mr Joseph Armitage holds by Lease a Messuage & one close of Land on the Owtwood of Wakefield containing by Estimation 4 acres & call'd by the name of the Lodge under the yearly Rent of Four pounds	4 0 0
Mr Abrm̃ Ratcliff holds by Lease a piece of Grown'd called Long Moor in Holmfirth containing by Estimation Thirty acres under the yearly rent of	2 10 0
Widw Abson holds at the Will of the Lord a hous called Newhous on the midle o'th Outwood formerly built by Sr Chr[ist]ofer Clapham when L[or]d of the Mannor w[i]th a designe to inclose severall acres to't & make it the Farme hous under the yearly rent of	0 8 0
Mrs Wheatley holds at the Will of the Lord a Shop in Sylver Street in Wakefield under the yearly rent of	0 2 6
Olery Stoops & Kirkhous are set in the Rentall at 6d p[er] ann[um] & are suposed to be for Stoops setting & incroching on the Streets but have not been paid of late years	0 0 6
John Walker holds at the Will of the Lord a Shop built on the Street under the Church yard Wall in Wakefield at the yearly rent of ..	0 1 0
Obadia Redhead holds another thereunder the yearly rent of	0 3 0
John Nevile Esq holds by Copy of Court Roll a Com̃on called Thurston Haynes [or Hagnes] in Fee under the yearly rent of	1 6 8
The Inhabitants of Rastrick hold by Lease of the Lord of the Mannor a Com̃on called Rastrick Moor which they have inclosed under the yearly rent of	1 0 0

D° 21 acres which were reserved in the said Lease & to be paid 1 s per acre for the Lord of the Mannor per annum whenever inclosed ..	1	1	0
Henry Raynor holds of the Lord of the Mannor by Lease a Tanyard taken off the Wast of Sandall Moor under the yearly rent of	0	0	6
Theophilus Shelton Esq holds by Lease some yeards of grownd that belong'd to the Moothall garth on which he has erected a Stable & other houseing adjoyning the Register	0	0	6
Caleb Batty holds by Lease of the Lord of the Mannor a Small hous and garth oth' Outwoodside under the yearly rent of	0	0	6
Totall of the yearly rent of the Inclosures	£10	14	2

COTTAGE RENTS

There are Certain Cottages erected in the severall Wast Grounds of the Mannor of Wakefield And some Garths or Crofts inclosed to severall of those Cottages of the said Wasts The Farmers of these Cottages and Crofts who are able pay the following yearly rents to the L[or]ds Receiver but a great many of them being Poor & relieved by the Parish in w[hi]ch they dwell are yearly returned in arrear such rents are also p[ar]ticuleriz'd as follow the Land being measured & the Rents sett by William Elmsall the Duke of Leeds Receivor at the time when his Grace purchased the Mannor of Wakefield.

Wakefield Outwood

South side. Edward Fostard a small Cottage on the South side at Newton Lain End ..	0	1	0
John Wood a good Cottage & a Garth about 1 r 29 pearches	0	5	0
Wm Brum̃it a Cottage & a Croft of 1 rood 12 pearches N.B. the Coals have since the setting of this Cottage been got soe near it that one p[ar]te of the Cottage is let downe	0	5	0
John Hartley a poor Cott[age] & a Croft of half an acre..	0	5	0
John Smith a poor Cottage & a small garth of 7 pearch..	0	1	0
Wid^w^ Wilkinson a very poor Cottage & a croft about a Rood	0	3	0
Samuel Smith a poor Cott[age] & a small garth of 5 pearch	0	1	6
Wid^w^ Spinke only a Cottage	0	1	0

Tho: Hall a Cottage joyning & of Widow Spinks w[hi]ch a Little garding of 6 pearch ..	0	1	8
Mary Barke a very small Cottage	0	0	4
Elkana Walsh a Cottage & 3 rood & ½ of grownde ..	0	6	8
Thomas Butterfield a poor Cottage & garden of 6 Pearch	0	1	6
East side. Robert Smith an Intack without any houseing of 3½ roods	0	6	0
North side. Thomas Glover a poor Cottage but a garth of 1a 1r of ground	0	7	0
John Dickinson an Intack of 3 roods full of pitholes ..	0	4	6
Wid[w] Burnhit a Cott[age] & garden of 25 pearch ..	0	4	0
Tho: Smith a Good Cott[age] & a Garth of 3 roods ..	0	6	8
Wid[w] Dickinson a very poor Cottage w[i]th a Garth 1r 20p	0	3	0
Benj: Wilkinson a good Cott[age] & 3 rhoods of land ..	0	5	0
Christofer Cass a Cott[age] only	0	1	8
W[m] Armitage an Intack of near 3 roods	0	3	6
Westside. Abr: & Thomas North a bad Cottage w[i]th a Croft of 1 acre	0	6	8
Wid[w] Fletcher now M[rs] Cooper a Cott[age] & above 3 roods in a croft	0	5	6
Thomas Richardson a very good Cott[age] & a Garth of 1 Rhood & 14 Pearch	0	6	8
Mathew Richardson he holds by Copy yet always collected by the Cott[age] Collector ..	0	10	0
John Wilks a Cott[age] & a Barne & 2 crofts of 2a 29p..	0	15	0
Stanley Towne 2 Cottages & a Garth w[i]th 2 poor people in & a croft of 29 pearch ..	0	2	6
Samuel Ward a poor Single Cottage	0	0	6
John Fletcher a Large old Cottage	0	1	0
Jonas Glover an Intack of 2R & 20p. bad land ..	0	2	6
Noah Syms a Small Cottage & a Croft of 1r & 21p ..	0	2	6
Nicholas Askwith a Cott[age] & a Croft of 1a 1r. & 6p bad land	0	6	8
Peter Andrew a Croft of ½ an acre & a bad Cottage ..	0	4	0
Thomas Thomson a Small Cott[age] & a Croft of 3 Rhoodes bad land	0	4	0
Wid[w] Dodgson a Small Cott[age] & a Croft of ½ an acre bad land now W[m] Adcock	0	3	0

Timothy Bowlin a good Cottage & a Croft 2a 2r of bad land	0	16	8
John Holdsworth now John Ledgard a Good Cott[age] w[i]th an acre & 1R. of a bad Croft ..	0	8	6
Jonas Glover a Cott[age] at Potovens & an Intack of 1½ acre here	0	8	6
Joseph Longley a good Cottage & a Croft 3r 16p ..	0	5	6
Thomas Glover an Intack of near 2 acres bad land ..	0	10	0
Jacob Chamlet a bad Cott[age] & a garth of 23P ..	0	2	0
Wid^w^ Gleadhill a bad Cott[age] & a Croft of half an acre	0	2	6
Richd Childe a bad Cottage & a Croft of half an acre ..	0	3	6
Timothy Deane a bad Cottage & a Croft of half an acre	0	2	6
John Saunderson D^o^	0	2	6
Wid^w^ Fox a bad Cottage & a Garth of 14 Pearch ..	0	2	0
Willm̃ Pickering a bad Cott[age] & a Croft near on acre & ½	0	6	8
Jonas Booth a Cott[age] & 3 R & 6 p of bad land ..	0	5	0
Samuel Winter a Barne	0	1	0
Mrs Cooper a Cott[age] in decay but 1 R 17 P of good land	0	3	0
Wid^w^ Aurgeley a Barne	0	2	0
Jno Wormall th' other p[ar]te of the Barne	0	2	6
Josias Lumbe for an Intack of 3 Roods	0	4	0
Wid^w^ Longley a Cottage	0	2	0
Saml Fox a Cottage	0	3	0
Potovens. Willm Sykes a poor Cottage	0	0	6
Anne Ramsden & a Croft 1r. & 34p...	0	2	6
Arthur Thomson a small Cott[age] & Garth of 1R 28p...	0	3	0
Tho: Willans a Cottage & a Garth of 1r & 31p ..	0	5	0
Wm Bryerley a Cottage & a Garth of 14P	0	2	0
Robt Colly Two Cottages..	0	3	0
Wid^w^ Powel a Cott[age] & a Garth of 26p.	0	2	6
Calep Glover a good Cott[age] & a garth of 18p ..	0	3	6
Joshua Glover a poor Cott[age] & a Garth of 20 p. ..	0	2	0
Wm Dodgson a poor Cott[age] & a Garth of 8p ..	0	0	6
Abrm̃ Peaker D^o^	0	0	6
Robt Willans a poor Cott[age] & an Oven hous ..	0	1	6
Joseph Thornton D^o^	0	1	0

James Willans D^{o}	0	1	0
Tymothy Glover D^{o}	0	1	0
Thomas Sharpus D^{o}	0	1	0
Henry Byerom a Cott[age] & a Garth of 25p.	0	2	0
Thomas Glover a very good hous & a garth of 1r 26p ..	0	6	8
Benj: Bevit a Cottage	0	2	0
Wid^{w} Whalley a Poor Cottage	0	0	6
Wid^{w} Mawd a Good Cottage	0	2	0
John Bevit D^{o}	0	2	0
Giles Bevit a Cott[age] & Smithy	0	1	6
Mathew Rigg a poor Cottage	0	0	6
Wid^{w} Glover a poor Cottage	0	1	0
Robt Rigg a Cott[age] and other houseing	0	2	6
Cornelius Glover a Cott[age] p[ar]te of Wid^{w} Glovers ..	0	1	0
James Bowling a good Cottage	0	3	6
Samuel Bowling a Cott[age] at Potovens & a barne oth' westend oth' Outwood	0	4	6
Thomas Glover a good Cottage	0	4	0
Richard Holyday a poor Cottage	0	1	6
Tho: Holyday D^{o}	0	1	6
Tho: Cartor now Richd Holyday a Poor Cott[age] & a Garth of 20p	0	2	0
Joseph Sadler p[ar]te of Wid^{w} Glover houseing ..	0	0	6
Daniel Glover a good Cottage	0	4	0
Robert Glover Junr D^{o}	0	3	6
Wid^{w} Gill a poor Cott[age] & a Garth of 1r 4p.. ..	0	2	6
Wm Fenay Two pore Cott[ages] & 2 Garths of 2r 18p ..	0	6	0
Thomas Kelshaw a poor Cott[age] & a Garth of 8p ..	0	1	0
Thomas Wilson a poor Cott[age] & a Garth of 13p ..	0	2	0
Christofer Elliot a Cott[age] at Bottom boat	0	2	0
Saml Winter & Robert Glover a Cott[age] & a Barne at upper Pottovens..	0	2	0
John Seel a Small Cottage	0	0	6
John Benton a Cott[age] next Wood	0	2	0
Matt: Glover a Cottage	0	1	0
Dewsbury. Ab. Beardshaw for 3 poor Cottages & a Garth of 1r 22 p adjoyning them ..	0	5	0

Jn° Knowles a poor Cott[age] & a Garth of 22p ..	0	2	6
Joseph Oldroyd a Small Cottage	0	0	6
Mathew Knowles a poor Cott[age] & a Garth of 19p ..	0	1	6
Sarah Fearnley 2 Cottages & 2 Garths adjoyning of 36p	0	3	6
Joseph West a small new Cott[age] & a Garth of 10p ..	0	1	0
John Ellis a new Cott[age] & a Garth of 19p	0	2	6
Joshua Fell a new Cott[age] with 2 Dwellings now Crawshaw	0	2	0
Mathew Ellis a poore Cott[age] & a Garth of 14 perches	0	1	6
Sam[l] Holdsworth now Thomas Wilby a poor Cott[age] & a Garth of 1r 19p	0	3	0
Richard Green a Cott[age] & p[ar]te of a Croft ..	0	1	8
John Coper Jun[r] a Cottage	0	1	0
John Dawson p[ar]te of Green Croft the whole being 2r 26p	0	2	2
John Coop[er] sen[r] a small Cottage	0	1	0
James Cooper a Small Cottage	0	1	0
Israel Awty a very poor Cottage & a Garth of 14p ..	0	1	0
Michael Awty D° and a Garth of 8p	0	0	8
Joshua Oldroyd a poor Cottage	0	1	0
Richard Robinson D°	0	0	6
Joseph Awty a good Cott[age] & a Garth of 1r 28p ..	0	6	8
James Green a Cottage	0	1	0
Wid[w] Hargraves D°	0	1	0
Joshua Ellis a Small Cottage	0	0	6
Moses Oldroyd a very poor Cottage	0	0	6
Robert Broadley a new Cottage	0	2	0
John Hirst a good Cott[age] & a Garth of 20p. ..	0	3	0
Heatonbank. John Hirst a small new Cott[age] & a Garth of 12p.	0	1	4
Joseph Field D° & a Garth of 22p.	0	2	2
Gawthrop. Thomas Kitson a poor Cottage	0	0	6
Abr: Philips a Cott[age] & a Garth of 8p.	0	1	0
James Firth a Small Cottage	0	0	6
Street. Wid[w] Shaw a Cott[age] & a Garden of 14 pearch	0	1	6
Sam[l] Barton D°..	0	1	6
John Wilson a Cott[age] & a Garth of 1r 24p.. ..	0	3	6
Osset. John Pickersgill p[ar]te of a Barne	0	0	6

Scamonden. Geo: Hoyl a Cottage..	0	0	4
Northowrom. a parcell of poor Cottages w[hi]ch are sett & vallewed together at 5^{s} but most of the people being kept oth' Towne none pay except: Mary Booth 2^{d} Jer: Robinson 6^{d} Geo: Oldfield 8^{d} Jno & Abr^{m} Brigs 1/-=2s 4d	0	5	0
Totall of the yearly Cott[age] Rents ..	19	19	0

RENT CHARGES

There are Severall Rent charges or reserved Rents out of Former Grants of Grounds & Lands which belong'd and were appurtenant to the Mannor as followe

Due yearly to the Lord of the Mannor out of Wakefield Ings formerly called Earls Ings now in the-poss[ession] of James Sill, Gent & John Smith, gent the Sume of	6	0	0
Also out of a certain peice of Pasture Grownd in Stanley called Wilbet in the poss[ession] of Henry Robinson, Clarke	6	0	0
Also out of a p[ar]cell of Pasture grownd upon the River of Calder near Wakefield called Disforth or Disford	0	6	8
Totall of the Yearly Rent charges.. ..	£12	6	8

Forfieted Lands

Three Closes in the Towne of Shelly were said to be Forfieted for that the Owner was convicted for stealling certain Fish and that one [*blank*] Allot compounded w[it]h the Crowne for those three Closes setling a Rent charge of £1 : 13 : 4 out of them & other Lands of his owne in Shelly all w[hi]ch are now called by the name of Allot Lands and are charged with the said yearly rent of	1	13	4
A Farme in Stanley now in the poss[ession] of John Sugden is said to have heretofore bene forfieted the owner being convict of a Capital crime farmed now by the said John Sugden at the Will of the Lord under the yearly rent of	5	0	0

	£	s	d
A Cottage hous & a Croft in Holmfirth now in the poss[ession] of John Lockwood was forfieted to the Lord for that about 20 years agoe [*blank*] Robinson, Clerke, the owner thereof was convicted for the Treason of counterfieting money & was executed at Yorke now farmed by the said John Lockwood under the yearly rent of	1	4	0
Totall of the yearly Rent out of the Forfieted Lands	7	17	4

Colieries

	£	s	d
A Coliery on Wakefield Outwood w[hi]ch is farmed by The Hon[ora]ble Thomas Earl of Westmoreland who holds it by Lease under the yearly rent of	140	0	0
A Coliery on Lawmoor in Holmfirth farmed by Jonas Kay, Gent who holds it at the Will of the Lord under the yearly rent of	2	0	0
A Coliery on a Comon called Lights in Osset farmed by Joseph Naylor p[er] Lease under the yearly rent of	0	10	0
A Coliery on Hartchstead Moor farmed by S[r] John Armitage Baronet who holds it by Lease under the Yearly Rent of	5	0	0
A Coliery at Dewsbury on that Comon farmed by Willm̃ Poplewell who holds it at the Will of the Lord at the yearly rent of	4	0	0
A lib[er]ty of soughing through the Hall Laine in Holme farmed by Edward Baraclough who holds it at the Will of the Lord under the yearly Rent of	0	5	0
Totall of the yearly Coliery Rents ..	151	15	0

Quaries and Stone Delves

	£	s	d
A Quarie or Stone Delf on the East of Wakefield Outwood farmed by Benjamin Wilkinson who holds it by Lease under the yearly rent of	2	10	0
A Quarie or Stone Delf on Warley Moor farm'd by John Gawkeroger at the Will of the Lord under the yearly Rent of	0	13	4
A Quarie on the West end oth'Outwood farmed by Richard Burnill at the Will of the Lord under the yearly rent of	0	6	8

A Quarie on the Wast at Newmiller Damm farmed by Wm Carr formerly is now dead & it stands	0 10 0
Totall ..	4 0 0

N.B. It may reasonably be suposed that there are great quantities of Coall & other mines in the great wasts within the Mannor wh[i]ch may by a diligent Scrutiny hereafter be found & gott

Potters

Amongst those who inhabit in the Cottages on the Outwood is a Manufactory of earthen Ware, Potts of all sorts being made there w[hi]ch require noe more than Clay & Lead. The Clay oth' Outwood is farmed by Four of the cheif of that Trade there (vizt) Thomas Glover, Robt Willans Daniel Glover & Robert Glover Junr who hold it by Lease under the yearly rent of	10 0 0

Bricks

There were formerly Brick Kilnes Farmed of the Lord of the Mannor on the East Moor of Wakefield now the Inhabitants make for their owne use & pay 4d p[er] 1000 to the Lord of the Mannor, but being [?seeing] the whole Mannor abounds soe much with good Stone the yearly profits communibus annis may amount to only ..	1 5 0

The Fishery

The Fishery is in the River of Calder in all such p[ar]tes & Branches of it as are w[i]thin the Mannor It is farmed now by John Anby Esq at the will of the Lord under the yearly rent of ..	3 0 0

Compounded Fines.

The Compounded Fines within this Mannor are very uncertain as to the yearly vallew By a comon Computation of severall years may be computed to communibus annis	38 0 0

Vncompounded Fines

They are more uncertain & scarce can be computed by Years for p[er]haps there may be a year in an Age that these Fines may hapen to be above £100 and other years not any at all. The nearest computation may be guest at the yearly value of	35 0 0

Vncompounded Lands

As to the uncompounded Lands of the Mannor they are very difficult to be found out. The unwaryness of the Stewards at the time when the Lands were compounded for of any dispute ariseing from their not nameing the perticuler Lands in the Rentall annexed to those Decrees has proved the occasion of soe many subsequent wrong Admittances many Lands being obscured under the Rents there mentioned & accordingly allowed to be Compounded w[hi]ch were none or any p[ar]te of those the Rents issued out of these originall mistakes make it a difficult matter to finde out those Lands: Soe far as a certainty may be depended on are hereafter incerted; the rest w[hi]ch are uncompounded may p[arte] of them if not most be found out accidentally or occasionally upon future admittances if the Tenure of such Lands for w[hi]ch they are required or demanded be duly inquired into.

Lands uncompounded within the Graveship of

Wakefield

Mary Raper a Small Parcell of Land with the buildings thereupon in a Street called Northgate

John Walker a Messuage in a Street called Northgate

Willm̃ Naylor a messuage in Northgate adjoyning on the Church yeard

Anne the wife of Mr Browne for certain Lands formerly Mr John Peables's. NB. these are intermixed with the Lord Rabys & Robt Muncktons Esqr that till a p[ar]ticuler of their Devision be had they can not be p[ar]ticulerizd under their respective heads

Willm̃ Midlebrook a mess[uage] in Northgate at the Bitchill

John Bromley, Gent one close of Land called Oliver Inge

James Scrivener a Small p[ar]cell of Land in Northgate to place Two Posts on

The Hon[ora]ble The L[or]d Raby all his Lands and Tenem[en]ts late Saviles

Robt Munckton Esqr all his Lands & Tenem[en]ts late Saviles

Isaac Gascone a Cottage & a small p[ar]cell of Land at Brooksbancke

Mercie Brook, widw a Messuage or Tenem[en]t near The Pinfold

Thornes

Grace Nayler Five Roods of Land in The Lawefield

Thomas Hawkins one Rood of Land in The Lawfield

John Bains for a Cott[age] & Garden in Thornes

Dorothy Armitage for one Rood of Land taken off the wast

The L[or]d Raby for Lands late Saviles

Robt Munckton Esqr for Lands late Saviles

Anne Browne the Daughter of Mr John Peables for Land late Saviles

Joseph Walmsley for one acre taken off the Wast
Martha Fairbanck for Five Roods in The Lawfield
Christofer Hargraves for one Rood & Twenty yeards in Length & Twenty six in breadth taken of The Wast

Sandall

Francis Duckenfield a Cottage & Garth & Twenty yeards of Land in length & Twenty yeards in bredth adjoyning to the said Cottage lyeing at Newbiggin Hill
Joseph Oxley a Cottage & a p[ar]cell of Land of Fifteen yeards in length & Foureteen yeards in bredth
Francis Duckenfield a Cottage on Outhous Garden & Croft to the same belonging at Humley royd
Richard Pearson a Cottage & Garth to the same belonging at Wood-moor side
Mary Hawksworth a Cottage at Woodmoorside
John Bedford a Cott[age] & a p[ar]cell of Land to the same adjoyning containing 30 yeards in length & 14 yeards in bredth
England Fyefield a p[ar]cell of Land of 1[d] Rent lyeing within a Close of Compoundid Land in Painthorp
Henry Raynor a Cott[age] & half a Rood of Land lyeing in Crigleston-Cliff
W[m] Norton a Cottage and Garden at Dawgreen
M[r] Joseph Wood, Cl[erk] One Cottage at Milnethorpegate & thirty yeards of Land in length & Ten yeards in bredth
Joseph Beever a p[ar]cell of Land containing Eight yeards in length & Tenn in breadth near Newmilner Dame
Anthony Kay a Cottage in Milnethorp
Samuel Norton, Gent his heirs a Cottage at Humley a Garden three Roods & Twenty pearches of Land to the same belonging
Edward Allot, Gent a parcell of Land late Godfrey Copley Esq
Elizabeth the wife of W[m] Webster a Cottage & Croft on Criggleston-Cliff
The Lord Raby for his Messuages & Lands late Saviles
Anne the wife of John Browne, Gent for her Lands late Saviles
Robert Munckton Esq for his Lands late Saviles
Thomas Lee a Cottage near new mill Dame & one parcell of Land adjoyning to the same containing Eight yeards in length & Six yeards in bredth
Barnard Parker a Cottage at Newbiggin Hill
Edw[d] Allot a Close of Land called Bryery Close
Robert Beckwith a Messuage or Cottage & Barne erected on the Wast in Milnethorp near the Highway leading between Wakefield & Royston
Willm̃ Preston Two Parcells of Land lyeing at Dircarr called Dockrey Roydes & Holes

Edward Beckit a Cottage at Newbiggin Hill near New mill Dam̃e & a garden to the same belonging

The heirs of Francis Nevile Esq a Cottage & parcell of Land by Robert Wright

Richard Haigh a Cottage at Newmiller Damme

James Swallow a Cottage & Croft at Hall Green

Edw[d] Allot, Gent a p[ar]cell of Land with w[i]th the buildings thereon at Newbigin Hill by Chr[ist]ofer Long

Heirs of Sam[l] Norton, Gent for a Close of Land called Cookson Inge containing four acres lyeing in Newsome

Richard Haigh a Cott[age] at Newbiggin Hill near New mill Damme

John Rayner the Northend of a Messuage and a Garden to the same adjoyning at Stanbridge

Robert Flower a Cottage and a Garden to the same adjoyning at a place called Oulerbrigg near the New mill Damme

Jeramia Milner Three Roods of Land in one close called Pitt Close lyeing in Criglestone

Cyrill Arthington Esq all the Coal Mines on the wasts off Crigleston Rent 5[s]

The Governors of the Poor of the Parish of Sandall for a messuage Orchard & Croft lyeing in Dirtcarr by Robert Oxley

Robert Kitson & Eliz: Wood, Widow a Cott[age] at Newbiggin Hill near Newmill Damme

Horbury

Thomas Pearson for p[ar]te of one close lyeing upon a Place called Old Cross in Stonebrigg feild rent 1[d]

Lawrence Cockill a Cottage & one Rood of Land in Horbury Towne & Two Roods of Land in the Westfeild upon Quarel Hill

Joshua, David, & Benjamin Coop for Lands late Rapers & Robinsons & formerly Radcliffs.

Thomas Hunt one Cottage & a Croft adjoyning upon the Hall Cliff

Thomas Birkhead a p[ar]cell of Land belonging to a Messuage att Streetside

Willm̃ Morkill for a mess[uage] & certain Feild Lands after the death of Mathew Tottie

John Carr a Rood of Land in the South feild

Richard Wormall Two Roods of Land upon the short Sowefeild Shutt in the Mill Feild

Samuell Thornes a Close of Land upon Litle Brigg Nook Shutt in the Stonebrig feild

John Dawson a Rood of Land upon a Shutt called Longsouth feild

John Carr a Close containing one acre called Longcroft

Willm̃ Curtis an old Cottage and p[ar]te of a Croft containing half an acre at Sowood Green

Rob̃t White a Small p[ar]cell of Land taken off the Wast at Sowood Green

John Issot Four half roods of Land in the Mill feild

John Pollard an acre in the Stonebridge Feild
Edmund Wood one half acre in the Stonebrigg feild near Goodall Cross
Wm Dawson Seaven Roods
Thomas Tottie Four acres & one Rood
Robt Leek, Geñ half an acre of Land in a Close called Bensill
Willm̃ Tottie a Cottage & Two Roods of Land in the Eastfeild
Elizabeth Portington one close called litle Benshall containing half an acre lyeing in the Stone brigg feild
Willm̃ Tottie & others Two Cottages & one acre of Land adjoyning the West Feild
Robert Leek, Gent Seaven Roods & the Thirde p[ar]te of a Rood in the Westfeild adjoyning on Denton Lane
John Carr One Cottage & a Barne & a Croft of half an acre of Land
Thomas Walker a Cottage & one Rood of Land
Elizabeth Sympson Two half Roods one in the Millfeild at the Mill Door th'other on Preistwell Shutt in the Westfield
Tempest Pollard the Mess[uage] & the Lands thereunto belonging now in his owne possession

Alverthorp

John Kirke a Cott[age] & Croft at Pinfold Hill & Two closes called Wallit Close &c Dog Croft late Wentworths
Daniel Mawd, Gent p[er] Currier Close & Lands in Shawfeild w[hi]ch were Sr Wm Wentworths
Eleazar Holdsworth a mess[uage] & Three Closes formerly Chr[ist]ofer Smiths
John Wormall a Cottage & Garden Stead
Richard Loxley a Cottage & an Intack joyning on Alverthorpe Green
Mary Kirke a Cottage & half a Rood of Land on Alverthorp Green
James Benton a Cottage & Garden stead p[er] Timothy Stead
Jno Dennison a Cottage, Shilveing Croft, Two closes called Crimbles & Toft Shove from his father also an old Messuage a Garden Stead an orchard a Croft & Five Closes of Land called the litle Hawks, the Long Close, The Well Close, the Eastfeild Close & Kelshaw Ing, a Reversion after the death of Beatrix Pollard
Anne the wife of Mr John Browne & daughter of John Peables Esq her Lands late Saviles
John Oldroyd for a small p[ar]cell of a Penny L[or]ds rent late Thorntons
Robert Clarkson a mess[uage] & Croft in Newton by Chr[ist]ofer Smith
Mrs Wheatley for Two Closes containing three acres adjoyning in Broadfoard a Parrock containing one Rood taken off Clif-feild Two closes containing Three acres called Humble jumble closes & 5½ acres near Cliff hill

Wm Dennison for the half of a close called Toft Shough
Wm Batty a Cott[age] with the appurt[enance]s called Fidling hous
John Keysar a close called Long Close containing three acres
The Lord Raby for Midletons, Fleemings, & Broome Lands late Saviles
Elizabeth Smith a Cottage & half a rood of Land lately inclosed at Alverthorp Green
Willm̃ Swinscoe one Rood of Land in Humble Jumble feild
John Foster 2 Cottages with a Garden Orchard & Backside
Richard Taylor a close called Cliff hill containing Eight acres by Willm̃ Oglethorp
John Mason a Cott[age] & Garden Stead by Tymothy Heald

Stanley

Samuel & Thomas Burgh hald an acre of Land in the Nether Feild abutting upon the old Parke Hedge
John Clarkson of Silkston Cl[erk] certain uncompounded Lands given him from Arthur Clarkson his father under the L[or]ds rent of £0. 1. 5.
Anthony Abson half an acre of Land by John Wilks
Thomas Smith a Parcel of Land in the Churchfeild upon a Shutt called Broadarse abutting upon the North hey Laine
David Law an acre of Land lyeing in Heath feild
George Teall a Cottage & Garth lyeing on the West of the Outwood late John Brownes
Oswold Hatfield, Gent & Jno Hatfield a mess[uage] a Croft & Garden to the same belonging in Stanley sur[rendere]d to them by Wm Copendall
Joseph Armitage, Gent 2 closes called Dewceroyd & Three nooked Close & 2 other closes called Flagg Close & Square close
Robt Watson, Gent a croft called Gun Croft & 2 acres in the midlefeild & Westfeild of Ouchthorp
Richard Shaw, Gent a p[ar]cell of Land where a Wall now Stands in Sladley Laine surr[endere]d to him by Alice Andrew
David Law 3 Butts & 3 Roods of Land in the Cross feild by Edwd Beckit
Samuel Copley a Cott[age] & Croft taken off the Wast oth' Outwood
James Browne, Gent a messuage & severall Closes of Land to the same belonging lyeing in Stanley & Ouchthorp
John Scott, Geñ a Cottage Garden & orchard at Eastmoor
John Harrison half an acre of land in the Netherfield
Thomas Smith Two half acres of Land in the Kirkfield lyeing on a Shutt abutting upon North hey Laine
Sr Lyon Pilkington Baront a Barne & 1 croft & 2 Lands in one close called the Paddock to the same adjoyning p[er] Jo: Richardson, Clerke, & others
Anne the wife of James Browne & daughter of Mr Peables her Lands late Saviles

Robert Glover a Cottage & parcell of Land taken off the Wast oth' Outwood by Timothy Glover
Robert Sellars a Cottage in Ouchthorp Laine
Hanna Moxon a Messuage at the Pinfold in Stanley
John Kent a small p[ar]cel of Land in Stanley by Inheritance
John Sunderland a Cottage at The Outwoodside
Sr Lyon Pilkington Baront a Cottage & 2 litle Crofts sur[rendered] to him by Saml Burgh
Charles Cooper a p[ar]cell of Land inclosed off the wast oth' Outwood
Anne & Willm̃ Casson a p[ar]cell of Land taken off the wast with all the buildings thereupon built containing 30 yeards in length & 12 in breadth at Browneshay Green
Sr Lyon Pilkington Baront a rood of Land in the Kirkfield surr[endered] to him by Samuel Firth
The Hon[ora]ble The L[or]d Raby all his Lands in Stanley late Wm̃ Saviles
Willm̃ Darley a Messuage & Croft at the Outwoodside by Toby Sill
Alice Smith an acre of Land in the Heathfield sur[rendered] to her by Richard Smith
Mathew Richardson a Mess[uage] & 5 acres of Land oth' west oth' Outwood sur[rendered] to him by Edward Rasing
Thomas Michill certain feild land sur[rendered] to him by Robt Law
Gervas Harrison a small p[ar]cell of Land in the Kirkfeild of a Farthing Lords rent
Sarah Oley a Cottage at Newton
Eliz: Smith a Cott[age] & Fold in Stanley
Daniel Oley 2 acres 3 roods in the Midlefeild
Tho: Birkhead by Inheritance a small p[ar]cell of Land in Stanley of 2d Rent
Thomas Denton the half p[ar]te of one Close called Quarrel Close & one Close called Coldholme & one Selion of Land in the North Feild
Robert Glover a p[ar]cell of Land at Lower Potovens & a New hous thereupon builded, & a building called a Cup Oven
John Longley a Cott[age] & 2 acres of Land at Stony Laine End
Robt Munckton Esq all his Lands in Stanley late Saviles
John Wilks a hous a Barne a Stable & 3 roods of Land at Carryate
Nicholas Cooper ½ acre of Land at the Outwood w[i]th buildings thereon
Mary Hick a close called burn't Close
Richard Cockill 2 closes in the Netherfield & Howroid Feild called Sweetercliff & midleflatts
Widow Hall ½ acre of Land & a Cottage at Kirkham Yate
Margret Broadhead Widow a messuage a Foldstead Garden, Orchard & Croft to the same belonging at Outwood-side also 3 closes of Roodland lately made into 5 Closes called by

the Names of Ruddings, Great Inge, Bothom Inge, Cockshutt, alias Brackin Closes, and also 1 close called Broad Close al[ia]s Mayne-Close, now made into 3 Closes—and 1 litle Close called Breck close

James Moxon 1 close called Ingroade close containing 3 acres

Thomas Dodgson one hous & Cottage & the 4th p[ar]te of a p[ar]cell of Land called Butler Carr & ½ acre of Land in Ouchthorp Westfeild

Sr Lyon Pilkington Baront 30 acres of Land in a Close called New Intack lately inclosed from the Kirk Feild sur[rendered] to him by Shefeild Clapham Sonn of Sr Chr[ist]ofer Clapham Knt

Richard Everingham for a certain Field Land in Stanley

Osset Graveship

Richard Speight a Cottage a Garth & a Shop lyeing under Earls Heaton Banck late Richard Allots

Henry Heald a Cottage in Gauthorp sur[rendered] to him by Henry Hudson

John Townend a Cottage & Croft on Osset Leights

John Netleton a p[ar]cell of Land at Sowood Green being 14 yards Square

Richard Kitson a Cottage in Gauthorp

The Governors of Wakefield Free Schoole a mess[uage] & 1 close of Land lyeing in Gawthorp containing 8 acres in the possession of Thomas Graves

John Wade a Cottage in Osset

Grace Ratcliff a small p[ar]cell of Grownd at Streetside

Thomas Birkhead a p[ar]cell of Land at Streetside

Thomas Sykes a p[ar]cell of Land 6 yeards in Length & 5 yeards in breadth

Thomas Shepley a Cott[age] in Earlsheaton

Daniel Sikes a peice of Land and a Cott[age] in the high Street of Osset

Richd Apleby a Cott[age] and Garden in Earlsheaton

Thomas Wilson a Cottage and Garden in Earlsheaton

Henry Heald a Cott[age] and Garden in Earls Heaton

Thomas Pashley a small p[ar]cell of Land taken off the Wast at Sowood green rent 6d

Robert Munckton Esq all his Lands in Osset late Saviles

George Pickard a small p[ar]cell of Land at Sowoodgreene

Robert Whittakers a Cottage & a Small p[ar]cell of Land at Heaton Banck Top

Richard Foster a Rood of Land on Osset Leights

Rastrick

Thomas Thornhill Esq 4 acres 3 roods of Land lyeing under a Hill called Tootill Hill & knowne by the name of Fletcher Lands Rent 9d Sur[rendered] to him by Mary Law

Benjamin Law a p[ar]cell of Land belonging to Vpper Woodhous L[or]ds Rent 10[d]
Joseph Bouthroid a p[ar]cel of Land called Madglaughton
Agnes Law one Close called Nether Inge one close & a Wood called Linland Roid Wood al[ia]s Overspring sur[rendered] to her by Richd & Alice Ramsden

Holme

Henry & Abel Jackson for an acre of Land among other Lands sur[rendered] to them by John Cusworth & wife
Bartholomew Bray one close of Land called Netherfeild lyeing near a mess[uage] called Stakelaine
John Roberts for Three acres in Holmfirth
Humphrey Hinchliffe 2 acres of Land at Bawshay w[i]th certain buildings thereon sur[rendered] from Thomas Booth
Godfrey Crosley 3 closes called Roger royds & Binns wood in Overthongue
Mary Heaton a Cottage in Synderhill browe
Jonas Kay, Geñ for a Close called Carr Inge in Holme at Wade place
John Tinker a Close of Land called the Hey in Foolstone
Martin Saunderson for the half p[ar]te of a mess[uage] & 7 acres of Land lyeing in Austonley
Joseph Earnshaw the other half p[ar]te
Henry & John Booth a mess[uage] & severall closes of Land in Vpper Thwonge
David Dickson a Close called Wolfe Bottom
Sarah Noble 3 Roods in Hepworth
Thomas Cuttill a Cottage called Binscoat & a Garth & a Fold to the said Cottage in Over Thwonge
John Cusworth a mess[uage] & a garden in Over Thwonge
Willm̃ Moorehous a mess[uage] a Garden & severall closes called the Croft the Great Inge, now made into 3 Closes the Pighel, the Stubbings brow, the Litle Ingewood, 2 closes called Nether & over Stubbing, The Hurnepike, The midle Hurne, & The Hurnend scituate in Fulstone
Thomas Cuttill for a Cottage & a Croft in Over Thwonge sur[rendered] to him by Robert Ray, Gent
John Holdsworth a p[ar]cell of Land called the Intack lyeing in a place called Bawshaw
Thomas Bray a hous at Synderhills one other hous wherein Amos Bower dwelt, another hous called the Turf hous, one Garden, one Fold, & one Croft & 6 Closes of Land called the Over Feild, Nether Feild, Nether & Over Tudehoile, Laith Croft, Little Lee, & the Furlong lyeing at Synderhill
Samuel Burslam a small peice of Wast grownds in Holme surr[endered] by Cusworth

Joshua Rhodes a mess[uage] called Woodhous & 5 closes of Land thereto belonging adjoyning to Cartworth moore

John Tinker one Bay of houseing called the Kitchin, & a chamber, over the same, Two Bays of the West End of a Barne, & 8 square yeards of one close called Midlefield, & a mess[uage] called Moor banks w[i]th 2 gardins & a Close of Shrubby or Wast Ground in Scholes

James Earnshaw severall Closes of Land called by the names of Towcroft, the Laith Croft, the Longroyd, & the Cliffe banck, sur[rendered] to him by Mathew Moorhous

Philip Burdit severall Closes of Land called by the names of the Dearn Flatt al[ia]s the Feild, The John Roid, the Marsh Inge, & the Narr & Farr Westringlees belonging to a messuage called the Hall sur[rendered] to him by Mathew Moorhous

James Bower a little Cottage called Buckley hous conteyning 6 yeards in length & 6 in breadth adjoyning to a Litle Close called Scutle Croft & one garden to the said Cottage adjoyning in Wooldale Rent 1[d] sur[rendered] by John Buckley

John Newton a mess[uage] w[i]th all the buildings Cottages Closes Lands Tennem[en]ts & premisses to ye same belonging called Stackwood hill Biggin & woodall scituate in Fulstone & Woodall

Richard Dixon severall Closes of Land called Butterlee, The Carr, The Gillroyd, the Gill Royd Inge, & the Stackwoodroyd lyeing in Fulstone sur[rendered] by Mathew Moorhouse

Philip Bray a Close of Land called Shelley sur[rendered] by Thomas Squire

John Micklethwaite ½ acre of Land abutting on the Closes late Jonathan & Chr[ist]ofer Micklethwaite

Joseph & Joshua Beever a mess[uage] at Hill w[i]th all buildings Closes & Lands to the same belonging scituate & being in Overthwonge

Mathew Moorhous a messuage called the Hall w[i]th the Lands thereunto belonging in Fulstone

Sarah Newton for an acre of Land being 4[d] L[or]ds Rent lyeing among other Lands belonging to her mess[uage] in Scholes sur[rendered] by Josias Newton

John Midgley 6 yeards in Length & 4 in breadth lyeing at the end of one close called Ellen Inge in Austonley

Luke Wilson a Barne called New Laith, a Litle Croft to the same adjoyning one close called Sinderhill, & one close called Round Close lyeing near Sinderhill in Wooldale

Abraham Green all the buildings at Nether hous & one Garden & the half p[ar]te of the Fold in Overthwonge

Luke Wilson a Close called Lee banck in Wooldale sur[rendered] by Eliz: Genn

John Roberts one close called Ryeroyds the 3[d] p[ar]te of the Tenter Croft & one close called Short butts in Thongue

Thomas Littlewood a mess[uage] called Damm house & a p[ar]cell of Land thereunto belonging

John Woodhead a mess[uage] & Lands thereunto belonging sur[rendered] to him by Michael Midgley

Mary Beaum[on]t 2 parlors, a chamber, a washouse, a mistall, an oxelaith, & 4 Closes of Land called the Two new Crofts, the Fairbroad Ing, & the Mouspike Hill in Fulstone sur[rendered] by Mathew Moorhous

Luke Firth a hous & Croft at Overthwonge

Tho: Littlewood a close called Flatt, a Close called Pighel, now devided into 2 closes, 1 rood of Land in the Barrcroft, & half of the Turney croft, & the half of the Turney croft wood by Jn° Castle

John Taylor the half of a mess[uage] called Called Carr, & the half of a Close called bankside, & severall other closes called the Narr heywood, the Whorestonewood, the Furwoodhey the Welcroft, & the Townefield in Overthwonge

James France an acre of Comon not inclosed in Fulstone

John Hirst a p[ar]cell of Land in Overthwonge

Alice Kenion half an acre of Land in Fulstone

Abrm̃ Hirst a small p[ar]cell of Land taken off the wast at Deinbridge in Hepworth

John Hinchliff a mess[uage] in Cartworth called Waterside w[i]th the Lands

John Green a mess[uage] in Cartworth w[i]th the Lands thereunto belonging sur[rendered] to him by Luke Firth

John Crosland a Close called Farrdowne shutt & a close called Ellen Inge in Austonley by John Charlesworth

Caleb Armitage a p[ar]cell of Land called Garden w[i]th 2 ways adjoyning to the same sur[rendered] to him by Jn° Hatfield

James Earnshaw a messuage called Bright hill & 3 Roods of Land in Cartworth sur[rendered] to him by Michael Eastwood

John Green a Litle Close called the Pingil sur[rendered] to him by Michael Eastwood

Jonas Charlesworth the half p[ar]te of a mess[uage] called Ryecroft in Scholes

Joshua Rhodes the half p[ar]te of a mess[uage] at Woodhouse in Cartworth sur[rendered] to him by James Roberts

Jane Bray & Joshua Rhodes the other p[ar]te of the said mess[uage]

Humphrey Roebuck a Close of Land called Marshing containing one acre

Jonas Kay, Gent a mess[uage] called Woodardhill & 4 closes called Moorhey, Hancockhill, Rushfield & Old Heywood

James Tinker a Parcell of Land taken off the Wast in Wooldall at a place called Bawshaw containing 2 acres

Thomas Litlewood 1 Cottage & Garden in Cartworth sur[rendered] to him by Chr[ist]ofer Kay

Luke Firth a close called Knowles Close lately made into 2 closes, the east end of a Barne, a parcell of Land called nether Sparr doalls, & a Close called litle Close lyeing in Overthwong

Chr[ist]ofer Kay 1 acre of Land & 2 Cottages thereon sur[rendered] to him by Thomas Cuttill

John Crosland ½ a rood of wast near Watergreen & ½ a rood in Holme

Sowerby

Geo: Raunsley a p[ar]cell of Land at Hardknott near a place called Farrheight in Soyland

Sarah Shakleton a Cott[age] at Hilleley Green

John Smith, Gent a peice of Land inclosed off Soyland Moore lyeing near Hardknott & Wren nest

Sarah Smithies a p[ar]cell of Land late taken off the wast & all the buildings thereupon builded in Stanningden containing ½ an acre sur[rendered] to her by Jon[athan] Smithies

John Hoile a mess[uage] called Highlumm & 22 acres of Land to the same belonging lyeing in Sowerby

George Hoyle & Anne Denton a Cottage 1 Close of Land in Soyland called Lowerfield & ½ a rood of land lately inclosed off the Wast sur[rendered] to them by Joseph Kershaw

John Sugden & John Ryley an acre & a half being 2 Closes at Feild End in Soyland.

Richard Holdroid a hous called Prison (?) house, a Barne, a Garth, & 2 crofts thereunto belonging in Staningden

Joshua Laycock a p[ar]cell of Land in Warley lyeing betweene a p[ar]cell of Woody grownde called Deanhouswood & Boothwood

Allen Whiteley a Cott[age] & Garth at Farraheight

Mary Thomas a Cottage in Sowerby called the Cobcastle

Samuel Hoyl a Cottage & a small p[ar]cell of Land taken off the Wast

Joseph Kirshaw 1 Close called Croft containing ½ acre, & 1 close, & a hous called Northfield, & another close called Goodfeild in Soyland

George Holdroyd a Close called New Close late inclosed off the Wast in Soyland

Susanna West a Close in Sowerby

John Crosley a p[ar]cell of Land of 2[d] rent belonging a mess[uage] called Moor

John Murgatroyd a Rood of Land in Warley

Symeon Dyson an acre of Land

Henry Wilson ⅔rd partes of a Rood of Land taken off the Wast on Soyland Moore

Jeremia Crosley a Croft & a mess[uage] or Cottage at Lighthazles by James Wofenden

John Ryley ½ an acre w[i]th the buildings thereupon at Maidenstone, 1 close called Swifter inclosed off Soyland Moor & ½ an acre in Stanninden of w[hi]ch one sixth p[ar]te is not compounded

John Ryley ½ an acre taken off the wast on Soyland Moor & a Cott[age] at Whitegate head

Michael Crosley a Rood of Land inclosed the wast called Netherend in Soyland

John Gawkeroger a Cott[age] & a Close containing 2 acres on Soyland moore

Joshua Horton Esqr 1½ acres of Land at the Waterstalls sur[rendered] to him by Henry Sutcliffe

Samuel Midgley a p[ar]cell of Land on w[hi]ch Ludenden Brook runns w[hi]ch reacheth from Patchets Close to the Waingate & the Dean Mills

John Marsden 3 Roods of Land on the wast of Soyland

John Eccles a Cottage & an acre of Land on Soyland Moore

Mary Feilding 3 acres of the Wast on Soyland Moor

James Sutcliff 1 acre of Land at Pikelaw

Henry Marsden an acre in Soyland

Joseph Holdroyd 2a 1r. in Soyland

Mathew Wilkinson a rood of Land between the two Highways leading to Soyland Mill

James Murgatroyd a Cottage at Lambhill end

Isaac Nayler a parcell of Land belonging to one messuage called Jackson Inge

Henry Smith 30 yeards in bredth & 2 in length in Soyland

Hipperholme

John Fletcher a Cottage & a parcell of Land adjoyning to the same containing 1 Rood in Northowrom

Willm̃ Gleadhill for an acre of Land taken off the wast of Northowrom & injoyed with 1 messuage being Freehold of the said W[m] Gleadhill's near a place called Ambler Sike

James Lister, Gent for Shibdin Mills & the Lands & Damm thereto adjoyning

Joseph Crowther, Gent a Cottage built on the wast of Northowrom

Jerramia Robinson a small Cottage at Begrinton

John Wilson a Cottage in Northowrom

Joseph Hall a Rood of Land inclosed off the Wast at a place called Blakehillside with the buildings thereon

Jonathan Gleadhill an acre of Land inclosed off the Wast in Northowrom sur[rendered] to him by Mearcy Longbothom

Willm̃ Walker a mess[uage] & 4 Closes of Land called the Great Brookfeilde, the Litle brookfeilde, the Midle Close, & the Inge, And one p[ar]cell of Land called the Calf Croft, lyeing in Lightcliffe

Willm̃ Richardson, Gent a mess[uage] called Lower Cliffhous & the Land thereto belonging in Lightcliffe

Abr^{m} Longley, Gent 2 Cottages & a p[ar]cell of Land containing 60 yeards in length & 20 yeards in breadth sur[rendered] to him by Wm̃ Walton

Joseph Crowther, Gent a small p[ar]cell of Land belonging to the Whitehill

Nathan^{l} Sowood a Cottage Fold & Garden at Amblerthorne

Mary Thornton a Cott[age] & 10 yeards of Land in length & 5 in breadth in High Preston

Mary Thornton Junio^{r} a Cott[age] lately built on the Wast at Begrington

Richard Hoyle a Small p[ar]cell of Land of 6 yeards in Length & 5 foot in bredth w[i]th a Well in it

Joseph Crowther, Gent a small p[ar]cell of Land containing 20 yeards in length & 20 in breadth lyeing upon a p[ar]cell of Land called the Green between Shibdin Brook & Symcarr Inge sur[rendered] to him by John Longley

Alice Crowther a Cott[age] & Smythy near Hallifax Northbrigg

Joseph Booth a Cott[age] Garden & Croft in Northowrom sur[rendered] to him by James Booth

Abr^{m} Longley, Gent a close called Quarlers in Lightcliff sur[rendered] to him by Henry Birkhead

Abr^{m} Shaw a Cott[age] in Northowrom

Joseph Briggs 4 Parcells of Land with the buildings thereon in Northowrom sur[rendered] by Edwd Bairstow

Joseph Crowther, Gent half a days worke of Land adjoyning to a place called Langshaw & another p[ar]cell lyeing near a Laine called Hall Laine

Mary Bowcock a Cott[age] & Garden in Northowrom

Daniel Walker a Close called Netherhilelee with all the buildings thereon now devided into 5 Closes containing 4 acres & called by the names of the Stony Close, The Inge, The Overhey, The Netherhey, & the Parrock rent 1^{s} 4^{d} to the Lord

John Best a Cott[age] at Laudymersike surrendered by John Gill

John Thomson 1 rood of Land w[i]th the buildings at a place called Ambler Sike Thorn Delves

James Oates a small p[ar]cell of Land lyeing by the Highway leading from Bradford to Hallifax

Scamonden

George Hudson a Cottage & 1 acre of Land to the same belonging on Scamonden Moore

COMONS & WASTS

Comons & Wasts not inclosed within the Mannor of Wakefield belonging to His Grace the Duke of Leeds & not claimed by other Lords with their number of acres computed

	acres	acres
Wakefield		
Wakefield Outwood lyeing within Wakefield Stanley, & Alverthorp	2500	
Westgate Moor	200	
Eastmoor	30	
		2730
Thornes		
Thornes Moor, & Whinny Moor		100
Sandall		
Wood Moor	50	
Humley Moor	20	
Crigleston Cliffe	20	
Part of Wooley Moor	50	
Sandall Moor	80	
Milnethorp Green	10	
Dirtcarr Green	10	
		240
Horbury		
Storshill		20
Alverthorp		
Alverthorp Green		5
Osset		
Osset Lights	350	
Heaton Banck	200	
Dewsbury Moor	400	
		950
Holme		
Thurstonland Banck	200	
Nabbs Cliff & Burn't Cumberworth ..	400	
Brown edge	500	
Crowedge & Whitcliffe	600	
Hay Slacks Moor	500	
Whitley Moors	350	
Bedding Edge	250	
Yoke Edge	80	
Law & Lawsike	500	
Snailsden & Dead Edge	600	
Harding	600	
Scoles Moor	1000	
Cartworth Moor..	1000	
Ramsden	200	
Harbridge & Twedall	400	
Lightings	300	

	acres	acres
Burley Banck & Burn't head	250	
Holme Moor & Hishays	900	
Good Bent, Broadslade, & Deanhead ..	1250	
Bradshaw & Reaphill	1250	
Holme Clough	1300	
Holme Mosse	1600	
Mount Comon	150	
Ridle Pitt	150	
		14280
Sowerby		
Soyland Moor, Baitings, Blackstone Edge & Sowerby Moor lying all contiguous	5500	
Warley Moor	3500	
Turley Holes	1000	
		10000
Hipp[er]holme		
Swales Moor	500	
Mickle Mosse	450	
Catherin Flack	150	
		1100
Scamonden		
Scamonden Moor	500	
Cowgate Hill	150	
		650
Normanton		
Normanton Moor		50
Hartchstead		
Hartchstead Moor		250
Totall of the computed acres		30375

NB. There are severall Highways of considerable breadths & Towne Greens &c w[ch] containe great quantities of acres & are not here taken notice off.

THE GENERALL RENTALL DRAWNE FROM THE PARTICULARS.

	£	s.	d.
The Vnder Stewardship as in	40	0	0
The Geole houseing	27	0	0
The Baylywick of Wakefield	42	0	0
The Baylywick of The Fee of Wakefield	16	0	0

	£	s.	d.
The Baylywick of Hallifax	50	0	0
The Baylywick of Holme	10	0	0
The Tolls	50	0	0
The Common Bakehous	25	0	0
Wakefield Graveship	7	7	9½
Sandall Graveship	19	19	9
Horbury Graveship	10	0	10
Alverthorp Graveship	8	3	0½
Stanley Graveship	14	4	3¾
Osset Graveship	11	13	7¼
Thornes Graveship	8	9	9
Holme Graveship	61	15	5¾
Sowerby Graveship	65	13	5½
Hipperholme Graveship	22	12	11¼
Rastrick Graveship	8	11	5¾
Scamonden	3	9	5
Inclosures	10	14	2
Cottages	19	19	0
Rent Charges	12	6	8
Forfeited Lands	7	17	4
Colieries	151	15	0
Quaries & Stone Delves	4	0	0
Potters Earth	10	0	0
Bricks	1	5	0
Fishery	3	0	0
Compounded Fines	38	0	0
Vncompounded Fines	35	0	0
Totall	£793	19	0¼

INDEX OF PERSONS AND PLACES

An asterisk (*) denotes that the name occurs more than once on the same page

For EU product safety concerns, contact us at Calle de José Abascal, 56–1°,
28003 Madrid, Spain or eugpsr@cambridge.org.

www.ingramcontent.com/pod-product-compliance
Ingram Content Group UK Ltd.
Pitfield, Milton Keynes, MK11 3LW, UK
UKHW010041140625
459647UK00012BA/1533

* 9 7 8 1 1 0 8 0 5 8 8 4 1 *